Which Side Are You On?

John W. Hevener

Which Side Are You On?

The Harlan County Coal Miners, 1931-39

University of Illinois Press

Urbana   Chicago   London

Permission to quote portions of the following songs is
gratefully acknowledged.

"Harlan County Blues" by George Davis. From George Korson,
*Coal Dust on the Fiddle: Songs and Stories of the Bituminous
Industry* (Philadelphia: University of Pennsylvania Press,
1943; reprinted, Hatboro, Pa.: Folklore Associates, 1965).

"Harry Simms" by Jim Garland. © 1947 Stormking Music, Inc.
All rights reserved. Used by permission.

"Which Side Are You On?" by Florence Reece. © 1947 Stormking
Music, Inc. All rights reserved. Used by permission.

Library of Congress Cataloging in Publication Data

Hevener, John W   1933–
    Which side are you on?

    Bibliography: p.
    Includes index.
    1.   Trade-unions—Coal-miners—Kentucky—
Harlan Co.—History.   2.   United Mine Workers of
America—History.   3.   Strikes ad lockouts—Coal
mining—Kentucky—Harlan Co.—History.   4.   Labor
policy—United States—History—Case studies.
I.   Title.
HD6515.M616H373   331.88′12′23309769154   78–16417
ISBN 0–252–00270–9

To Mary

Contents

List of Illustrations

Preface

Among the many labor struggles of the Depression decade, none attracted more national attention than the prolonged and violent conflict between the coal miners and operators of "Bloody" Harlan County, Kentucky. Unemployment, irregular employment, plummeting wages, short-weight, the cleanup system, arbitrary work rules, and coal-company domination of their economic, social, and political destiny quickly converted a majority of the miners in this former nonunion bastion to unionism. Fearing for their job security and their personal safety, however, and unable to establish lasting contact with an outside union, they were long prevented from successfully organizing. The coal operators, fearing that their poorly located industry could not survive both regulation of freight rates and union-imposed wage and hour stabilization, adamantly resisted unionization. In control of county politics, they used privately paid mine guards to bar union organizers from entering the county and to disrupt local union rallies. They also exercised their control of employment and relief funds to deter miners from joining the union and to break strikes. Within weeks after passage of the National Industrial Recovery Act in 1933, the United Mine Workers of America had organized 92 percent of the country's coal miners; but for six long years thereafter, the powerful Harlan County coal operators fought John L. Lewis's union to a stalemate.

In a county that during the peaceful and prosperous twenties had produced the highest homicide rate of any rural county in the United States, the ensuing struggle between union miners and the operators resulted in thirteen deaths and shocked the national conscience. After deputy sheriffs had ransacked her miner's shack in search of either her union husband or radical literature, Florence Reece ripped a sheet off her calendar and angrily scrawled her view of the struggle. Her outcry, "Which Side Are You On?," became one of the most enduring protest songs born of the labor struggles of the thirties:

> If you go to Harlan County
> There is no neutral there.
> You'll either be a union man
> Or a thug for J. H. Blair.
>
> Which side are you on?
> Which side are you on?

Having established beachheads in neighboring Bell County, Kentucky, and Jellico, Tennessee, the United Mine Workers, between 1931 and 1937, launched four unsuccessful invasions of Harlan County. Finally, between 1937 and 1939, the national government decisively intervened to open the county to successful organization, to create a new balance of economic and political power, to increase the dimensions of labor's civil liberties, and to achieve twenty years of industrial peace. The extent of the national government's involvement in Harlan County provides a unique opportunity to observe in microcosm the practical workings of the entire New Deal labor policy.

Which Side Are You On? tells how Harlan was organized and analyzes the causes of the miners' conversion to unionism, of the retardation of local unionism, of the strenuous opposition of the coal operators, of the persistent efforts by the union to organize the field, of the ensuing violence, and of the ultimate success of the union. While focusing central attention upon the union campaigns, the study deals with the political, economic, and social forces that affected unionism and that were, in turn, affected by it. I hope that the human element—hunger, despair, fear, greed, religious faith, and violence—has been sharpened, rather than obscured, by the union focus.

Finally, the study attempts to separate fact from myth and reality from rhetoric, no easy task in a controversy so rich in myth, song, and legend. Until the recent excellent but brief accounts by Tony Bubka, Theodore Draper, F. Ray Marshall, and George Tindall, public knowledge of Harlan's labor-management relations rested primarily upon two propagandistic documents: Theodore Dreiser's *Harlan Miners Speak* and the reports of the La Follette Civil Liberties Committee. Since people act as often upon myth as upon reality, misinformation about the past can do great contemporary harm. Modern industrialists still shun what they believe to be Harlan County's excessively militant and troublesome labor force, thereby casting a pall upon the county's present and future. Neither the tough talk of old union men nor the enduring silence of surviving operators has helped dispel the "bloody" image of Harlan. If, as some believe, violence thrives upon a violent tradition, a more accurate understanding of and a new perspective on Harlan's past may contribute to a more peaceful and prosperous future. Thus far, as Barbara Kopple's documentary film, *Harlan County, U.S.A.*, so poignantly demonstrates, there have been no happy endings in Harlan County.

Acknowledgments

A scholar incurs numerous debts that unfortunately can be repaid only by a warm expression of appreciation. The late Professor Foster Rhea Dulles of Ohio State University first aroused my interest in labor history, and Professor Glenn Miller of Wichita State University enthusiastically cultivated that interest. Professor Robert H. Bremner of the Ohio State University focused my attention on Harlan County and patiently guided the study through the dissertation stage. In addition to their knowledge and wisdom, all three offered warm and continued friendship. Professor David Brody of the University of California at Davis steered me to several rewarding sources, and he, Professor Donald Sofchalk of Mankato State University, Professor Warren Van Tine of the Ohio State University, and Professor Richard Stites of Georgetown University read the manuscript and offered numerous valuable suggestions for improvement in both style and interpretation. Professor David Overy of Saint Cloud State University, Professor David Walker of the University of Northern Iowa, and Patricia Rohrbaugh read the manuscript for style and offered many helpful suggestions.

Grants from the Graduate School at the Ohio State University and Mankato State University facilitated my research in the manuscript collections. Archivists at the State Historical Society of Wisconsin, Indiana University, the University of

Virginia, West Virginia University, the University of Pennsylvania, the Ford Archive at Dearborn, Michigan, and especially Joseph D. Howerton at the National Archives and Moreau B. C. Chambers at the Catholic University of America were most helpful. The efficient and cooperative interlibrary loan staffs at the Ohio State University, the University of Kentucky, and the University of Tennessee speeded and eased the newspaper research. The *Knoxville News-Sentinel* and the Louisville *Courier-Journal* generously shared with me the contents of their photographic archives. The late George Titler, whose successful organizing campaign in Harlan County ultimately propelled him to the vice-presidency of the United Mine Workers of America, unselfishly shared with me his then-unpublished account of his Harlan County experience, "Hell in Harlan."

Richard Wentworth and Judith McCulloh of the University of Illinois Press generously encouraged, guided, and assisted throughout the project. Several typists, most notably Helen Sofchalk of Mankato, Minnesota, and Katherine Bigelow and Judy Von Blon of Lima, Ohio, worked quickly and efficiently to help me meet various deadlines.

All of the above contributed greatly to the book's merits. I, alone, am responsible for its flaws.

Finally, I express my deepest gratitude to my wife, Mary, and to my children, John and Anne, who sacrificed much to make this study possible.

Chapter *1*

Harlan's Industrial Revolution

1911-31

For nearly a century after its founding in 1819, Harlan County, Kentucky, lay shrouded in an isolation unique even among Southern Appalachian coal counties. Located just north of historic Cumberland Gap, where southeastern Kentucky bounds Virginia and Tennessee, the county is tucked away in a narrow valley between the Pine and Black mountains, both ranges of the rugged Cumberlands. The mountainous terrain rises from 1,200 feet at the county seat, Harlan, to 4,260 feet atop Benham Spur, Kentucky's loftiest peak. Three headwaters of the Cumberland River—Clover Fork, Poor Fork, and Martin's Fork—geographically divide the county. Save for primitive wagon trails from Hagen, Virginia, and Pineville, in neighboring Bell County, no railroad or highway penetrated the secluded valley until 1910, when the Louisville & Nashville Railroad extended a spur line into Harlan. Not until 1928 did the first automobile enter the county. Because of its isolated location, the county remains a land of mystery to many modern residents of the Bluegrass, and certainly in the 1930s it retained a foreboding air of being a law unto itself.

Although Harlan's abundant timber and coal resources were discovered as early as 1750,[1] industrial development was delayed until the last decade of the nineteenth century. Despite the rugged terrain and marginal soil, until 1911 subsistence

1

agriculture remained almost the sole basis of the county's economy. Ginseng, yellow root, and furs were bartered for labor and supplies, and acorn-fattened hogs were driven to distant markets to pay for salt, almost the sole import. Local carpenters and itinerant cobblers fashioned furniture and shoes from home-grown raw materials, and housewives wove fabric for clothing from homespun woolen yarn. In 1848, an eastern traveler contrasted the county's wealth of resources with the poverty of her people, who were "attempting to force from nature products that are not hers to give."[2] By 1890, the county's rigorous and unrewarding environment had attracted only six thousand inhabitants.

Social and political life was as primitive and provincial as the economy. Marital alliances were often arranged between large and locally prominent families. Prior to the wedding, neighborhood men gathered to "raise" a house, and their wives showered the couple with homemade quilts. A local midwife delivered the couple's children, and "natural" doctors treated the family's illnesses with herbs and home remedies. Fundamentalist sects of the Pentecostal Holiness, Baptist, and Methodist churches were most popular; their "speakin's," frequently lasting eight hours, were well attended. The fatalistic and religious mountaineers stoically attributed poverty, illness, and death to "the Lord's will." As a result of the mountain region's antislavery and Unionist tradition, until the Great Depression county politics were staunchly Whig and then Republican; contests between rival Republicans were usually decided by the number of votes a candidate could command from family connections.[3]

During the 1890s, lumbermen began to exploit the county's most accessible tracts of timber. Four lumber companies purchased several thousand acres of timber land bordering the Cumberland River and its tributaries and floated logs to their Pineville and Williamsburg mills. After the railroad's arrival in 1910, additional local mills expanded the lumbering industry; yet as late as 1938, more than one hundred thousand acres of virgin timber remained unharvested. By the turn of the century, the demand for loggers, buyers, and surveyors had increased Harlan's population to ten thousand, where it remained until 1910, on the eve of the county's coal boom. But Harlan's seclusion remained undisturbed.

During the first decade of the twentieth century, native and northeastern entrepreneurs laid the foundations for Harlan's later development. James Eads founded a weekly booster newspaper, the *Harlan Enterprise,* which in 1928 began daily publication. A. B. Cornett and Judge W. W. Lewis, along with Massachusetts businessman Charles Henry Davis, organized the First State Bank, and local investors established a telephone company. In 1902, the heirs of Philadelphia businessman Edward M. Davis, who in 1870 had purchased eighty-six thousand acres of coal and timber land in Harlan and Bell counties, inaugurated a geological survey and formed the Kentenia Corporation to clear title to the property through a series of civil suits. In 1910, Kentenia enlisted the aid of influential local citizens in petitioning the Louisville & Nashville Railroad to enter Harlan County. The rapid development of one of the nation's major coal fields was thus assured, and Kentenia shared the benefits. In the 1930s, the corporation owned thirty-eight thousand Harlan County acres, seventeen thousand of them covered with virgin timber, and leased coal properties to several of the county's largest operators.[4]

The railroad's arrival ushered in the rapid development of the county's coal industry. From 1911, when three new mines produced 17,860 tons of bituminous coal worth $21,000, the mining industry quickly expanded until 1928, when fifty-nine mines produced nearly 14,500,000 tons valued at $25,531,000. On the eve of the Great Depression, previously impoverished Harlan ranked among Kentucky's three or four wealthiest counties. The county's population tripled during the coal boom's first decade, from ten thousand in 1910 to thirty-one thousand in 1920, and then doubled in the next decade, to sixty-four thousand by 1930. Between 1911 and 1930, the number of employed miners expanded from 169 to 11,920; but because the miners were largely recruited from the surrounding mountainous counties of Kentucky, Virginia, and Tennessee, the county's population retained a remarkable homogeneity. In 1930, 90 percent of the county's 64,557 residents were native-born whites; only 9 percent were black; and 1 percent were foreign-born whites. Many of the 5,879 blacks and nearly all of the 822 immigrants lived at United States Steel Corporation's large camp at Lynch. Thus, even during its population explosion, Harlan County attracted largely its own kind. The late-comers introduced few alien ideas or customs, and the county's isolated provincialism remained intact.

Prior to the Great Depression, the rapid expansion of Harlan's coal industry rested largely on three factors: high-quality coal, low in sulphur and ash content, which found a ready market as a special-purpose coal; the absence of union-ism, which permitted uninterrupted operation, a lower wage scale, and nonunion work rules; and, until 1929, a more favorable freight rate structure than thereafter prevailed.

The special characteristics of its coal and the absence of unionism induced several corporate giants to develop in Harlan captive mines whose entire output, rather than being sold on the commercial market, was utilized by the parent company's manufacturing or power-generating plants. Between 1911 and 1920, International Harvester, Koppers Company, Detroit-Edison, United States Steel Corporation, Peabody Coal Cor-poration, Insull, and Ford Motor Company opened ten subsidiary mines in the county.[5] In 1920, after Henry Ford began producing his own iron ore and steel, he found it ad-vantageous to produce his own coke. Commercial coke price fluctuations frequently cost the company dearly, railroad car shortages and labor strikes often interrupted coal supply, and Ford was unable to obtain a dependable supply of uniform-quality coking coal. The company's blast furnaces and foundries required a metallurgical coal that was low in sulphur and ash content and hard and strong-bodied enough to support the charge of ore while the air blast passed through freely. Ford also preferred drift or horizontal mines to deep or vertical-shaft mines because their superior ventilation made the formation of gas pockets, and consequently explosions, less likely and be-cause transportation costs from mine to tipple were lessened by the absence of an uphill haul. Because Harlan's drift mines offered all these advantages, in 1920 the Ford Motor Company purchased the first two of its fifteen coal mines from the Banner Fork Coal Corporation at Wallins Creek, in Harlan County.[6]

Similar advantages lured other firms to develop mining subsidiaries there, and throughout the 1920s and 1930s, such captive mines produced about three-eighths of Harlan's output.[7]

Because of the absence of union pressure and competition from high-wage manufacturing employment, Harlan wages were lower and more flexible than in most other coal fields. In 1922, when the United Mine Workers was still powerful throughout the northern coal fields, Harlan coal loaders earned 42 percent less per day than an Illinois miner, 35 percent less than an Indiana miner, 24 percent less than an Ohio miner, and 5 percent less than a Pennsylvania miner. Much of the northern miners' advantage was dissipated after 1927, when the northern operators abrogated the Jacksonville Agreement; but in 1929, Harlan's coal loaders still earned 32 percent less per day than an Illinois or Indiana miner, 2 percent less than a Pennsylvania miner, and 3 percent more than an Ohio miner.[8] Because labor costs accounted for about 70 percent of production costs,[9] Harlan operators could offset their higher freight costs with lower wages and thus undersell their northern competitors.

Regular running time was another important cost advantage in the highly competitive coal industry. During the 1920s, while production and running time steadily dwindled in the northern union fields, both mounted in Harlan. The Harlan miners' number of days worked rose from 105 days in 1922, to 209 in 1924, to 259 in both 1926 and 1929. The absence of strikes increased running time and ensured renewal of sales contracts as well. Steady operation redounded to the advantage of both the operator, who enjoyed lower operating costs, and the Harlan miner, whose annual income, despite lower daily earnings, mounted from approximately $578 in 1922 to $1,235 in 1929.[10] Regularity of nonunion operation constituted one main reason for the operators' and many miners' opposition to unionization of their field.

Despite some earlier union success in United Mine Workers District 19, which included Tennessee and five counties in southeastern Kentucky, mining in Harlan began in a nonunion era. A 1907 union contract signed with a majority of District 19's operators was abrogated by them in 1910, and by the eve of World War I, the district's union membership of five thousand had dwindled to forty-eight. The first brief interlude of Harlan County unionism was largely the product of government fiat. During World War I, the demand for coal, a mine-labor shortage, and the Wilson administration's encouragement gave impetus to coal-field unionism. In the spring of 1917, Van A. Bittner, William Turnblazer, Sr., David Robb, and William Feeney recruited fifteen hundred Harlan miners into three UMW locals. When local operators refused to recognize the union, in August, 1917, most county mines were closed by a strike. In view of the wartime crisis, National Fuel Administrator Harry Garfield summoned representatives of the Harlan operators and the union to Washington, D.C., to negotiate a settlement. While the operators refused to recognize the union, they agreed to a wage increase, a shorter workday, election of checkweighmen, and establishment of mine committees to adjudicate local grievances. On October 8, pending final agreement on wages and hours, work resumed; on November 1, the two parties signed a final agreement, which would terminate at the war's end. By July, 1918, Harlan mines were solidly organized with the exception of two giant captive firms: Wisconsin Steel Company, International Harvester's subsidiary at Benham, and U.S. Coal & Coke Corporation, U.S. Steel's subsidiary at Lynch.[11]

Never having officially recognized the union, the powerful Harlan operators had no intention of long suffering its interference once the war ended. Simultaneously, the union's district dissipated its strength. On March 1, 1919, District 19 miners elected as president S. A. Keller, who had been a union member only six months. Keller's administration threw the district into conflict with the international organizers assigned to the field, exhausted the district's treasury, and plunged it heavily into debt. The union was ill prepared to confront the hostile coal operators.[12]

On November 1, 1919, the United Mine Workers called a nationwide strike, which ended on December 12 when both sides agreed to arbitration by the Bituminous Coal Commission. In March, 1920, the commission awarded the miners a two-year contract that provided for a forty-eight-hour week and a 27 percent wage increase. In Harlan County, thirty-nine hundred union members halted 60 percent of the county's production and closed all major mines except those of Wisconsin Steel Company and U.S. Coal & Coke Corporation. The Harlan operators, however, rejected the national award, removed the checkweighmen from their tipples, refused to deduct union dues, discharged and evicted union miners,[13] and raised wages four cents per ton above the union scale for loaders and thirty-five cents to one dollar per day above the union's daily wage scale.[14] Finally, on August 13, 1920, national organizer Van A. Bittner induced the Harlan County Coal Operators' Association to sign a contract, but it proved completely unsatisfactory to local rank-and-file unionists, who charged that it paved the way for expulsion of the union from the Harlan field. The agreement did not cover powerful nonmembers of the operators' association such as Ford, Wisconsin Steel, and U.S. Coal & Coke, and covered only those mines where a majority of miners clearly wished to work under it. The contract did not provide for union recognition; it called for election of checkweighmen in open meetings at the mine mouth rather than by secret ballot in closed meeting at the union hall and established a daily wage scale between thirty-five cents and a dollar lower than the prevailing Harlan scale. The contract seemed to offer the union nothing more than a remaining toehold in Harlan County; and the miners, who perceived no advantage in it, forced the transfer of Bittner to Maryland.[15] In 1922, when the agreement expired, a feeble strike curtailed local production by only 21 percent and failed to win a union agreement. Except at Black Mountain Coal Corporation, union-management relations in Harlan County essentially ended with the war.[16]

In 1924, the last vestige of unionism was driven from the county when the Black Mountain Coal Corporation, a Peabody Coal Corporation subsidiary, abrogated its union contract and destroyed that nine-hundred-member local union. A year earlier, officials of the parent company had ordered Black Mountain's superintendent to terminate his union agreement unless other county mines were organized. When the agreement expired on March 31, 1924, the local union struck; but on September 1, the company discharged, evicted, and black-listed forty-two union miners, among them all the officers and committeemen of the local union. The company then surrounded its property with fifteen private mine guards and resumed operation as an open shop. Many former Black Mountain unionists left the county in search of employment, but a few remained at the incorporated town of Evarts, near Black Mountain's camp, where they retained membership in UMW Local 5355, a recruiting local without a single contractual relationship.[17] Only this tiny nucleus of unionism survived—to become the storm center of labor agitation in 1931.

In 1923, and again in 1926, organizers attempted to revive unionism in Harlan County, but in both campaigns they were quickly expelled from the area by operator-controlled county officials. In the latter campaign, Sheriff George S. Ward, concurrently employed as assistant secretary of the Harlan County Coal Operators' Association, drove the organizers from the county. In 1927, a third organizing effort recruited one thousand members and briefly established locals at nearly every county mine, but later the same year, the campaign had to be abandoned. During 1929–30, the Harlan miners supported national government regulation of their declining industry, the policy then being advocated by the now nearly defunct UMW. But only after the Great Depression resulted in severe unemployment and underemployment and after the first drastic wage reduction in February, 1931, did local miners mount a sustained effort to rebuild their union.[18]

The coal operators and miners were jointly responsible for the elimination of local unionism. Handicapped by disadvantageous fixed transportation costs, the operators fiercely resisted any attempt by either the union or the federal government to achieve an industry-wide standard for wages and hours as well. The Harlan operators viewed unionism as a northern conspiracy to destroy the southern coal industry. The archconspirators, they believed, were the northern coal operators who, saddled with union wages and hours, sought to utilize the Interstate Commerce Commission to obtain a freight-rate advantage for themselves and who also encouraged the northern-based United

Mine Workers to organize the southern coal fields to standard-
ize wages and hours. If unable to organize the South, the UMW
could periodically agitate labor disturbances. Either higher
wages or strikes would cause southern operators to lose sales
contracts to their northern competitors. Thus, caught in a vise
between higher freight rates and standardized wages and
hours, the southern coal industry would face liquidation.[19]
Local operators rhetorically justified their antiunionism to their
employees with the argument that nonunion southern miners
could profit from northern union work stoppages. Northern
strikes would result in increased production, regular employment, and, consequently, higher annual earnings in the South.
Harlan operators also warned their miners that union efforts
to organize southern workers were solely motivated by a
hunger for additional dues payments.[20]

During the 1920s, Harlan miners generally prospered. While
daily wages and working conditions gradually eroded, running
time and annual earnings increased. At the same time, the
almost certain prospect of discharge, eviction, and blacklisting
in retaliation for union activity acted as a powerful deterrent
to organization. Many earlier unionists were disillusioned with
the union's response to the post–World War I situation. Re-
inforcing this was the psychology of the typical Harlan miner.
A first-generation industrial worker drawn from the impoverished hillside farms of the surrounding region, he possessed a
fiercely independent spirit and had not yet accepted the idea
of permanent working-class status. The new housing and bus-
tling activity of the coal camp was superior to the isolated
mountain cabin he had fled. His desertion of a hillside farm
had decidedly enhanced his economic fortune. Economically
unsophisticated, he could not comprehend that increased production of cheap southern coal would glut the already saturated
coal market, undermine union strength in the North, hasten
the depression of the entire coal industry, and ultimately bring
unemployment and substandard wages home to Harlan. Not
until he experienced firsthand the impact of the Great Depression with deteriorating work conditions, inadequate wages,
and severe unemployment resulting from economic forces

beyond the control of either himself or his paternalistic employer would the Harlan County miner be prepared to join the union.

While the Harlan operators were able to stave off the union's conquest of county miners until 1937, just prior to the Depression they lost the sectional battle over freight rates. Harlan County's geography proved both an asset and a liability. Blessed with abundant high-quality coal reserves, the county was at the same time plagued by the absence of local, industrial markets for its coal and by its distance from major industrial centers. During World War I, the Interstate Commerce Commission had stimulated southern coal production by imposing only a minimal freight-rate differential on southern shippers, an advantage that Harlan producers enjoyed right up to the eve of the Depression. Throughout the 1920s, despite an energetic mechanization program, northern coal producers, burdened with higher union wage scales and frequent strikes, relinquished a steadily increasing share of the national coal market to their southern competitors. In 1927, the United Mine Workers, whose strength was concentrated solely in the northern coal fields, joined Illinois, Ohio, and Pennsylvania coal producers in successfully petitioning the ICC for a larger North-South freight-rate differential. On January 1, 1929, the Harlan operators' rate differential was increased from twenty-five to thirty-five cents per ton.[21]

After 1929, the deterioration of its wage advantage over northern producers, the hike in southern freight rates, and the Great Depression combined to disrupt Harlan's steady industrial progress. Production plunged from 1929's 14,093,453 tons worth $24,432,000 to 9,338,951 tons valued at $13,598,000 in 1931. Although work-sharing permitted Harlan mines to employ a record 11,920 miners in 1930, nevertheless, over the two-year period 1929–31, employment fell from 10,831 to 9,932, days worked from 259 to 175, average daily wages from $4.77 to $4.28, and average annual earnings from $1,235 to $749.[22]

Low wages, irregular employment, and unemployment quickly brought poverty, hunger, and disease in their wake. By March, 1931, a Knoxville coal operator who owned mines in

Harlan County reported that "conditions are bad. . . . The miners' families are still able to eat and keep warm, but I don't pretend that they are living as they ought to live." [23] Fred C. Croxton, district representative of the President's Emergency Employment Commission, visited Harlan and discovered that "conditions were deplorable," the miners having little more than shelter and fuel.[24] A visiting federal labor conciliator discovered a "distressful condition" accompanied by widespread despair because miners were unable to properly feed their families.[25] The number of children dying of malnutrition-induced diseases mounted from fifty-six in 1929 to ninety-one in drought- and Depression-stricken 1930 and eighty-four in depressed 1931.[26] Had it not been for the American Friends Service Committee's child-feeding program launched in the fall of 1931, the latter figure would have been far higher.

When these conditions were further aggravated by a 10 percent wage reduction on February 16, 1931, local miners decided that they "might just as well die fighting as die of starvation." [27] They launched a decade-long struggle for unionization of their county to resist deterioration of working and living conditions and to redress long-standing grievances.

NOTES

1. Willard Rouse Jillson, "A History of the Coal Industry in Kentucky," *Register of the Kentucky State Historical Society*, 20, no. 58 (1922), 25.

2. Herbert Carleton, *Eastern Kentucky News*, Aug. 24, 1894, quoted in John A. Dotson, "Socio-Economic Background and Changing Education in Harlan County, Kentucky" (Ph.D. diss., George Peabody College for Teachers, 1943), p. 20.

3. John H. Fenton, *Politics in the Border States* (New Orleans, 1957), pp. 23–24.

4. This discussion of preindustrial Harlan County is primarily based on Elmon Middleton, *Harlan County, Kentucky* (Big Laurel, Va., 1934), pp. 43–53; Dotson, "Education in Harlan County," pp. 15–23; and Mabel Green Condon, *A History of Harlan County* (Nashville, 1962), pp. 132–44.

5. U.S., Congress, Senate, Committee on Manufactures, *Conditions in Coal Fields in Harlan and Bell Counties, Kentucky, Hearings* on S.R. 178, 72 Cong., 1 sess. (1932), addendum (hereafter cited as *Conditions in Coal Fields*); minutes of the meeting of the Board of Directors, Banner Fork Coal Corporation, July 30, 1920, Henry Ford Museum, Ford Archive, Banner Fork Coal Corporation Corporate Record, pp. 77–78.

6. Ford Motor Company, *The Ford Industries: Facts about the Ford Motor Company and Its Subsidiaries* (Detroit, 1924), pp. 73, 77.

7. U.S., Congress, Senate, Committee on Education and Labor, *Violations of Free Speech and Rights of Labor, Hearings* on S.R. 266, 75 Cong., 1 sess. (1937), pt. 10, Exhibit 1175, p. 3655. These are the La Follette Committee hearings, hereafter cited as LFCH.

8. U.S., Dept. of Labor, Bureau of Labor Statistics, *Hours and Earnings in Bituminous Coal Mining: 1929*, Bulletin no. 516 (May, 1930), p. 27.

9. Albert Pearce, "The Growth and Overdevelopment of the Kentucky Coal Industry, 1912–1929" (M.A. thesis, University of Kentucky, 1930), n.p.

10. For 1922: 105 days x $5.51 average daily wage = $578; for 1929: 259 days x $4.77 daily wage = $1,235; testimony of Howard N. Eavenson, *Conditions in Coal Fields*, p. 212.

11. George J. Titler, *Hell in Harlan* (Beckley, W.Va., n.d.), pp. 3–7; telegram, John P. White to Van A. Bittner, Sept. 24, [1917?], Van Amberg Bittner Papers, West Virginia University.

12. Titler, *Hell in Harlan*, p. 7; Frank Walters to Bittner, Aug. 4, 1920; John L. Lewis to Bittner, Aug. 6, 1920, Bittner Papers.

13. Titler, *Hell in Harlan*, pp. 7–10; Walters to Lewis, June 1, 1920, Bittner Papers.

14. Walters to Bittner, May 21, 1920; E. L. Reed to Bittner, Sept. 15, 1920, Bittner Papers. Contrary to the letters from union officials in the Harlan field asserting that the question of a union contract was complicated by the fact that Fordson Coal Company had raised loaders' wages by 4¢ per ton and daily wages by $1.00 per day and that the Harlan firms in general had raised daily wages between 35¢ and $1.00 per day, George Titler contends that Harlan operators slashed wages by 27 to 30 percent (*Hell in Harlan*, p. 10).

15. S. A. Keller to Lewis, Aug. 13, 1920; Keller to Bittner, Sept. 30, 1920; Lewis to Bittner, Aug. 6, 1920, Bittner Papers.

16. Titler, *Hell in Harlan*, p. 10.

17. Ibid., pp. 11–12.

18. Ibid., pp. 14–19.

19. Editorial, *Pineville* (Ky.) *Sun*, Apr. 23, 1931; editorials, *Courier-Journal* (Louisville, Ky.), May 7, July 4, 1931; editorial, *Cincinnati Enquirer*, reprinted in *Pineville Sun*, May 14, 1931.

20. Charles Barnes to Richard Brown, Feb. 21, 1935, U.S., National Archives, Record Group 9, National Recovery Administration, Bituminous Coal Labor Board, Division no. 1—South, Correspondence File; Resolution, James Westmoreland, Mar. 17, 1934, National Archives, Record Group 9, National Recovery Administration, Bituminous Coal Labor Board, Division no. 1—South, Case Files, Case no. 373; editorials, *Pineville Sun*, Jan. 2, 1936, Jan. 7, Feb. 18, 1937. These National Archives Record Groups are hereafter cited as NA, RG/9, NRA, BCLB.

21. Pearce, "Growth and Overdevelopment," n.p.; editorial, *Courier-Journal*, July 4, 1931.

22. U.S., Dept. of Labor, Bureau of Labor Statistics, "Wages and Hours of Labor," *Monthly Labor Review*, 33 (Oct., 1931), 914; for 1929: 259 days x $4.77 average wage = $1,235; for 1931: 175 days x

$4.28 average daily wage = $749. A 1931 study by the Harlan County Coal Operators' Association of miners' earnings at nine commercial mines showed average annual earnings of $777; see testimony of Eavenson, *Conditions in Coal Fields,* p. 199. The operators' figure of $777 differs slightly from the Bureau of Labor Statistics' figure of $749 because the bureau's figure covers only coal loaders for the entire state of Kentucky, whereas the operators' figure covers only nine Harlan County mines and includes some more highly skilled and higher-paid employees.

23. *Knoxville* (Tenn.) *News-Sentinel,* Mar. 1, 1931. The unidentified coal operator was probably Edward C. Mahan.

24. *Courier-Journal,* Apr. 4, 1931.

25. U.S. conciliation commissioner to Hugh L. Kerwin, Mar. 10, 1931, U.S., National Archives, Record Group 280, Federal Mediation and Conciliation Service, "Coal Miners (Southeastern Ky.) Pineville, Ky.," Box 294 (hereafter cited as NA, RG/280; other National Archives record groups will be similarly cited).

26. Testimony of Arthur T. McCormack, *Conditions in Coal Fields,* p. 157.

27. William Turnblazer, circular letter in U.S., Congress, House, *Congressional Record,* 71 Cong., 3 sess. (1931), vol. 74, pp. 4069–70.

Chapter 2

Unsettled People

The Harlan miners' struggle for unionization in the 1930s was both an attempt to remedy unsatisfactory working conditions and a miners' revolt against the Harlan mine owners' arbitrary economic, political, and social power. The *Cincinnati Enquirer*'s Kentucky correspondent, Wilmer G. Mason, a perceptive but conservative journalist by whose values the Harlan operators wished to be judged, thought that Harlan miners, in the 1930s, faced three basic problems: the uneconomic nature of their coal field, the mine owners' political control of the county, and the coal companies' monopoly of miners' housing that had evolved into a powerful social control. In Mason's opinion, trade unionism offered no solution to any of these essential problems. Union leaders, however, stressed especially their intention and their ability to change the coal operators' paternalistic political and social control, a paternalism that stifled the miners' independent thought and free expression. The union sought to "free the miners from an archaic system in which liberty has no place." [1]

Early in the county's two-decade transformation from an isolated agrarian community of ten thousand inhabitants into an interdependent, semiurban, industrial society of sixty-four thousand persons, the new coal barons wrested political control from the family factions that had ruled during the county's agrarian era. First, the mine owners assumed control of town government. The operators housed the influx of new miners and their families, 61 percent of the county's population, in unincorporated company towns ranging in size from a few dozen souls to ten thousand residents at Lynch. The mine superintendent governed these camps and policed them with deputy sheriffs who were appointed and commissioned by the county sheriff and county judge but paid and controlled by the mine superintendent. The coal operators also chose the precinct committeemen from these camps, which allowed them to exert a powerful control over both county party organizations.[2]

The coal operators also had a vital interest in numerous functions of county government: the assessment of property for taxation purposes, the levying of property taxes, the location of county and state highways, the county court's execution of eviction proceedings against occupants of company houses, the circuit court's criminal prosecutions during labor disputes, the sheriff's enforcement of the law, and the sheriff's and county judge's appointment of deputy sheriffs.

Formed in 1916, the Harlan County Coal Operators' Association, including all major local firms except U.S. Coal & Coke and Wisconsin Steel, greatly facilitated the operators' political takeover of county government. After 1932, the association's secretary, George S. Ward, served as chairman of the dominant Republican party. Robert Tway, a former president and the most active member of the association, served for a time as state Republican chairman. When the Democratic party finally emerged as a strong contender for public offices by 1936, association president S. J. Dickenson was chosen county Democratic chairman. During the Democratic governorships of Ruby Laffoon and Albert B. Chandler (1931–39), Herbert Smith, who leased coal properties to Harlan operators, emerged as county Democratic boss and a statewide political power.[3] As a long-time county politician explained, "The coal operators have a hell of a lot of influence in the elections. If they are not for you, it is too bad. . . . They want to build up the community so long as it does not cross their interest. The labor question is the only touchy point." [4]

In the process of gaining and retaining political control, the coal barons and their allies corrupted the political process.

Votes were bought, ballot boxes were stuffed and stolen, and fraudulent returns were submitted. Harlan's entire 1931 gubernatorial vote was invalidated because of irregularities in Harlan-Wallins Coal Corporation's camp at Verda. During the next gubernatorial election, Governor Laffoon thrice dispatched the National Guard to Harlan to prevent an expected attempt to steal the election. A special circuit court judge invalidated the county's 1937 election for sheriff, county attorney, coroner, and jailor because of widespread irregularities practiced by both parties. A federal district court convicted forty-four county election officials of fraud in connection with the 1942 United States senatorial election.[5] These incidents are but a few examples of the political corruption so common in the county. Republican county chairman George Ward explained how the coal operators retained political control. "They [the miners] never have stuck together. They can always be bought by the side that has the most money."[6] In this single-industry county, no one doubted who could afford the luxury of political dominance.

During the labor struggles of the 1930s, most county officials were allied with the mine owners. Sheriff John Henry Blair (1930–33) publicly asserted that, during the strikes of 1931–32, "I did all in my power to aid the coal operators."[7] A state investigatory commission reported in 1931 that Blair's deputies, among them numerous coal-company officials, antiunion partisans, and men with criminal records, had enforced the law "in a lawless manner in Harlan County."[8]

Coal miners helped elect Blair's successor, Theodore Roosevelt Middleton (1934–37), who promised to reform the deputy sheriff system and to give union organizers and members equal protection under the law. Once elected, however, several antiunion coal operators posted his official bonds, and while in office, he greatly increased his personal fortune and acquired five coal mines and an interest in a coal-camp commissary and a leased coal property. Thereafter, he exerted the full power of his office to prevent unionization of the county's mines. His running mate on the reform ticket, County Judge Morris Saylor, became a partner with the sheriff and an antiunion operator in the commissary and coal-land leasing venture and commis-

sioned all the sheriff's deputy appointments.[9] Among their 169
deputy appointees were sixty-four indicted and thirty-seven
convicted felons and several notorious enemies of the union.[10]
All but a handful of these deputies were paid by the coal
operators, stationed on their property, and controlled by them.

The operators used the deputies, for one thing, to exclude
union organizers from company property. Howard N. Eavenson, owner of Clover Splint Coal Company and one of Harlan's
fairest operators, used his deputies to expel "outside agitators"
from his company camp, Closplint. Asked by a Senate committee to define those subject to expulsion, he explained that
Harlan operators ran open shops and defined as an agitator
anyone "who comes in there and tries to get them to do it some
other way." [11] Beyond that, Sheriff Middleton, the Harlan
County Coal Operators' Association's chief deputy Ben Unthank, or another of the sheriff's trusted deputies organized
the deputies into roving gangs that barred union organizers
from entering the county and disrupted miners' meetings. By
Sheriff Middleton's fourth month in office, a county grand jury
noted that, since the first of the year, "in practically every
homicide which has occurred in Harlan County . . . , officers
figured prominently." [12] A 1935 state investigatory commission
reported that "in Harlan County there exists a virtual reign
of terror, financed in general by a group of coal mine operators
in collusion with certain public officials; the victims of this
reign of terror are the coal miners. . . . *There is no doubt* that
Theodore Middleton, sheriff of Harlan County, is in league with
the operators and is using many of his deputies to carry out
his purposes." [13] The sheriffs and their privately paid deputies
formed the keystone of the operators' resistance to unionism,
and until the private deputy system was abolished in 1938, the
United Mine Workers devoted a major share of its effort to
ridding Harlan County of this archaic institution.

Miners suspected that the coal barons controlled the courts
as well. Davy Crockett Jones, Harlan County circuit court
judge (1928–33), was married to the former Nellie Hall, part-
owner of Three Point Coal Company. Commonwealth's Attorney W. A. Brock (1928–33) instructed a 1931 jury to "put
the cold chills of steel down the backs of the criminal element

in this county," by which he was assumed to mean the union element. Brock's successor, Daniel Boone Smith (1934–45), received $2,100 in annual retainer fees from Harlan-Wallins Coal Corporation, Mary Helen Coal Corporation, and R. C. Tway Coal Company while serving as prosecutor. While their connections did not necessarily prohibit these officials from rendering evenhanded justice, they greatly impaired the public's belief in their integrity. Because the miners rented company houses and paid no property taxes, they were barred from jury service. Grand and petit juries were therefore dominated by coal-company officials, merchants, and farmers. Perjury and bribery and intimidation of witnesses frequently marred the administration of justice, and miners were often afraid or believed it futile to testify before local juries.[14] Their readiness to carry their case outside Harlan County, to testify before a state commission, a United States Senate committee, or a federal district court, attests to the miners' conviction that justice was unattainable at home.

Via their ownership of the unincorporated company towns that housed nearly two-thirds of the county's population, the mine owners exerted a powerful combination of economic, political, and social control over the lives of miners and their families.

Some miners had little quarrel with the physical aspects of company houses or with rents. Because Harlan was a newly developed field and its large rail mines were fairly permanent in nature, the county's company housing was generally superior to that found in competitive fields. Harlan-Wallins's largest camp, Verda, an average Harlan mining community, was considered superior to coal towns in the adjacent Hazard, Kentucky, field and in the Southern Appalachian field to the south. Because of the unavailability of level land, the typical company house was built on a hillside. Set on a wooden post foundation, it had a weatherboarded, regularly painted exterior. Interior walls and ceilings, though occasionally plastered, were usually finished with wallboard or wood. Each room was lighted by a single electric drop cord suspended from the ceiling. An outdoor hydrant, one for each six or eight families, supplied water. Toilet facilities consisted of an outdoor privy. The company furnished free water, collected the garbage, cleaned the privies, and repaired and painted the houses. These three- to five-room houses rented for two dollars per room per month, less than half the amount charged for comparable housing in the county's incorporated communities. The median monthly rental for the county's 8,779 nonfarm homes in 1930 was under ten dollars.[15]

A few Harlan camps, such as Lynch and Closplint, offered accommodations far above average for the nation's coal fields. All three hundred houses at Closplint, the county's newest camp, were plastered and contained bathrooms. The town lit its streets and provided fire hydrants and an excellent sewage system. Because of its superior accommodations, the company charged $2.50 monthly rental per room. Lynch offered tree-lined streets, a company movie theater, and a company store that was reputed to be eastern Kentucky's best department store.[16]

A few Harlan mining camps were primitive slums, where two-room, unpainted shacks housed as many as ten or twelve people. A nearby mountain spring or creek furnished the only water supply, and the roads and yards were strewn with garbage. Such camps usually furnished free electricity and rented their houses for one or two dollars per month.[17]

The county's provisions for sanitation, disease prevention, and health care were generally poor. Only the four incorporated towns and a few larger company towns provided a sewage system, and these generally emptied into small rivers and streams, posing a health hazard. Few of the outdoor privies, though periodically cleaned and disinfected, were sanitary. Most camps provided an adequate supply of water, but few piped it inside the houses. Not until World War II, when more than one-third of Harlan's first draft call-up was rejected because of venereal disease, did Harlan become the last of Kentucky's counties to organize a health department.

Company doctors treated minor illnesses and injuries, but if a patient required hospitalization, the county's two facilities provided only ninety-four beds to serve sixty-four thousand people. When the Great Depression struck, Harlan possessed no county welfare agency, no trained social workers, and no well-established and trusted relief organization. During the 1930s, several meningitis epidemics swept the county, and in the first three years of the Depression, malnutrition-induced diseases killed 231 children.[18]

Although the miners seldom complained of the physical shortcomings of their communities, they rebelled against the mine owners' abuse of property rights and local government to control their lives. The operators fancied themselves as benevolent patriarchs caring for their children; so long as the camp's occupants did not violate the operator's moral code that prohibited prostitution, theft, and, in some camps, drunkenness, and did not flirt with unionism, they provided them a reasonable amount of social security. Residents who either violated moral sanctions or joined the union were discharged and evicted from the camp.[19] The operators closely supervised the goings and comings of their employees and their families. From what appeared to be an innocent tree-house, actually a guardhouse, erected near the only entrance to Verda, Harlan-Wallins's mine guards noted everyone's movements and ejected anyone from company property whose presence could not be satisfactorily explained. In one instance, Deputy Sheriff Bob Eldridge and his son pistol-whipped and marched a job applicant at gunpoint to the nearby railroad depot because he came from adjacent UMW District 30 and was, therefore, assumed to be a union intruder. U.S. Coal & Coke guards expelled a Berea coed from Lynch because her sister's husband was president of the local union. Anyone wishing to drive an automobile into Louellen, Cornett-Lewis's camp, had first to obtain from Superintendent "Uncle Bob" Lawson a key with which to unlock a heavy steel cable stretched across the camp's only entrance. The owners even sought to control residents' thoughts. During the 1931–32 strike crisis, at least seven companies prohibited delivery in their camps of the miners' favorite paper, the *Knoxville News-Sentinel,* because it was critical of the local operators.[20] Partly with company funds and partly with payroll deductions, the mine owners built churches and schools and paid teachers to extend the school term for two months beyond the regular state-supported seven-month term. The operators, however, exercised at least veto power over the selection and retention of both teachers and ministers. Payroll deductions financed burial insurance and medical care, but the mine owner selected the company doctor. In the 1930s, all employees were required to rent a house in one of these tightly controlled camps and, preferably, to live in it. This company monopoly of miners' housing was an abuse the UMW obviously intended to abolish.

Beyond obtaining a voice in wage decisions, union miners sought to abolish various nonunion work practices. After the operators removed union checkweighmen following World War I, and after the Depression intensified pressure on wages, coal loaders frequently complained that some firms short-weighed and thereby underpaid them. The charge was most often leveled at Harlan-Wallins Coal Corporation, where one miner charged that he loaded four- and five-ton cars but was paid for loading two and a half or three tons. A National Recovery Administration code inspector, who as a railroad employee until 1931 had been in a position to check Harlan-Wallins's weights against railroad weights, asserted that the company's scale, by which it paid employees, underweighed its production by three or four thousand tons per month. A state mine inspector informed union official George Titler that false weights cost Harlan-Wallins's loaders pay for 850 tons of coal per day. Other Harlan operators commonly believed that the firm cheated its employees. Although state law required that miners who wished to employ and pay a checkweighman were entitled to one, any Harlan-Wallins employee who agitated for a checkweighman was promptly fired.[21]

Miners also complained that Harlan-Wallins and Black Mountain enforced the cleanup system that required loaders, paid by the ton, to remain on the job until they had thoroughly cleaned up all dust and rock and set timbers and that required day men to work between nine- and twelve-hour days for seven or eight hours' pay. Black Mountain also forced its loaders to "buck coal": the company delivered two cars at a time to each loader, who had to load the nearest car and then reload the coal from the first into the second car for no extra pay.[22] Harlan operators fought adamantly for the right to continue such work practices, which shaved the cost of production as effectively as

lower tonnage or daily rates. The UMW, by contrast, tradi-
tionally required pay for all such "dead work."

Some local firms required their employees to purchase all
groceries, clothing, and supplies at the company store, and
New York Times reporter Louis Stark discovered that in 1931
many Harlan mines were turning their only profit at the commissary. Although U.S. Coal & Coke's commissary reduced food
prices by 37 percent and clothing prices by 28 percent during
the first two years of the Depression, between 1934 and 1937,
Verda's commissary, jointly owned by Harlan-Wallins superintendent Pearl Bassham, Sheriff Theodore Middleton, and
County Judge Morris Saylor, produced a 170 percent annual
profit. Clover Splint did not force employees to patronize its
company store, but Black Mountain sent its miners a letter that
they interpreted as a warning to either buy at the company
store or seek employment elsewhere. Clover Fork's superintendent bluntly told his employees: "If you trade at Piggly
Wiggly's, you can get your job at Piggly Wiggly's." [23]

Harlan's coal firms were not just running a business in
Harlan County: they were running the county. More than just
a simple economic struggle to raise wages, shorten hours, and
gain job security, the union movement of the 1930s was a
power struggle to curb the operators' authoritarian control of
the county's economic, political, and social life. Miners sought
to regain control over their lives and destiny that had been
usurped by the coal barons during the course of two decades.
Since the mine owners' use of wealth, corruption, and loyalty
to the dominant Republican party prohibited any successful
political revolt, miners were forced to wage their power struggle
through the institution of unionism.

Unlike typical middle-class American society, Harlan County
lacked any sizable disinterested middle class to moderate and
adjust conflict between the elite and the disinherited. Two-
thirds of the county's labor force mined coal, and the coal
companies employed and controlled most lawyers, ministers,
teachers, mercantile clerks, and law-enforcement officials. The
few small farmers were about the only truly free people in the
county. Although not all miners, merchants, ministers—or
operators, for that matter—were of a single mind, the struggle

came down to a bare-knuckled conflict between "us" and "them."

With local power and opinion so arrayed against them, and lacking any significant uncommitted local body politic to bring about internal change, the miners were forced to seek external intervention—from the state's governor and legislature or from the federal courts, Congress, or Justice Department—to effect a change. The coal barons also sought the state's aid—the National Guard—to suppress the rebellion when necessary.

Harlan County's general level of violence helped insure that the bitter labor-management conflict of the 1930s would be bloody. During the 1920s, a decade of labor-management peace, Harlan's homicide rate surpassed that of any other county in the United States. The county's rate of 77.6 homicides per 100,000 population was twice as high as that of the most violent state, Florida, and seven times as high as in Al Capone's Chicago. Contemporaries often considered Harlan just another "rough" coal county, but even in the company of other "bloody" coal counties, Harlan's homicide record was unique. "Bloody" Mingo and Logan counties, West Virginia, during the decade of the Mingo miners' march, possessed homicide rates of 49.5 and 33.9, respectively; "Bloody" Williamson County, Illinois, in the decade of the Herrin Massacre, had an annual rate of only 14.[24] Clearly, something other than Harlan's large mining population caused its violence.

Contemporaries, recalling the famous Hatfield-McCoy feud that had erupted on the nearby West Virginia–Kentucky border, frequently attributed the county's violence to the Southern Appalachian feud tradition. Harlan, however, had experienced only one brief family feud in its entire history.[25]

A 1932 study of homicide blamed the common custom of "pistol toting" south of the "Smith and Wesson Line" for the South's higher homicide rate.[26] An estimated one of every five Harlan residents carried a pistol; and no doubt many of the county's political, religious, and labor quarrels would have vented themselves in a nonfatal affray had not the ever-ready revolver been close at hand. But residents of the nearby southern West Virginia coal fields also commonly carried guns and retained a far lower homicide rate. Pistol toting also fails to explain the more frequent eruption of conflict that led to killing.

Because the national homicide rate for blacks exceeds that for whites, and because the proportion of blacks in the population is highest in the South, numerous analysts have blamed the region's racial composition for its violence. Sheldon Hackney has shown, however, that because both the white and black southerner are more violent than their northern counterparts, the region's racial makeup does not determine its higher murder rate.[27] Harlan experienced no unusual racial violence, and certainly its tiny 9 percent black population did not produce its excessive violence.

Although some scholars attributed the South's high homicide rate to its disproportionate share of poverty, studies of Minnesota's welfare recipients and Seattle's impoverished Japanese minority have shown the poor to be no more violent than the general population.[28] Harlan's homicide rate peaked in the 1920s, its most prosperous era. The county's homicide rate was low during its impoverished preindustrial era, declined somewhat during the depressed 1930s, and plummeted in the late 1950s, when 11 percent of its labor force was unemployed and 40 percent of its population was existing on pensions and welfare programs.

Some analysts have argued that the South's higher share of perceived low-status occupations causes its high rate of violence, but Sheldon Hackney discovered that violent southern cities had fewer lower-status jobs than their northern counterparts.[29] With a majority of its labor force engaged in semi- and unskilled mining jobs, Harlan certainly possessed an unusually high ratio of low-status occupations. This condition, however, was no more prevalent in the violent 1920s than in the peaceful post–World War II era.

Southern violence has also been explained in terms of the region's predominantly rural character. Hackney demonstrated, however, that the urban South was more violent than the rural South and that the eleven ex-Confederate states were more violent than the eleven most rural nonsouthern states.[30] Harlan's homicide rate had been far lower in its pastoral past and peaked in its first decade as a semiurban society.

If one eliminates feuding, pistol toting, racial composition, poverty, low-status occupations, and ruralness as causes for Harlan's excessive homicide rate, what other factors might have spawned the county's violence?

Sheldon Hackney demonstrated a high correlation between the South's lower level of educational attainment and its higher homicide rate. He contends that educational deficiency accounts for much of the region's higher murder rate. Although Harlan's schools remained open two months beyond the regular state-supported term and offered a model vocational-oriented curriculum geared to student needs at Benham High, the rapid influx of so many undereducated adults from surrounding tri-state counties with inferior educational opportunities perpetuated a low level of education. In 1920, 12.3 percent of the county's population over ten years of age was illiterate; in 1930, 10.6 percent could not read and write. Educational deficiency probably did, as many local contemporaries suspected, contribute to Harlan's violence.[31]

Comparative international studies of homicide indicate that the disruptive process of rapid industrialization and urbanization is productive of violence. Mature, modern industrial and urban nations enjoy the lowest level of violence. The most backward undeveloped countries enjoy the second lowest homicide rate, and the emerging, rapidly developing nations experience the highest level of homicide.[32] Harlan's homicide rate remained low during its agrarian era, peaked during its rapid two-decade transformation from a rural, agrarian county to a semiurban, industrial society, and then declined as its modern society matured.

The rapid, six-fold population increase and the wrenching transformation of thousands of independent farmers living in lonely mountain cabins into work-disciplined miners dwelling in crowded coal camps produced serious social disorganization. The basic social unit of earlier times—the family—was thoroughly disrupted. The family pattern changed from patriarchal to matriarchal because fathers who had once toiled long hours in the fields alongside their children now spent long hours absent in the mines and no longer actively participated in family life. By the 1930s, one of every four local marriages ended in divorce, a situation almost unknown in the preindustrial era, and child desertion had emerged as a social problem of serious proportions. By 1942, venereal disease afflicted one-third of the adult male population, probably indicating a greater degree of sexual promiscuity than in earlier times.

Secondary social institutions—church, school, and community—did not satisfactorily supplant the family as a social cement. Religious values weakened as miners withdrew from company churches and young people deserted because the churches' fundamentalist creeds prohibited dancing in either church or school. Beyond the Harlan County Coal Operators' Association, two Kiwanis clubs, and three American Legion posts, civic and social organizations were totally lacking. The first Boy Scout troops were organized only during 1931–32 to combat the Communist threat, and the first 4-H clubs and Girl Scout troops were formed during the WPA era. Youth abandoned the old community-oriented house-raisings and quilting bees to compete in high school sports, listen to the radio, and speed aimlessly about the county in automobiles. Many adults frequented the county's forty-two roadside taverns that offered liquor, dancing, gambling, prostitution, and brawling. These taverns quickly emerged as the county's major crime centers. Labor conflict split both the family and community when sons joined the union and their fathers did not, and some neighbors joined but good friends in the neighborhood refused to affiliate. At school, union miners' sons taunted nonunion miners' children with cries of "little yellow-dogs" and "scabs." [33] Nowhere in camp or county could one discern a genuine sense of social cohesion or community.

Emile Durkheim, in *Suicide* (1898), argued that rapid industrialization, urbanization, population growth, heterogeneity, and the resultant conflict between new and old values often produced anomie, a state of restless, drifting, valueless uncertainty and anxiety; anomie, in turn, frequently resulted in deviant behavior such as suicide or homicide.[34] This was indeed Harlan's pattern: its rapid development created a high level of conflict and anomie that frequently culminated in homicide.

Educational deficiency and serious social disorganization,

then, accounted for much of Harlan's high level of homicide. A bitter labor-management conflict conducted within such a violent environment could not be peaceful. The eleven deaths that directly resulted from a decade-long labor-management war, however, pale by comparison to the approximately fifty homicides that occurred during each of those years.

All the historic causes of violence specific to American labor disputes were present in Harlan County in the 1930s. The demand for a fundamental change in the condition of employment—establishment of a union and collective bargaining—has been historically the greatest such cause, and this was the key issue in dispute throughout Harlan's decade-long labor conflict. Employers' attempts to operate their businesses with nonunion employees in the face of strikes by their regular labor force frequently breed violence; nonunion operation during strikes was common practice in Harlan. Employers' use of a private army—privately paid deputy sheriffs or plant guards—often provokes violence; throughout the 1930s, privately paid deputies acted as the main bulwark against union organization. When laborers widely share feelings of resentment and injustice because of business's control of local government and law enforcement, violence often erupts; Harlan's miners dramatically exhibited such feelings.[35]

The Harlan operators, the Harlan and Pineville newspaper editors, and many others viewed unionism as part of a northern conspiracy to destroy the southern coal industry. Whether the UMW succeeded only in periodically stirring up labor trouble that would cause southern operators to lose sales contracts or successfully organized the field and standardized wages, hours, and working conditions, the Harlan coal industry would be destroyed.[36] In addition to viewing union agents as outside conspirators, the operators thought of them as reckless and irresponsible agitators, dues-hungry racketeers, radicals, and violence-prone disturbers of the peace. The *Harlan Daily Enterprise* editor portrayed the outside labor organizers as "destroying influences," "foreign radicals," and "a menacing hand that threatens" to destroy Harlan's bright future.[37] The operators used all necessary means to exclude such threatening influences from the county.

The operators employed deputy sheriffs to bar organizers from the county and from company property. The deputies owed economic allegiance to the mine owners who paid them. In addition, because one of the UMW's major goals was abolition of the private deputy system, the deputies sought to defeat the union in order to preserve their own positions. Beyond that, as several studies of law enforcement have demonstrated, policemen develop certain personal or occupational goals in addition to their legally defined duties. Officers see the public at its worst and develop a cynical view of society. Viewed by the public with varying degrees of hostility—uncomfortableness, disrespect, suspicion, fear, and hatred—the officers develop a defensive posture toward society. They create particular enemies among the public, usually those who frequently exhibit disrespect for the officer and his authority or who pose a threat to the officer's safety. The enemies must also be so poor, weak, and powerless, or so ostracized by society that they cannot rally public support when abused by officers. Dangerous criminals, sex offenders, blacks, students, and liberal newsmen have all at one time or another served as targets of police attack. Officers freely use force against such persons to punish them, to protect their own and fellow officers' lives, and to compel obedience and respect of themselves.[38]

Harlan deputies viewed union members and, especially, union organizers as such an enemy. Miners commonly exhibited disrespect for the deputies by calling them "gun thugs." After 1931, when union miners ambushed ten deputies, killing three and wounding two, the deputies in turn viewed them as "cop killers." Consequently, deputies killed, wounded, beat, and spied on union organizers and members to defend themselves, to punish the unionists for suspected crimes, and to compel respect. By abusing union men, the deputies simultaneously satisfied their own personal and occupational needs and the operators' economic and political requirements. Their violence was rewarded by pay and plaudits from the county's elite. In the course of the decade, deputies and National Guardsmen killed six miners and wounded thirteen miners and two newsmen.

Another powerful occupational need prohibits an officer from informing on or testifying against a fellow officer.[39] Fellow-officer secrecy, combined with the miners' fear of testifying in local courts, explains why so few deputies were indicted and none convicted for violently abusing miners.

The miners stereotyped the deputy sheriffs as criminals, spies, enemies of the union, cold-blooded killers, and tools of the mine owners who were enforcing coal operators' law. In the decade-long union campaign, miners killed five deputy sheriffs and wounded three deputies and two National Guardsmen. All eight deputies were killed or wounded during the spontaneous, nearly leaderless uprising of 1931. During the remainder of the conflict, when district union leaders were in firm control, miners wounded only two National Guardsmen in self-defense in what should be classified as a police riot. This pattern of labor violence suggests that Harlan's elite, by using injunctions and violence to exclude the hated district organizers from the county, increased rather than diminished the possibilities for violence.

Coal miners' strikes often assume a standard ritualistic pattern that includes picketing, armed marches, "baptizing" non-unionists, "belling" unpopular company doctors, gathering and distributing strike relief (including robbing, if the need is desperate enough), and sometimes dynamiting mines, tipples, or mining machinery. These seemingly frivolous and irresponsible acts have a deadly serious purpose. In a power struggle where business-dominated law officers and courts are arrayed against them, the miners use numbers and arms to display labor's power. The union thereby presents itself as a viable, powerful institution, impressing some and intimidating others. Picketing deters nonunion miners from working or replacing striking employees, thus insuring the strike's effectiveness. Such activities give every striker a role to play and bolster morale. When law officers, especially company-controlled officers, disrupt this routine by evicting miners from company houses, smashing picket lines, introducing strike-breakers, halting marches, or disrupting the food supply, miners frequently retaliate by using their only power: direct action and violence. This pattern unfolded in Harlan during the major strikes of 1931 and 1939; and in both cases, violence followed.

One should bear in mind, however, that this bitter labor-management war, lasting for nine years, exacted eleven lives in a county where some fifty persons met violent death each year. The labor war may have brought the county national notoriety as "Bloody Harlan," but it was not labor that most bloodied its record.

NOTES

1. Wilmer G. Mason, *Cincinnati Enquirer,* Apr. 13, 1932; F. Raymond Daniell, "Behind the Conflict in 'Bloody Harlan,'" *New York Times Magazine,* June 26, 1938, p. 11.

2. Editorial, *Courier-Journal* (Louisville, Ky.), Mar. 29, 1932.

3. Testimony of George S. Ward, LFCH, pt. 10, p. 3525; testimony of A. J. May, LFCH, pt. 12, p. 4201; John H. Fenton, *Politics in the Border States* (New Orleans, 1957), pp. 23–25.

4. Anonymous, interviewed by John A. Dotson, Apr. 23, 1942, quoted in Dotson, "Socio-Economic Background and Changing Education in Harlan County, Kentucky" (Ph.D. diss., George Peabody College for Teachers, 1943), p. 35.

5. *Harlan* (Ky.) *Daily Enterprise,* Nov. 11, 18, 23, 1931, July 1, Aug. 4, Sept. 6, 1935, Mar. 31, 1938; U.S., Congress, Senate, Special Committee to Investigate Presidential, Vice Presidential and Senatorial Campaign Expenditures, 1940, *Investigation of Presidential, Vice Presidential and Senatorial Campaign Expenditures, 1940,* S. Rept. 47, 77 Cong., 1 sess. (1941), p. 63; "99 Are Indicted in Kentucky Vote," *New York Times,* June 6, 1943, p. 41; "33 Vote Officials Sentenced," ibid., July 29, 1945, p. 41.

6. George Ward, quoted by Steve Humphrey, *Knoxville* (Tenn.) *News-Sentinel,* May 7, 1931.

7. J. H. Blair, quoted in *Courier-Journal,* Mar. 28, 1932.

8. Report of the Hays-Bablitz Commission, quoted in *United Mine Workers Journal,* Jan. 15, 1932, p. 6.

9. Testimony of Theodore Middleton, LFCH, pt. 12, pp. 4142–62; testimony of Lawrence Dwyer, ibid., pt. 10, p. 3470; Charles Barnes to Richard Brown, Feb. 21, 1935, NA, RG/9, NRA, BCLB, Correspondence File.

10. Jerold S. Auerbach, *Labor and Liberty: The La Follette Committee and the New Deal* (Indianapolis and New York, 1966), pp. 117–18.

11. Testimony of Howard N. Eavenson, *Conditions in Coal Fields,* pp. 210–11.

12. Final Report of the Harlan County Grand Jury, May 5, 1934, LFCH, pt. 10, Exhibit 1214, p. 3730.

13. Report of the Denhardt Commission, U.S., Congress, House, *Congressional Record,* 74 Cong., 1 sess. (1935), vol. 79, pp. 8987–88.

14. Henry Harvey Fuson, "History of Harlan County, Kentucky: Some Chapters" (unpublished ms., University of Kentucky Library); W. A. Brock, quoted in *Harlan Daily Enterprise,* Aug. 17, 1931; testimony of Daniel Boone Smith, LFCH, pt. 12, pp. 4310–12; testimony of Kelly Fox, ibid., pt. 13, pp. 4435–36.

15. A. B. Culton to F. L. Poindexter, Apr. 7, 1934, NA, RG/9, NRA, BCLB, Case Files, Case no. 585; testimony of Eavenson, *Conditions in Coal Fields,* pp. 191–92; Dotson, "Education in Harlan County," pp. 47–48.

16. Culton to Poindexter, Apr. 7, 1934, NA, RG/9, NRA, BCLB, Case Files, Case no. 585; Paul Floyd Taylor, "The Coal Mine War in Harlan County, Kentucky, 1931–32" (M.A. thesis, University of Kentucky, 1955), pp. 36–37; Dotson, "Education in Harlan County," p. 48; testimony of Eavenson, *Conditions in Coal Fields,* p. 19.

17. Taylor, "Coal Mine War," pp. 37–38.

18. Dotson, "Education in Harlan County," pp. 25, 38, 42; testimony of Eavenson, *Conditions in Coal Fields,* p. 200; testimony of Dr. Arthur T. McCormack, *Conditions in Coal Fields,* p. 157; *Harlan Daily Enterprise,* Feb. 7, 1937.

19. Daniell, "Behind the Conflict," pp. 2, 11; testimony of McCormack, *Conditions in Coal Fields,* pp. 158–59.

20. George J. Titler, *Hell in Harlan* (Beckley, W.Va., n.d.), pp. 48–49; C. W. Pierce to Hugh S. Johnson, Aug. 21, 1934, NA, RG/9, NRA, BCLB, Case Files, Case no. 585; testimony of James Westmoreland, LFCH, pt. 11, p. 3907; testimony of R. E. Lawson, ibid., pp. 3841–42; *Knoxville News-Sentinel,* June 10, Dec. 17, 1931.

21. Richard Lunsford to Mrs. Franklin D. Roosevelt, Jan. 27, 1934; Culton to Poindexter, Apr. 7, 1934; telegram, William Turnblazer to Barnes, Apr. 7, 1934, NA, RG/9, NRA, BCLB, Case Files, Case no. 585; Titler, *Hell in Harlan,* p. 43.

22. Turnblazer to J. Will Taylor, n.d., U.S., Congress, House, *Congressional Record,* 71 Cong., 3 sess. (1931), vol. 74, p. 4070; Culton to Poindexter, Apr. 7, 1934, NA, RG/9, NRA, BCLB, Case Files, Case no. 585; anonymous, interviewed by Paul F. Taylor, Aug. 16, 1954, quoted in Taylor, "Coal Mine War," p. 67.

23. Louis Stark, *New York Times,* Sept. 27, 1931; testimony of Eavenson, *Conditions in Coal Fields,* p. 192; testimony of Pearl Bassham, LFCH, pt. 10, p. 3583; Black Mountain Coal Corporation to John Burton, quoted in National Committee for the Defense of Political Prisoners, *Harlan Miners Speak: Report on Terrorism in the Kentucky Coal Fields* (New York, 1932), p. 30 (hereafter cited as *Harlan Miners Speak*); Irving Bernstein, *The Lean Years: A History of the American Worker, 1920–1933* (Boston, 1960), p. 365.

24. H. C. Brearley, *Homicide in the United States* (Chapel Hill, N.C., 1932), pp. 220–23 (table 12), dust jacket.

25. Dr. J. W. Nolan, interviewed by John A. Dotson, May 14, 1942, quoted in Dotson, "Education in Harlan County," p. 12.

26. Brearley, *Homicide in the United States,* pp. 72–73; Paul Frederick Cressey, "Social Disorganization and Reorganization in Harlan

County, Kentucky," *American Sociological Review,* 14 (June, 1949), 390; editorial, *Pineville* (Ky.) *Sun,* Jan. 18, 1934; *Courier-Journal,* May 9, 1931; testimony of McCormack, *Conditions in Coal Fields,* p. 156.

27. Sheldon Hackney, "Southern Violence," *American Historical Review,* 74 (Feb., 1969), 908–9.

28. Ibid., pp. 912, 920–22.

29. Ibid., pp. 909–10.

30. Ibid., pp. 910–12.

31. Ibid., pp. 912–15; U.S. Dept. of Commerce, Bureau of the Census, *Fifteenth Census of the United States: 1930: Population,* Vol. 3, pt. 1, *Alabama-Missouri* (Washington, D.C., 1932); Wilmer G. Mason, *Cincinnati Enquirer,* Apr. 8, 1932.

32. Hugh Davis Graham and Ted Robert Gurr, *The History of Violence in America: Historical and Comparative Perspectives* (New York, 1969), p. 571.

33. Dotson, "Education in Harlan County," pp. 25–26, 36, 43–47; Cressey, "Social Disorganization," pp. 391–92.

34. Hackney, "Southern Violence," pp. 915–17.

35. See Philip Taft, "Violence in American Labor Disputes," *Annals of the American Academy of Political and Social Science,* 364 (Mar., 1966), 134–35, 140.

36. Editorial, *Pineville Sun,* Apr. 23, 1931; testimony of McCormack, *Conditions in Coal Fields,* p. 153; editorial, *Cincinnati Enquirer,* reprinted in *Pineville Sun,* May 14, 1931; editorial *Courier-Journal,* July 4, 1931.

37. Editorials, *Harlan Daily Enterprise,* Dec. 13, 1934, June 7, 1935.

38. William A. Westley, *Violence and the Police: A Sociological Study of Law, Custom, and Morality* (Cambridge, Mass., and London, 1970), pp. ix, xii–xvi, 7–8, 16, 59, 68, 72, 82, 121–22, 127, 131, 136, 142–43, 145, 147, 151, 168; Rodney Stark, *Police Riots: Collective Violence and Law Enforcement* (Belmont, Calif., 1972), pp. 40, 61.

39. Westley, *Violence and the Police,* pp. xiv–xvi, 5, 7.

Chapter 3

Strike!

February - July, 1931

In the early spring of 1931, the Depression, a mild winter, and the seasonal hiatus in the lake cargo trade combined to severely depress the Harlan coal industry. In these straits, on February 16, local coal operators declared a 10 percent wage reduction.[1] Because of irregular employment and reduced wages, many miners and their families began to experience the pinch of abject poverty. Just as the miners' need for relief reached its peak, local funds were exhausted. For the first time in its history, the county appealed for outside assistance, and the national Red Cross attempted to come to the rescue. The Red Cross restricted its funds, however, to relief of drought victims, although Harlan's predicament was largely caused by industrial depression.[2]

The wage cut triggered an immediate union organizational campaign and a futile, violent strike that initiated a nine-year effort to unionize the county's miners. Seizing upon this opportunity to reestablish the United Mine Workers in the county, district officials and local unionists sprang into action. District 19 president William Turnblazer circulated a handbill throughout southeastern Kentucky and eastern Tennessee urging the miners to organize to resist wage reductions, to abolish the cleanup system, to elect checkweighmen, and to improve working and living conditions. The circular placed responsibility for the wage cut on the operators, who persisted in selling coal for less than the cost of production, a policy that would fail to obtain a larger market for the fuel. Turnblazer encouraged the miners to "fight and fight and fight against this terrible degradation that is being heaped upon you and your families." [3]

On Sunday, March 1, more than two thousand Harlan and Bell County miners attended a rally in a Pineville theater where UMW national vice-president Philip Murray urged reorganization of District 19. Attributing the industry's ills to cutthroat competition, he pleaded with operators and miners to attack their mutual problems in "a spirit of cooperation, in a reasonable, intelligent manner," and emphasized that the union did "not intend to precipitate strikes or create an industrial catastrophe. . . . We are not radical or revolutionary." [4] After the speech, Lawrence "Peggy" Dwyer, a one-legged, militant national organizer, enrolled hundreds of members. [5]

The next morning, several Harlan firms, whose spies had reported the names of local miners attending the rally, began discharging and evicting members. The Harlan-Wallins Coal Corporation dismissed 49 employees, Black Star 60, and the Black Mountain Coal Corporation more than 175. [6] Manford Maupin, a young miner at the Mary Helen mine at Coalgood, was a typical victim of the purge. On Sunday, March 29, he joined the union. The next day the mine foreman ordered him out of the camp immediately and warned that if he continued to reside at home his father would also be discharged and evicted. [7] By April 8, seven or eight Harlan firms had discharged several hundred employees, [8] although a spokesman for the operators assured a federal labor conciliator that the numerous discharges had been mainly for effect and that all but some fifty of the most troublesome agitators would ultimately be reemployed. [9] Thus, eleven months of almost continuous labor trouble began with a partial lockout of union employees. Not until major violence erupted and the National Guard arrived in early May did the miners convert the struggle into a major strike.

Most of the discharged and evicted miners moved with their families to Evarts, one of the county's three incorporated, or noncompany, towns; by May 5, they had swelled that village's normal population of fifteen hundred to approximately five thousand inhabitants.[10] There, the evicted unionists occupied vacant houses, garages, barns, and sheds provided by sympathetic miners, farmers, aspiring politicians, and independent merchants who hoped through unionism to break the company stores' monopoly of the miners' trade. Among the most generous provisioners was Joe Cawood, an Evarts landlord and merchant and member of one of the county's pioneer families. In 1929, Cawood had won the Republican nomination for county sheriff in the primary election but had lost the nomination to his opponent, John Henry Blair, when the latter contested the election in the local court. Cawood apparently hoped to repair his political fortunes by befriending union miners.[11] Evarts officials, Mayor Bradley Burkhart, Police Chief Asa Cusick, and Assistant Police Chief Al Benson, an active member of UMW Local 5355, also sympathized with the union. Evarts already had a reputation as a "tough" town; but when it emerged as the center of union agitation and relief distribution and the scene of starving miners' raids on company stores and private groceries, it represented, to county officials and coal operators, a powderkeg placed right at the heart of the rich Clover Fork coal field.

Even before the Pineville rally, local unionists had begun the clandestine revival of the United Mine Workers. In early February, fifty-three miners had attended a secret meeting in an abandoned mine entry at Black Mountain. Continuing their furtive gatherings in the dark woods of Pound Mill Hollow, by March 1, the date of the Pineville meeting, they had recruited five hundred members. By that time, however, the local had been infiltrated by Sheriff Blair's spies and had nothing to gain by continued secrecy. In mid-March, UMW Local 5355 opened a public headquarters in Evarts. Crowds of miners and sympathetic farmers, merchants, and lumbermen, ranging from three hundred to two thousand persons, gathered regularly in the Evarts schoolyard or, during inclement weather, at the Blue Front Garage. One room in the home of William B. Jones, the local secretary, served as union headquarters and distribution center for strike relief gathered by local relief committees. This aid, unionists maintained, consisted of contributions from farmers, merchants, and gardeners in the surrounding counties of Kentucky and Tennessee.[12] Union opponents, on the other hand, charged that the supplies were stolen during a series of store and commissary robberies in late April and early May.[13]

During February and March, until he moved to Bell County, the fiery George Burchett served as local union president. Briefly, in April, an itinerant member of the Industrial Workers of the World, Lee Lively, succeeded Burchett as president, but district union officials quickly deposed him when he began soliciting IWW memberships.[14] In late April, William Hightower, an illiterate, seventy-seven-year-old miner who in March had been discharged by the Harlan-Wallins Coal Corporation for union activity, was appointed president.[15]

But William B. Jones, the exceptionally able forty-eight-year-old secretary of the local, was the real leader. After fleeing mine closures in southeastern Ohio in 1930, Jones was employed as a coal loader at Black Mountain; on March 8, 1931, because he attended the Pineville rally, the company discharged him. A UMW member for twenty-nine years before he arrived in Harlan, Jones had attended the early, secret union meetings at Black Mountain and Pound Mill Hollow; and during Burchett's presidency, the local elected the forceful speaker and energetic organizer secretary. A week after his eviction from the Black Mountain camp, he moved to Evarts and established local union headquarters at his home.[16] Although the union's enemies accused Jones of secretly advocating radicalism and violence, his public statements again and again reiterated the theme of peaceful organization.

The local union conducted a series of weekend marches to solicit members in surrounding coal camps. On Sunday, March 15, twenty-seven hundred miners marched from Evarts to a meeting on the L & N right-of-way near Harlan-Wallins's camp at Verda where three hundred miners joined the union. In early April, twenty-five hundred marchers recruited 275 members at High Splint and 272 at Louellen.[17] On April 8, a similar group passed through Back Mountain's camp en route to Disney, where thirty or forty miners joined the union. Flag bearers and one automobile carrying local president Lee Lively, armed with a shotgun, led the procession. Although unionists contended that Lively carried the only weapon in the march, Black Mountain superintendent E. B. Childers charged that half of the marchers carried arms, which they fired once or twice.[18] Armed or unarmed, by early May the marchers had successfully recruited eight to nine thousand members into their local.[19]

Black Mountain Coal Corporation, because of its proximity to Evarts and its unrelenting nonunion policy, led the operators' attack on unionism. According to the company superintendent, between March 1 and May 5, one thousand of its employees were either discharged or struck in sympathy with those dismissed. By early May, only three hundred miners, apparently most of them newly hired nonunion employees, out of a normal one-thousand-man work force were still working. Officials of the parent firm, Peabody Coal Corporation of Chicago, ordered the mine closed for the duration of labor troubles but yielded to Superintendent Childers's plea to continue operation. "My boss wanted me to shut down," Childers explained after violence erupted. "I begged him not to. I had good men and I didn't want to lose them. If you shut down they drift away. We weren't making any money but we were working about 300 men." [20]

The eviction of miners and their families without adequate provision for food, clothing, and shelter created an explosive situation. On February 17, the day after the wage cut took effect, the Harlan County Health and Welfare League disbanded and transferred its nearly depleted treasury to the local Red Cross chapter. The national Red Cross contributed $3,000 to the local chapter but, refusing to interfere in an industrial dispute, consistently denied relief to striking miners.[21] A combination farmer-miner who could supplement his meager mine wages with home-grown vegetables was entitled to Red Cross assistance, while an unemployed or striking miner who suffered far greater privation was not.

The bankrupt United Mine Workers was unable and unwilling to contribute strike relief to an unauthorized walkout.[22] The coal operators, the only source of local relief funds, of course refused to contribute to their own defeat. F. D. Perkins, a mine owner who relinquished his position as chairman of the local Red Cross chapter when labor troubles began, succinctly summed up the operators' position: "The men refused to work. You can't get contributions for men who won't work." [23] On March 24, District President William Turnblazer visited Harlan for the only time during the course of the strike. He found that the discharged miners and their families who were denied local, Red Cross, or union assistance were "actually starving" [24] and described a meeting with twelve hundred "keenly agitated" unionists in the county seat as a "spasmodic" gathering. [25] Union appeals to National Red Cross chairman John Burton Payne and to Governor Flem Sampson and President Herbert Hoover to intervene with Payne failed to produce a reversal of the Red Cross's noninterventionist policy. [26]

Hungry strikers finally began to loot grocery stores and company commissaries in the Evarts vicinity. On Thursday night, April 23, thieves nearly emptied the shelves of the Evarts A & P store. Restocked on Friday, the grocery was looted a second time. The following evening, East Harlan Coal Company's commissary was robbed. The next Tuesday night, another of East Harlan's company stores was looted. On Wednesday night, April 29, thieves plundered John Powell's grocery and, for the third time within a week, the A & P store. [27] On April 24, following the first robbery, an alarmed Turnblazer dashed off a second appeal for relief to President Hoover. He described the Harlan miners as "very, very hungry" and consequently "dangerous," and voiced his fear of impending "riot and bloodshed." [28] In a last-minute appeal to the National Red Cross chairman, Turnblazer warned that local miners could not "understand the difference in starving to death from drouth and starving to death from depression within the coal industry. . . . When people become hungry and see their loved ones crying for food in a land of plenty, they become mad. The spirit of revolt is nursed within their breasts; they lose faith in our American principles and institutions. Common sense and judgment do not prevail and sometimes the people themselves get beyond our control." [29]

Other than writing letters, however, Turnblazer was powerless, for the United States District Court issued temporary injunctions that removed the last vestige of the district union chief's moderating influence. On Saturday, April 25, the court granted temporary restraining orders to Black Mountain and PV & K Coal Company that prohibited Turnblazer, Dwyer, and Milt Harbin, the union's county field representative, from either entering company property or talking to or in any way influencing company employees to strike. On the following Wednesday, the court granted a similar order to Harlan-Wallins and extended its prohibitions beyond the three district officials to apply to 397 specific unionists. The judge did, however, reject Harlan-Wallins's plea to enjoin any violation of yellow-dog contracts, a severely restrictive injunction frequently granted in the West Virginia coal field.[30]

Simultaneously, local unionists and county officials attempted to restore order. On Saturday, May 2, Evarts police chief Asa Cusick arrested eight persons, curiously none of them union members, and charged them with the April 29 robbery of the local A & P store; over the weekend, Jones and Hightower organized an armed patrol of union miners ostensibly to guard Evarts's stores. On Monday, May 4, in response to both robbery and violence, Circuit Judge D. C. Jones summoned a special grand jury to convene two days later to investigate "a state of lawlessness" that existed in Harlan County.[31]

In addition to hunger, the miners were goaded to anger by real and fancied abuses suffered at the hands of mine guards employed by the coal companies to protect working miners and company property. During 1931 and early 1932, Sheriff John Henry Blair had 170 deputies at his command, all but about 6 of them in the pay of the coal companies.[32] By his own admission, he had at least 86 more than were normally necessary to police the county.[33]

More provocative than the intimidating number of guards employed was their disreputable character and the county's partisan use of them in law enforcement. A year after the strike, Sheriff Blair clearly stated his position during the controversy: "I did all in my power to aid the coal operators. . . . There was no compromise when labor troubles swept the county and the 'Reds' came into Harlan County." [34] Blair freely deputized company officials. During March, 1931, he appointed as deputies E. B. Childers, Black Mountain superintendent; Pearl Bassham, vice-president of Harlan-Wallins; L. P. Johnson of Crummies Creek Coal Company; Charles Guthrie of Harlan Fuel; and Bill and Ed Whitfield of Clover Fork Coal Company. Among the other deputies, Ben Unthank, who was directly employed as chief detective by the Harlan County Coal Operators' Association, George Lee, Lee Fleenor, Frank White, Jim Daniels, Bill Randolph, and John Hickey ultimately achieved notoriety for their antiunion activity.[35] Of the 169 deputies still serving in 1937, many of them on the force in 1931, 64 had been indicted and 27 convicted of felonies, 8 of them for manslaughter and 3 for murder.[36] Their substantial criminal records and unsavory reputations as gunmen merited the miners' characterization of them as gun thugs. One miner's wife, asked to explain her conception of the abstract term *law* replied, "The law is a gun thug in a big automobile." [37]

In May, 1931, during a National Guard investigation of the strike, the most frequently voiced miners' complaint was of mistreatment by the deputy sheriffs.[38] By mid-April, nineteen thousand persons had signed a union-sponsored petition requesting the governor to remove Sheriff Blair, County Judge H. H. Howard, Circuit Judge D. C. Jones, and all the deputized mine guards.[39] During the course of the strike, three mine guards were wounded and four killed, and after the Battle of Evarts, the emphasis of strike demands shifted from preoccupation with union recognition to an equal, if not greater, insistence on removal of armed guards. The guards' forcible evictions of miners from company houses provoked intense hostility; and numerous unsubstantiated rumors circulated alleging that the guards ran miners and their families off the public highways, intimidated them by displaying firearms, and abused miners' wives and children.[40] Clearly, their very presence was abhorrent. "They put guards over us," Evarts miners protested. "We're free men and we don't wear stripes." [41]

As early as March 20, friction between miners and deputies began to build. Within days after Black Mountain hired Estes

Cox as a night watchman, an unidentified sniper wounded him in the leg.⁴² On April 17, a squadron of deputy sheriffs halted in Evarts to serve warrants on several unionists charged with assaulting Charles Carpenter, a black nonunion miner, at a union meeting the previous day. While the deputies were making an arrest, Bill Burnett, an armed miner who was not among the suspects, left the crowd of miners and walked behind a coal gondola on his way home. Deputies Jess Pace and Frank White pursued him with drawn guns. Pace allegedly opened fire and thrice wounded Burnett, who only then drew and killed Pace. Turning, he saw Frank White firing at him from the other end of the coal car and drove him into flight.⁴³ That same afternoon, when a sheriff's posse halted to question eight armed miners walking along a railroad grade, the deputies were fired upon, one of the bullets passing through the hat of Deputy Robert Blair, the sheriff's son.⁴⁴ That Sunday, during a union rally in the county seat, Sheriff Blair and his deputies, armed with tear gas, kept the gathering under strict surveillance. Although William B. Jones urged the miners to continue their fight for union recognition "peacefully and without use of arms," a visiting reporter noted that his followers were generally armed and in an "ugly frame of mind"; and a *Knoxville News-Sentinel* headline warned, "Flare-Up in Harlan Area Is Expected." ⁴⁵

On Monday morning a dynamite blast destroyed a mine entry at Shields, and on Thursday night an almost continuous succession of robberies began. At dawn on Tuesday, April 28, approximately fifty union miners hidden in the dense foliage on Black Mountain fired on nonunion miners on their way to work. Deputy sheriffs rushed to the scene and for over an hour strafed the mountainside with nearly two thousand rounds of automatic rifle fire to no effect.⁴⁶ Sheriff Blair warned strikers who resorted to violence they could expect no quarter from his forces. "Hell, yes, I've issued orders to shoot to kill," he bellowed at a reporter. "When ambushers fire on my men, they'll shoot back, and shoot to kill. That's what we use guns for here." ⁴⁷ On Thursday night, at Cawood, arsonists burned sixteen company houses that only that day had been vacated by evicted strikers. Adding to the horror of the conflagration, gunmen drove back and forth through the village for two hours, firing into the post office, two homes, and a restaurant.[48]

On Monday evening, May 4, three hundred members of Local 5355 assembled in the Evarts theater. Although Tuesday and Friday were the regular meeting nights, unionists asserted that the gathering was a special aid meeting. According to the union version, the group elected two committees, one to administer strike relief at Evarts and one to aid Verda. After a brief discussion of mine-guard abuse, the group selected a third committee to call on Sheriff Blair the following day to request impartial police protection for residents of Evarts and Black Mountain. If the sheriff refused to intervene, the committee was instructed to proceed to the state capital to appeal directly to the governor. Their business concluded, the meeting adjourned.[49]

Union opponents contended that the theater meeting was called to hatch a conspiracy to ambush a number of Black Mountain deputies as they passed through Evarts next morning. The two committees were appointed, they charged, not to solicit and distribute relief, but to journey to Bell County to obtain guns and ammunition for the attack. The third committee was selected, not to seek the sheriff's intervention, but to lure him into the trap set for his deputies.

At the later trial of William B. Jones for conspiracy to murder, three brothers, Fred, John, and Hugh Lester, gave a dramatic prosecution account of the theater meeting held on the eve of battle. The Lesters testified that Jones urged the three hundred miners present to gather by the roadside below Evarts the next morning to ambush the Black Mountain guards as they journeyed to Harlan to testify at the scheduled arraignment of Bill Burnett, charged with the murder of Deputy Jess Pace. According to the Lesters, Jones told the miners to gather with their rifles and "all that has not got high-power rifles . . . , take shotguns, and them that has not got shotguns to take pistols, and anybody that hain't got any gun at all, get some rocks, and . . . if there is any of you not able to throw rocks . . . , get a red handkerchief, you can wave it." Jones cautioned the miners that because the deputies wore bullet-proof vests, they should aim high. "Shoot to get meat, shoot their God damned heads off." [50]

Then, said the Lesters, President William Hightower put the proposal to a vote; after it passed, he covered his mouth with his hand and ordered all present to "keep this shut, hear nothing, see nothing and know nothing." [51] An elderly black miner-preacher then said he was sorry that, being a man of God, he could not participate in the blood-letting, but he would pray for their success. [52]

Did Jones and Hightower hatch a murder plot before an audience of three hundred known to be infiltrated with the sheriff's spies? Did they believe that so many loyal unionists would deny the conspiracy that conviction would be impossible? If the ambush was so openly conceived in the presence of the sheriff's undercover agents, why did his deputies fall so innocently into the trap? Why were they not forewarned? Eight juries, confronted with diametrically conflicting testimony, chose to believe the Lesters' story and sentenced Jones, Hightower, and six other miners to life imprisonment for conspiracy to murder.

Early Tuesday morning, May 5, Black Mountain superintendent E. B. Childers notified Roy Hughes, a newly employed nonunion miner, that he was dispatching a truck to transport the miner's household effects from Verda to the Black Mountain camp, Kenvir. [53] Shortly after the truck passed through Evarts at 7:30 A.M., a mob of fifty or seventy-five miners, nearly half of them armed with rifles and shotguns, began congregating around the Evarts railroad depot. The station agent, anticipating trouble, telephoned a warning to Childers. [54] The superintendent called for the assistance of Sheriff Blair, who immediately dispatched fifteen deputies to intercept the company truck at Verda and escort it back through Evarts. Childers then sought out his chief mine guard, Jim Daniels, who had already learned of impending trouble and was organizing a ten-man posse to meet the truck at Verda. The first of three cars was driven by J. P. Evans and carried Jim Daniels and George Dawn. Sherman Percival, Pat Moran, and Doc Evans rode with Bill Sears in the second car. Estes Cox and Howard

Jones, a deputized commissary clerk, accompanied Otto Lee in the third automobile, a company car normally driven by Daniels, the most hated Harlan mine guard. About 9:30, the motorcade drove slowly through Evarts en route to Verda.[55]

Two hundred yards below Evarts, the highway passed through a cut. On one side of the highway a bank rose to a height of four feet; on the opposite side in a low spot stood a water birch tree. As the front car reached the tree, one shot rang out, and concealed miners unleashed a withering barrage of rifle and shotgun fire at the vehicles.[56] The three cars halted abruptly. The third car, ordinarily driven by Daniels, bore the brunt of the attack; it was struck by thirty-nine rifle bullets and more than sixty shotgun pellets. The driver, Otto Lee, was fatally shot in the head before his car stopped rolling. Commissary clerk Howard Jones was killed before he could open the front door. As Estes Cox crawled from the rear seat, eighteen shotgun pellets nearly severed his left arm.[57] As soon as the front car halted, Jim Daniels and George Dawn leaped out and took cover behind a mound of earth in front of the birch tree. As they peered over the bank, a black miner rose up and shot Daniels directly in the face with a shotgun blast. George Dawn squeezed off a few shots from his Browning automatic that may have killed Carl Richmond, a white miner later found dead under the birch tree.[58] Just as the second car stopped, Sherman Percival was wounded in the left arm. He leaped from the car and as he rounded the rear of the vehicle was hit a second time. Suffering from two dozen wounds, he crawled up the hill to a nearby house only to find it swarming with ambushers. A man seized his rifle and declared, "If you were thugging for Black Mountain, you are a goner." Somehow, Percival convinced him to the contrary, and he was permitted to escape.[59] After about a thousand shots were exchanged in the course of thirty minutes, the firing tapered off. The two Evans brothers, Pat Moran, George Dawn, and Estes Cox fled in the first two cars, leaving Jim Daniels and Howard Jones dead, Otto Lee to die in an ambulance en route to a Harlan hospital, and Sherman Percival bleeding on the field.[60] Even after Sheriff Blair flooded the Evarts region with special deputies under orders to arrest all persons bearing arms, violence continued; when the Black Mountain truck bearing Roy Hughes's furniture passed through Evarts that afternoon, it was greeted by sporadic rifle fire from the distant mountains. For two days a virtual state of anarchy reigned in Evarts. The public schools closed, and a number of families fled the county.[61]

Sheriff Blair and Governor Flem Sampson attributed responsibility for the Evarts ambush to radicals who had infiltrated the UMW local at Evarts. Relying on information allegedly contributed by informants planted within the local union, the sheriff blamed the outbreak on an "IWW organization in the . . . town of Evarts. Don't confuse the union organization there with the regular labor unions. I believe this is a separate group causing the present trouble." [62] In his order dispatching troops to Harlan County, Governor Sampson asserted that "several undesirable citizens from other states . . . have taken up their abode at Evarts and are inciting and leading the trouble. . . . Some are said to belong to those societies called 'Reds' and 'Communists,' and are opposed to the regularly constituted authority and to law and order." [63] Thus, as was so often the case, the violence was viewed as the work of outside agitators rather than the result of legitimate local grievances. On one count, at least, the governor was correct; law and order as administered in Harlan County was indeed the central target of the strikers' attack.

In a major study of violence in labor-management relations, Philip Taft asserts that he discovered not a single case where ideological radicalism, so often blamed for labor riots, caused violence; and the Harlan County bloodshed seems to be no exception to the rule.[64] Colonel Daniel M. Carrell, who conducted a National Guard investigation of the ambush and the violence that preceded it, flatly contradicted the governor's and sheriff's statements. Carrell asserted that prior to May 7, no radical activity, Communist or IWW, existed in Harlan County. Radical agitation and circulation of literature began only after the Battle of Evarts and the troop occupation and after it became crystal clear that the UMW strike had failed.[65] As late as November, 1931, when radical agitation in the county had reached its peak, a second National Guard investigation revealed "little or no activity" by radicals in the Evarts vicinity.[66]

Allan Taub, a New York attorney for the International Labor Defense, and Jim Garland, a local leader of the Communist-led National Miners Union, both testified before a United States Senate committee that Communist activity began only in late July and August after the UMW strike was broken.[67] When William Hightower was arrested ten days after the ambush, a cartoon depicting the Battle of Evarts was discovered on his person. In the cartoon, four assailants wore shirts significantly labeled "UMW," not "IWW." [68] Although an IWW pamphlet states that the organization chartered a Harlan County local as early as February, 1931, Harlan deputies allegedly confiscated a local IWW charter that was not issued until May 18, thirteen days after the ambush.[69] Not until June 2, four weeks after the battle, did *Industrial Solidarity*, the official IWW organ, first mention the Harlan strike.

Only after the battle, when the United Mine Workers refused to contribute strike relief, joined with county officials in a call for troops to quell the disturbance, and abandoned its campaign to organize the miners, did radical unionism, both IWW and Communist, gain a foothold in the county. Hunger, the abusive actions of private deputies, importation of non-union labor, the operators' unrelenting opposition to union recognition, and the spontaneous and uncontrolled nature of the strike, rather than radical harangues, produced the Battle of Evarts.

The violent climax of May 5 transformed the Harlan lockout into a full-scale strike that spread rapidly to twenty-three mines in the Clover Fork and Martin's Fork sections of Harlan County and to others in Bell County. On the day of the battle, 1,800 miners were out; six days later, 5,800 Harlan miners were on strike, leaving only 913 at work.[70] Strike demands now focused primarily on removal of armed guards.[71] On May 16, at a UMW rally in Pineville, eight hundred Bell County miners vowed, almost to a man, to mine no more coal until the Harlan guards were removed. They wildly cheered George Burchett's threat to "go up and shoot them off," [72] and in Harlan County several hundred miners turned out to pay their last respects to the one ambusher slain in the Battle of Evarts, Carl Richmond, who had attempted to do just that. Harlan operators attributed

the UMW's later failure in Harlan County to its violence and
radicalism during the 1931 strike, but no such conclusion can
be drawn from the events that followed the Evarts ambush.
Indeed, at this point the union seemed to enjoy its greatest
popularity and support. Only after the union adopted a compromising position and abandoned the campaign did the miners
grow disillusioned with the organization. Most miners seemed
more impressed by the futility of the UMW's effort than by the
trouble it caused.

In the wake of the Evarts ambush, county authorities, district union officials, and county residents, including many union
miners, joined in petitioning the governor for troops to restore
order. Aware that the organizing campaign was doomed and
military occupation was a certainty, district union officials and
Peter Campbell, secretary of the Kentucky Federation of
Labor, conferred with the governor's representatives to salvage
what they could. The governor promised that during the military occupation importation of strikebreakers would be prohibited, that all privately paid mine guards would be discharged
and disarmed, that evicted miners would be fed and housed,
and that the organizing campaign would be permitted to continue as long as no night meetings were held.[73] On May 7,
370 National Guardsmen, under the command of Colonel
Daniel M. Carrell, disembarked at the Evarts depot, where
they were enthusiastically greeted by a union band and a march
of two hundred union miners. The guard was instructed to
restore order, to protect lives and property, to investigate and
arrest all participants in the recent robberies and "assassina-
tions," and to use all lawful means to rid the area of outside
radical agitators.[74] The soldiers' arrival had an immediate quiet-
ing effect. On Friday, Evarts families who had fled the disturbances returned to their homes, and on Monday the public
schools reopened.

Despite the governor's quite generous agreement, no such
equitable solution was forthcoming. On May 11, Turnblazer
and "Peggy" Dwyer met privately with Governor Flem Sampson and attempted to gain his support for a settlement that
would substitute the open shop for the former nonunion shop;
in other words, county operators, without granting recognition

to the union, would henceforth employ both union and non-union miners. The agreement would provide for the reemployment of all discharged unionists without discrimination, the removal of armed guards, the dissolution of outstanding court injunctions, and the provision of food for starving miners and their families. For its part, the union would abandon its organizing campaign, exert every effort to prevent the growth of radicalism in the aftermath of the strike, and cooperate with the operators on any program that would mutually benefit both the industry and the miners.[75] The union was virtually offering a formal capitulation, but the next day, the Harlan County Coal Operators' Association met and dashed any hope for compromise.[76] In a later meeting that Governor Sampson arranged between Turnblazer and R. C. Tway, a powerful Harlan operator and Republican state chairman, Tway refused to discuss the unions' proposal with the governor's representative or even to enter the same room with Turnblazer.[77] Thus, through a combination of union impotence and management's firm position, the strike failed to gain anything.

As for relief of hungry miners, on May 8, Red Cross officials reiterated their refusal to interfere in an industrial dispute and recommended use of local contributions.[78] Because the coal operators refused local funds, the Red Cross's suggestion was an empty gesture. When strikers urged Colonel Carrell to request relief funds, the officer retorted that Black Mountain and Harlan Collieries needed five hundred miners, and if the miners badly needed food, they should work for it.[79] Ultimately, the miners were to be starved back into the pits.

The privately paid deputies were neither discharged nor disarmed. On May 11 and 12, however, at the owners' request, soldiers replaced private guards at Harlan Collieries, Black Mountain, and King Harlan, where only 11 of the firm's regular 280 employees were working; the reason for the transfer boded ill for the strikers. Colonel Carrell ordered the substitution of soldiers for private guards in order "to remove every possible trace of intimidation which we understand has kept men from seeking available work." The soldiers quickly halted picketing. On May 12, when union pickets stopped a Black Mountain truck that was transporting another nonunion employee's furniture to Kenvir, the guardsmen dispersed the pickets and escorted the truck through Evarts. Two days later, soldiers halted a march of three hundred union miners to non-union Crummies Creek mine.[80] Although many miners resumed work under troop protection, others saw "no difference be-tween working under the guns of 'tin hats' (troopers) and working under the guns of 'thug' mine guards." [81] It was a moot point because Sheriff Blair, asserting that "nobody is running this sheriff's department but me," refused to dismiss or disarm private deputies.[82]

While hunger and military occupation were undermining the strikers' morale, the special county grand jury's indictments and mass arrests dispensed with local union leadership. Four days after the Battle of Evarts, William B. Jones, Evarts police chief Asa Cusick, assistant police chief Al Benson, and Joe Cawood, the Evarts merchant and politician who had housed evicted unionists, were arrested and charged with three counts of murder in connection with the deaths of Jim Daniels, Howard Jones, and Otto Lee. Five days later, the union's president, William Hightower, was arrested on identical charges. On May 26, Jack Griffin, who succeeded Jones as act-ing secretary, was arrested on charges of banding and con-federating. Later, William Turnblazer, District 19's president, who had entered the county only once during the course of the strike, was indicted on three counts of conspiracy to murder on the basis of a letter he had written to Local 5355 before the ambush praising the Harlan miners for their fine spirit and urging them to keep up the good fight.[83] Forty-three unionists were eventually indicted and jailed for the slaying of the three deputies, and more than a hundred on charges of robbery and banding and confederating.

Not satisfied to stigmatize the union only with murder, robbery, and intimidation, on May 16 deputy sheriffs raided William B. Jones's house in Evarts, which also served as UMW headquarters, and allegedly discovered IWW literature, mem-bership lists, application cards, and dues books. The sheriff's undercover agents asserted that they had joined the UMW in Jones's front room and then had been taken into a back room for initiation into the IWW.[84] A Knoxville editor's suggestion that the evidence of radicalism might well have been planted by the same spies who discovered it in an effort to discredit respectable trade unionism did nothing to soften the blow.[85] Sheriff Blair's disclosure provided the county's operators, editor, and middle class with both a simple and a palatable explanation of the miners' past disaffection and a convenient rationalization for their own future violent reprisals against unionism, whether moderate or radical. Sheriff Blair first aroused a vicious antiradical hysteria and fastened upon the United Mine Workers an odium of radicalism and violence from which it required a decade to escape.

A week later, on Sunday, May 24, when the UMW convened a rally at the courthouse in Harlan, deputies tossed tear-gas canisters from the courthouse roof to disperse the orderly crowd, and Sheriff Blair proclaimed that no further rallies would be permitted.[86] Six years passed before Harlan County miners would again feel free to assemble. Thus, the last of the governor's promises—the union's right to assemble in daylight for organizational purposes—had been denied, and the United Mine Workers' 1931 campaign was clearly ended.

Their families starving, the members forbidden to picket or assemble, their leadership jailed and denied bail, and their union stigmatized as radical, union miners who were not permanently blacklisted gradually drifted back to work. At seventeen mines where only 913 miners were working when the troops arrived, 3,766 of the regular 6,800 employees were working two weeks later.[87] By June 17, when the R. W. Creech Coal Company, the county's most thoroughly organized mine, resumed operation, the strike was dead. When the last soldiers departed the county on July 23, all but 800 of 6,800 employees at seventeen mines were back at work.[88]

Between nine hundred and one thousand determined strikers who refused to relinquish their unionism and sign yellow-dog contracts were blacklisted and left to either starve or flee Harlan County. Both IWW and Communist organizers were already actively recruiting followers among the desperate and embittered minority. In mid-July, before the troops left, twenty-seven local National Miners Union members attended a Pittsburgh convention to help lay plans for another organizational campaign and strike. While any economic threat to Harlan's powerful nonunion operators was past, more trouble lay ahead for Harlan's citizens.

NOTES

1. George S. Ward, *Harlan* (Ky.) *Daily Enterprise*, May 14, 1931.
2. *Harlan Daily Enterprise*, Feb. 18, 22, 1931.
3. William Turnblazer, circular letter in U.S., Congress, House, *Congressional Record*, 71 Cong., 3 sess. (1931), vol. 74, pp. 4069–70.
4. *United Mine Workers Journal*, Mar. 15, 1931, p. 12.
5. *Knoxville* (Tenn.) *News-Sentinel*, Mar. 2, 1931.
6. Ibid., Mar. 23, 1931; U.S. conciliation commissioner to Hugh L. Kerwin, Mar. 10, 1931, NA, RG/280, "Coal Miners (Southeastern Ky.)," Box 294.
7. Manford Maupin to Herbert Hoover, Apr. 7, 1931, NA, RG/280, "Coal Miners (Southeastern Ky.)," Box 294.
8. U.S. conciliation commissioner to Hugh L. Kerwin, Apr. 8, 1931, ibid.
9. George S. Ward to U.S. conciliation commissioner, Mar. 31, 1931, ibid.
10. George Sweeten, interviewed by Paul F. Taylor, Apr. 15, 1954, cited in Taylor, "Coal Mine War in Harlan County, Kentucky, 1931–32," (M.A. thesis, University of Kentucky, 1955), pp. 60–61.
11. *Conditions in Coal Fields*, p. 203; Taylor, "Coal Mine War," p. 118.
12. Kentucky, Montgomery County Circuit Court, *Commonwealth of Kentucky* v. *W. B. Jones*, trial transcript (NA, RG/60, Classified Subject Files, Enclosures), vol. 7, pp. 981–86, 990–91, 993–94, 1012–13 (hereafter cited as *Commonwealth* v. *Jones*); Taylor, "Coal Mine War," p. 118.
13. Steve Humphrey, *Knoxville News-Sentinel*, May 8, 1931.
14. *Commonwealth* v. *Jones*, vol. 13, pp. 1908–9, vol. 7, pp. 985, 1109.
15. Kentucky, Montgomery County Circuit Court, *Commonwealth of Kentucky* v. *William Hightower*, trial transcript (NA, RG/60, Classified Subject Files, Enclosures), vol. 8, pp. 1052–60, 1082–83.
16. *Commonwealth* v. *Jones*, vol. 7, pp. 978–85.
17. Lawrence Dwyer to editor, n.d., *United Mine Workers Journal*, Apr. 15, 1931, p. 4; Al Benson, interviewed by Paul F. Taylor, Sept. 7, 1954, cited in Taylor, "Coal Mine War," p. 64.
18. *Commonwealth* v. *Jones*, vol. 1, pp. 154–58, vol. 7, pp. 1016–19.
19. Testimony of Jim Cawood, *Commonwealth* v. *Jones*, vol. 2, p. 171. An undercover agent for the county sheriff, Cawood probably estimated union membership conservatively.
20. Testimony of E. B. Childers, *Commonwealth* v. *Jones*, vol. 1, pp. 146–49; Childers's statement about closing is quoted by Steve Humphrey, *Knoxville News-Sentinel*, May 8, 1931.
21. *Harlan Daily Enterprise*, Feb. 18, 22, 1931; Louis Stark, *New York Times*, Sept. 27, 1931.
22. At this time, John L. Lewis, president of the United Mine Work-

ers, wrote: "Our organization affairs are such that it is simply impossible for me, at this time, to follow out your suggestion. . . . We are finding it necessary to conserve every dollar and, at the best, our accounts have been in the red for many months" (Lewis to W. Jett Lauck, Apr. 27, 1931, W. Jett Lauck Papers, University of Virginia). A year later, the president of District 2, UMW, wrote: "Of course, as you know our financial condition, we are unable to assist anyone on strike in the manner in which they request us to do so" (James Mark to Philip Murray, May 28, 1932, John Brophy Papers, Catholic University of America).

23. Louis Stark, *New York Times*, Sept. 27, 1931; F. D. Perkins, quoted by Steve Humphrey, *Knoxville News-Sentinel*, May 6, 1931.

24. William Turnblazer, quoted in *Knoxville News-Sentinel*, Mar. 25, 1931.

25. Turnblazer to U.S. conciliation commissioner, Mar. 24, 1931; see also telegram, Dwyer to U.S. conciliation commissioner, Mar. 17, 1931, NA, RG/280, "Coal Miners (Southeastern Ky.)," Box 294.

26. *Knoxville News-Sentinel*, Apr. 18, 1931; telegram, Turnblazer to Herbert Hoover, Mar. 31, 1931, quoted in *United Mine Workers Journal*, Apr. 15, 1931, p. 4.

27. *Knoxville News-Sentinel*, Apr. 26, 28, 1931; *Harlan Daily Enterprise*, Apr. 27, 28, 29, 30, 1931; Melvin P. Levy, in *Harlan Miners Speak*, p. 21.

28. Turnblazer to Hoover, Apr. 24, 1931, NA, RG/280, "Coal Miners (Southeastern Ky.)," Box 294.

29. Turnblazer to John Burton Payne, n.d., quoted in *United Mine Workers Journal*, May 1, 1931, p. 8.

30. *Knoxville News-Sentinel*, Apr. 27, May 1, 1931; *Harlan Daily Enterprise*, Apr. 27, 29, 1931.

31. *Knoxville News-Sentinel*, May 3, 1931; *Harlan Daily Enterprise*, May 4, 1931.

32. *Conditions in Coal Fields*, p. 204.

33. *Harlan Daily Enterprise*, Mar. 31, 1932. After dismissing eighty-six deputies as a result of a political quarrel in March, 1932, Sheriff Blair assured county citizens that his force was still sufficient to cope with any eventuality.

34. J. H. Blair, quoted in *Courier-Journal* (Louisville, Ky.), Mar. 27, 1932.

35. *Harlan Daily Enterprise*, Mar. 31, 1932; *Knoxville News-Sentinel*, Apr. 3, 1932.

36. Jerold S. Auerbach, *Labor and Liberty: The La Follette Committee and the New Deal* (Indianapolis and New York, 1966), pp. 117–18.

37. *Harlan Miners Speak*, p. 35, n. 1.

38. *Conditions in Coal Fields*, p. 120.

39. *Commonwealth* v. *Jones*, vol. 7, pp. 1045–47, 1056, 1112.

40. Ibid., vol. 1, pp. 142–43; *Conditions in Coal Fields*, pp. 120, 203.

41. Steve Humphrey, *Knoxville News-Sentinel*, May 6, 1931.

42. *Harlan Daily Enterprise*, Mar. 22, 1931.

43. *Commonwealth* v. *Jones*, vol. 6, pp. 962–67; *Harlan Daily Enterprise*, Nov. 20, 22, 1931, Sept. 25, 1932.

44. *Harlan Daily Enterprise*, Apr. 19, 1931.

45. *Knoxville News-Sentinel,* Apr. 19, 20, 1931.
46. *Harlan Daily Enterprise,* Apr. 20, 28, 1931; *Pineville* (Ky.) *Sun,* Apr. 30, 1931.
47. *Knoxville News-Sentinel,* Apr. 29, 1931.
48. *Harlan Daily Enterprise,* May 1, 1931.
49. Testimony of William B. Jones, *Commonwealth* v. *Jones,* vol. 7, pp. 1002–6.
50. Ibid., vol 3, pp. 369–70, 397–98, 400–401, vol. 2, pp. 313–14, 321, 346.
51. Ibid., vol. 2, p. 315, vol. 3, pp. 370–71.
52. Ibid., vol. 3, p. 371.
53. Testimony of Roy Hughes, *Commonwealth* v. *Jones,* vol. 4, p. 557. Some have contended that the miners were congregated on May 5 to picket and prevent the entry of Hughes, a nonunion miner, into the Black Mountain camp, but even Hughes himself was not informed of the move until that morning.
54. Testimony of Orville Howard, ibid., vol. 1, pp. 112–15, 120.
55. Ibid., pp. 141, 146, 152–53.
56. Testimony of Colonel Daniel M. Carrell, *Conditions in Coal Fields,* p. 120.
57. Testimony of E. M. Cox, *Commonwealth* v. *Jones,* vol. 1, pp. 77–80, 92, 94.
58. Testimony of George Dawn, ibid., vol. 2, pp. 258–63.
59. Testimony of Sherman Percival, ibid., pp. 231–35.
60. Testimony of Cox, ibid., vol. 1, pp. 82–83, 100–101.
61. *Harlan Daily Enterprise,* May 5, 1931; *Knoxville News-Sentinel,* May 8, 1931.
62. J. H. Blair, quoted in *Courier-Journal,* May 6, 1931.
63. Governor Flem D. Sampson, quoted in *Harlan Daily Enterprise,* extra edition, May 7, 1931.
64. Philip Taft, "Violence in American Labor Disputes," *Annals of the American Academy of Political and Social Science,* 364 (Mar., 1966), p. 130.
65. Testimony of Carrell, *Conditions in Coal Fields,* pp. 121, 125; idem, quoted in *Courier-Journal,* May 9, 1931.
66. Testimony of Major George M. Chescheir, *Conditions in Coal Fields,* p. 145.
67. Testimony of Allan Taub and James C. Garland, ibid., pp. 11, 46–47.
68. *Commonwealth* v. *Jones,* vol. 4, p. 580.
69. E. J. Costello, *The Shame That Is Kentucky's!* (Chicago, n.d.), p. 5; *Harlan Daily Enterprise,* Sept. 11, 1931.
70. Telegram, U.S. conciliation commissioner to Kerwin, May 6, 1931, NA, RG/280, "Coal Miners (Southeastern Ky.)," Box 294; testimony of Carrell, *Conditions in Coal Fields,* pp. 119, 121; George S. Ward, quoted in *Courier-Journal,* May 29, 1931.
71. Testimony of Carrell and Howard N. Eavenson, *Conditions in Coal Fields,* pp. 120, 203.
72. *Pineville Sun,* May 21, 1931.
73. Ibid., May 7, 1931; memorandum of agreement signed by William

J. Turnblazer, Lawrence Dwyer, Peter Campbell, Corbette Gillette, and Russell D. Miller, May 6, 1931, NA, RG/280, "Coal Miners (Southeastern Ky.)," Box 294.

74. Governor Flem D. Sampson, quoted in *Harlan Daily Enterprise,* extra edition, May 7, 1931; *Harlan Daily Enterprise,* May 7, 1931; *Knoxville News-Sentinel,* May 8, 1931.

75. U.S. conciliation commissioner to Kerwin, May 12, 1931, NA, RG/280, "Coal Miners (Southeastern Ky.)," Box 294.

76. D. B. Cornett, quoted in *Courier-Journal,* May 13, 1931.

77. U.S. conciliation commissioner to Kerwin, May 12, 1931, NA, RG/280, "Coal Miners (Southeastern Ky.)," Box 294.

78. *Harlan Daily Enterprise,* May 10, 1931.

79. *Courier-Journal,* May 14, 1931.

80. *Harlan Daily Enterprise,* May 12, 13, 15, 1931; *Conditions in Coal Fields,* p. 118.

81. William Hightower, quoted by Foster Eaton, *Knoxville News-Sentinel,* May 14, 1931.

82. *Knoxville News-Sentinel,* May 8, 1931.

83. Ibid., May 10, 1931; *Courier-Journal,* May 15, 27, 1931; *United Mine Workers Journal,* Jan. 1, 1932, pp. 6, 20.

84. *Harlan Daily Enterprise,* May 17, 1931; Foster Eaton, *Knoxville News-Sentinel,* May 16, 1931; testimony of Carrell, *Conditions in Coal Fields,* pp. 125–26.

85. Editorial, *Knoxville News-Sentinel,* May 17, 1931.

86. *Knoxville News-Sentinel,* May 25, 1931.

87. U.S. conciliation commissioner to Kerwin, May 25, 1931, NA, RG/280, "Coal Miners (Southeastern Ky.)," Box 294.

88. Testimony of Carrell, *Conditions in Coal Fields,* pp. 119, 121.

Union of the Damned

June, 1931 - July, 1932

In 1932, Harlan County's coal depression struck bottom. Coal production, which in 1929 had topped 14,093,453 tons valued at $24,432,000, plunged to 6,888,875 tons worth $7,765,000. Of 11,920 miners employed in 1930, only 7,838 were working two years later. The county's four thousand unemployed miners formed part of a nationwide pool of two hundred thousand surplus coal diggers. Miners who in 1929 had labored 259 days now worked 156 days, for two dollars per day. Losing money and watching mines close all about them, the operators were in an uncompromising mood; and their political servant, Sheriff Blair, his hand strengthened by the public outcry against violence and radicalism, would tolerate no further labor agitation. The time was inauspicious for a second miners' strike.

Although experienced UMW leaders recognized the futility of striking under such circumstances, the earlier, spontaneous Harlan miners' revolt had drawn the reluctant union into ostensible leadership of a strike that culminated in violence, mass arrests, total defeat, and the permanent blacklisting of nine hundred or a thousand miners. Most Harlan miners had had their fill of unionism and strikes for the moment; but the desperate blacklisted men, who had little more to lose, and miners in the surrounding southeastern Kentucky counties who had not yet revolted felt compelled to launch a second effort.

They believed themselves betrayed by the UMW, which had shown reluctance to lead them, had refused strike relief, had offered only meager legal assistance to the victims of the first strike, and had finally abandoned them altogether. These desperate souls turned for guidance to the UMW's more militant and daring Communist rival, the National Miners Union. The Communists, who in more prosperous times had few followers and who concerned themselves less with winning strikes and improving conditions than with radicalizing workers, did not shrink from combat during the Depression. They scorned the defeatist idea that unions could not organize and strike during such periods and deliberately defied past experience. They berated cautious party members for betraying a lack of faith in "the growing radicalization and revolutionizing of the masses in the U.S.A." [1]

In 1931, the National Miners Union organizers arrived in Harlan County exhausted and chastened by their recent experience in leading forty thousand miners of western Pennsylvania, eastern Ohio, and northern West Virginia in the largest strike ever conducted under the auspices of the Communist party. In the Pittsburgh strike, the first large strike the union had conducted alone, the NMU had demonstrated that it knew how to start but not to end a strike; it suffered a stunning defeat, which, in party chairman William Z. Foster's opinion, "dealt the N.M.U. a fatal blow." [2]

The union had little chance for success in Kentucky. It lacked the local cadre of disciplined Communist party leadership that it had enjoyed in the northern coal fields; when the union arrived, there was not a single functioning Communist party unit in the state of Kentucky, and at no time were there more than twenty local or outside trained party members operating in the field. The union's sizable contingent of immigrant leaders, bearing names like Borich, Kemenovich, and Wagenknecht, were at a disadvantage among a native-born, Anglo-Saxon, Protestant population who were suspicious even of WASP labor organizers from Pennsylvania. The Communists' atheist, interracial, collectivist, and pro-Soviet views, once known, directly affronted the Harlan miners' fundamentalist religion, racism, individualism, and patriotism. Because the governor and sheriff had attributed earlier violence to radical activity, antiradical hysteria was already building and soon reached fever pitch. The Communists confronted a wave of repression and vigilantism beyond anything the UMW had recently experienced. Reluctant to burn their fingers again on a strike, NMU leaders procrastinated, but impatient local miners ultimately propelled them into the unpromising struggle.[3]

During the UMW strike in Harlan County, from May 26 until late June, 1931, the National Miners Union was preoccupied with its northern strike and took little notice of the Kentucky struggle. Not until May 21, seventeen days after the Battle of Evarts, did the Communist press first mention the Harlan struggle. In mid-June, J. Louis Engdahl, chairman of the Communist relief auxiliary, the International Labor Defense, journeyed to Harlan to offer legal assistance to Jones, Hightower, and other defendants in the Evarts murder case, but the UMW men rejected his offer. In late June, a week after the R. W. Creech Coal Company resumed operation and the UMW strike was definitely lost, the first NMU organizer, Dan Slinger, alias Dan Brooks, and a young female representative of the ILD, Jessie Wakefield, were sent to Harlan County. They went at the behest of a tiny group of strikers who had been impressed by the militant rhetoric of the *Daily Worker* and who in early June had asked its editor to send NMU organizers. While the National Guard remained in the county, radical literature—the *Daily Worker, Southern Worker, Labor Unity,* and *New Pioneer*—was widely circulated, and the NMU established seven soup kitchens, a most effective recruiting device for starving miners. By early July, ten NMU local unions had been formed.[4]

On July 15, twenty-seven southeastern Kentucky delegates, led by Dan Brooks, Bill Duncan, Jim Grace, and Jim Garland, attended an NMU convention in Pittsburgh. One of the Harlan delegates assured the group that "nobody has any use for the UMW after seeing how they've done us in Harlan. Everybody is wanting to join the National Miners Union." [5] Jim Grace, a Holiness preacher from Harlan, emotionally depicted the starvation of the Kentucky miners and the Red Cross's and UMW's refusal to assist them. Grace urged the delegates to "take our guns and pistols out of their hiding places, and use them on traitors and gun-men who represent our present form of Government" and brought the delegates to their feet wildly applauding when he described the recent Battle of Evarts, "when several gun-men bit the dust of Kentucky, at the hands of the mining slaves." Frank Borich, the NMU's national secretary, reported that since the UMW strike had failed and the miners had been disillusioned with the compromising AFL union, the NMU had been actively organizing in Kentucky; he promised relief to Harlan strikers and asserted that a strike would be called at the next convention.[6] On July 22, the NMU issued a charter to the Harlan County miners.[7]

The Harlan coal operators, county officials, and the local press quickly acted to make the union's Communist connections the central issue. Instead of feeding people, alleviating suffering, and attempting to secure employment for blacklisted miners, the Harlan powers chose to suppress ideas, to halt distribution of relief, and to jail or expel from the county both the radical organizers and their followers. Erroneously attributing the earlier violence to radical agitation rather than to starvation and repression, county leaders sought to prevent a second outbreak of violence by using hunger and coercion, the causes of the first. Rationalizing their actions as necessary for social peace and the preservation of their very civilization, the coal operators, the sheriff, the courts, the press, civic groups, veterans' organizations, vigilantes, and the United Mine Workers combined to destroy the radical movement.

The local press helped establish a climate favorable to ruthless suppression. As soon as he learned there was a Communist in the county, editor Alverson asserted that *"an iron heel must be used to stamp out the foul growth."* And the editor of the *Pineville Sun* urged Bell County officials to crush communism without "too many scruples as to the methods." [8]

At the same time, every effort was made to squelch outside journalistic criticism of either hunger or repression. From across the mountain at Norton, Virginia, *Crawford's Weekly*, edited by Bruce Crawford, a member of the National Committee for the Defense of Political Prisoners, directed a steady barrage of criticism at Harlan operators and county officials. On July 28, when Crawford and a friend visited Harlan to gather news, a hidden assailant shot the editor in the ankle. In mid-August, Boris Israel, a twenty-one-year-old reporter for the Federated Press, a radical labor news service, arrived in Harlan to report the Evarts murder trial. On opening day, three men, one of whom Israel identified as Deputy Sheriff "Two-Gun" Marion Allen, abducted him from the courtroom, drove him to the top of a hill overlooking the county seat, threatened his life, and shot him in the leg as he ran from the hill. After having his wound dressed in Pineville, he fled Kentucky and failed to return to Harlan to press charges.[9] Federated Press replaced Israel with Mrs. Harvey O'Conner. On the day of her arrival, she received a note from "100% Americans and we don't mean maybe," warning her that she had "been here too long already" and to "remember that the other red neck reporter got what was coming to him, so don't let the sun go down on you here." [10] She did not.

Censorship was not confined to the radical press. The *Knoxville News-Sentinel*, which boasted a county circulation of six thousand compared to the hometown daily's four thousand, favored unionism, UMW or NMU. During the troubled summer of 1931, at least seven large coal companies prohibited circulation or possession of the Tennessee daily. "Uncle Bob" Lawson, superintendent at Cornett-Lewis, barred the paper at his camp because he believed it to be a "Red" or "Bolshevik" journal that published false and "dark pictures" of Harlan County.[11] When the Knoxville paper published a series of particularly critical articles by Benton J. Stong, the Harlan Kiwanis Club and the *Harlan Daily Enterprise* organized a boycott of the *News-Sentinel* and against the wholesale merchants of Knoxville until the newspaper ceased publishing "twisted, distorted, misrepresented and misinterpreted" views of Harlan County.[12]

Utilizing Kentucky's statute on criminal syndicalism, the sheriff attempted to jail or expel radical leaders. Soon after Bill Duncan and Jim Grace returned from the NMU convention, deputies raided their homes in search of radical literature. Duncan was arrested, and warrants issued for Grace's arrest forced him to pursue his activities in some other southeastern Kentucky county and eventually in New York City, where he solicited miners' relief. After having her automobile dynamited on August 6, ILD representative Jessie Wakefield was arrested on a charge of criminal syndicalism, as was Arnold Johnson, a seminary student representing the American Civil Liberties Union. Failing to post a $10,000 bond, the pair were held in the Harlan County jail for five weeks. Given their choice of transferring to an isolated Jackson County jail or leaving the state, on September 12 they departed Kentucky.[13]

The NMU's seven soup kitchens became favorite targets of suppression. Interestingly, the feeding stations posed a special problem for the Communists, who insisted on feeding white and black miners under the same roof and at the same table. Black miners, knowing that it would invite attack by county officials as an affront to community customs, strenuously opposed the practice and insisted on taking their meager allotments home for consumption. On August 11, deputies arrested Finley and Caleb Powers, who operated one of the feeding stations, on charges of banding and confederating; early the same morning, dynamite destroyed the Evarts kitchen. Two weeks later, deputies jailed Debs Moreland, proprietor of the Pansy feeding station. Released a month later, Moreland reopened the kitchen for two weeks. Again, deputies took him into custody, allegedly beat him, and forced him to flee the county. On Sunday evening, August 30, the Clovertown soup kitchen was the scene of two deaths. Having driven out to inspect the kitchen, Deputy Lee Fleenor focused his car headlights on the building and stepped out into the shadows. Three frightened men, Joe Moore, Julius Baldwin, an NMU local secretary, and his brother, Jeff Baldwin, rushed out into the headlights' glare with guns drawn and fired at Fleenor. Escaping injury, Fleenor killed Moore and Julius Baldwin and seriously wounded Jeff. Tried for murder only after a county political shakeup a year later, Fleenor was acquitted by a jury after a five-minute deliberation.[14]

Florence Reece, a balladeer whose husband joined the NMU, later recalled the repression. "When the thugs were raiding our house off and on, and Sam was run off, I felt like I just had to do something to help. The little children, they'd have little legs and a big stomach. Some men staggered when they walked,

they were so hungry. . . . We didn't even have any paper, so
when I wanted to write "Which Side Are You On?" I just
jerked the calendar off the wall and sat down and wrote the
words down on the back." [15] She scribbled a militant strike call:

> With pistols and with rifles
> They take away our bread
> And if you miners hinted it
> They'll sock you on the head.
>
>   Which side are you on?
>   Which side are you on?
>
> Gentlemen, can you stand it?
> Oh, tell me how you can?
> Will you be a gun thug
> Or will you be a man?
>
>   Which side are you on?
>   Which side are you on? [16]

This rarely militant folksong, carried east by the visiting organizers, was to become one of America's most popular and
enduring labor songs.

By late October, the raids had taken their toll. "Relief cut
down to practically nothing," reported a Communist field organizer to New York headquarters. "All the kitchens but one
closed in the last few weeks, the one operating is operating on
credit." [17] The remaining kitchen was undoubtedly located beyond Harlan's borders. Earlier, the same source had reported:
"Everything collapsed for a time; there was no functioning
Party, no meetings of miners' locals, nothing in fact except sub-
mission to repeated raids upon miners' homes, searches, sei-
zures, shootings, etc." [18]

Before the local movement collapsed, however, Harlan residents feared an outburst of violence when the Harlan County
Circuit Court convened on April 17 to try the Evarts murder
cases. A week earlier, the same day the Evarts soup kitchen
was destroyed, a stink bomb was detonated in the automobile
driven by the miners' defense attorneys, Ben Golden of Pineville and United States Congressman John M. Robison. That
weekend the ILD called for miners and their families to stage
a mass demonstration in front of the Harlan jail and courthouse

when court convened. The ILD demanded a jury composed solely of laborers, immediate release of all prisoners of the class war, dismissal of all company-paid mine guards, and freedom for the miners to organize, picket, and strike. Sheriff Blair publicly assured miners that the Evarts defendants would receive a fair trial and banned all public demonstrations for its duration. On Friday and Saturday nights the glare of flaming crosses illuminated the mountains overlooking the county seat, and ominous booms of exploding dynamite echoed across the valley to call attention to the spectacle. Although the local editors seemed puzzled by the exhibition, its meaning could not have been lost on the miners and Communists who watched through the barred windows of the Harlan County jail or who scurried furtively about the county to organize Monday's demonstration. Local citizens nervously awaited the opening of court.[19]

When court convened, Commonwealth's Attorney W. A. Brock requested a change of venue for the eighteen Evarts defendants, and on August 24, Judge D. C. Jones transferred the cases to the distant Bluegrass counties of Montgomery and Clark. This surprise action removed from Harlan County the most obvious rallying point for radical agitation, and NMU support there all but collapsed.

Although the Harlan miners were severely suffering, their mood had grown fatalistic. "It's possible to be bitter hungry most all of the time and still keep alive. That's what most of us do, I guess," a Harlan miner's wife explained. Having suffered one disastrous defeat, most Harlan miners had been rehired and had grown fearful of unions, investigations, and strangers.[20] As a result of the intensity of the antiradical campaign, the transfer of the Evarts murder cases to distant parts, and the unresponsiveness of the Harlan miners, the National Miners Union transferred its base of operations to neighboring Bell County around September 1.[21] In the Straight Creek section of Bell County and the Brush Creek section of Knox County, the NMU enjoyed a far greater response; thereafter, those counties served as the focal point of radical agitation, strikes, demonstrations, and investigations.

To revive waning interest in the NMU's organizing campaign

and potential strike, the ILD invited another new Communist auxiliary, the National Committee for the Defense of Political Prisoners, to investigate and publicize conditions in the Harlan and Bell County coal fields. Angered by the earlier shooting of his NCDPP colleague, Bruce Crawford, and alarmed by the ILD's contention that Harlan operators and county officials were perpetrating a "reign of terror" upon starving miners, the novelist Theodore Dreiser, currently serving as NCDPP chairman, and eleven other left-wing writers conducted a two-day investigation in early November.[22] Involved were Dreiser, author of *Sister Carrie* and *An American Tragedy;* John Dos Passos, author of the *U.S.A.* trilogy; Samuel Ornitz, author of *Haunch, Paunch and Jowl;* Lester Cohen, author of *Sweepings;* Bruce Crawford, editor of *Crawford's Weekly;* Charles Rumford Walker, later author of *American City;* Walker's wife, Adelaide, a former actress; Harry Gannes, *Daily Worker* editor; Melvin P. Levy, NCDPP secretary; George Maurer, ILD representative; Dreiser's secretary, Julia Parker (alias Celia Kuhn); and his friend Marie Pergain.

Governor Sampson's military observer who accompanied the committee on its rounds judged the group as "decidedly radical or communistic. . . . They are certainly anti-capitalistic and believe that the system of the United States Government is wrong, and that one must not be too cautious in bringing about a change." [23] A member of the American Friends Service Committee, which fed Harlan children that winter, thought the writers demonstrated a preference for "changing horses and dumping their rider into the stream." [24] Although a few members of the committee were committed radicals, most were troubled liberals stung by the Depression-induced poverty, the unemployment, and the apparent breakdown of capitalism. Many were wrestling with the whole question of the artist's role in society: should he stand above it, completely committed to art for art's sake, or should he become actively involved in shaping a better civilization? All were seeking an answer, but few had yet found any. Their observations among the Kentucky miners had an important impact on these sensitive individuals.

When Dreiser visited Kentucky, he stood at a crossroads of his career. Earlier in the year, at the behest of Communist party boss William Z. Foster, he had investigated the NMU's Pennsylvania coal strike and produced a report condemning the quiescent UMW and praising its aggressive Communist rival, the NMU.[25] For him, the Kentucky investigation and report, *Harlan Miners Speak*, represented a repeat performance that merely confirmed his deeply held prejudices. His most recent biographer believed that when Dreiser reached Kentucky, "he was unrivaled in his violence, his misinformation and his blind hatred for capitalists" whom he had formerly respected as "ruthless but essential" men of action.[26] Malcolm Ross astutely observed that had Dreiser in 1932

> approached Harlan people in the creative mood of *Sister Carrie*, he might have written something to be remembered long after the last load of Harlan coal has been mined. But Dreiser today is a bitter man. He is sickened by observing decades of injustice with the sensitized vision of an artist. When in the coal fields he closed his eyes to everything except the most dire wretchedness his guides could find for him. He snubbed the rather racy individuals who run things in those parts, and consequently they besmirched him with an immorality charge wholly irrelevant to the issue. This confirmed Dreiser's preconceived opinion of them. He was satisfied, for he had come to make war.[27]

In 1931, Dreiser's observations of capitalist failure in Pennsylvania and Kentucky and the apparent Communist economic stability he saw during a winter tour of the Soviet Union convinced him that communism was the solution for the United States' social and economic ills. Thereafter, he abandoned his literary career for that of pamphleteer and agitator. The following year, he began seeking membership in the Communist party; but because of his inability to accept party discipline, he was long denied admission. In 1945, long after most other American literary radicals had grown disenchanted with communism, Dreiser was at last admitted to the CPUSA.[28]

As a result of the Kentucky experience, John Dos Passos veered in the opposite direction. Since the Sacco and Vanzetti executions in 1927 he had moved steadily leftward, but in Kentucky, he watched Communist organizers manipulate the miners' misery to promote the party's cause, abuse the sincere

IWW and UMW members, and deny legal assistance to imprisoned miners who refused to join their movement. Convinced that the Communists were using the miners as "pawns" and "making monkeys of the warmhearted liberals" like himself, he edged away from them and moved gradually to the political right.[29]

Harry Gannes, George Maurer, and Celia Kuhn were already directly affiliated with one or another organization of the Communist party apparatus; and Sam Ornitz, later a defendant in the Hollywood Ten trial, had already expressed his revolutionary views before reaching Harlan in a strident *New Masses* article entitled "Bleeding Bowels in Kentucky."

At formal hearings in Pineville and Harlan, Mrs. Jim Grace, a local NMU organizer, had carefully preselected friendly witnesses and freely prompted those who faltered in their testimony. Two outside NMU organizers, Ruth Decker and Mrs. Tom Myerscough, conducted the committee on a tour of the left fork of Straight Creek, Bell County, an older coal field where most mines had been exhausted and the camps abandoned. Unemployed and blacklisted miners and their families had occupied the rent-free, deserted dwellings. This area and the adjoining Wallins Creek section of Harlan County, where the closure of two huge Ford Motor Company mines in 1929 and 1931 had left large numbers of miners unemployed, possessed the worst housing and dietary conditions in southeastern Kentucky.[30] John Dos Passos portrayed these miners' houses as Florida shanties, constructed of thin sheathing lined with newspapers to break the wind, roofed with tar paper, and floored with rotten and broken boards. "The first step I took into the cabin," he wrote, "the floor creaked so I put my hand against the wall to steady myself. The rotten boards gave. With several people crowding into it, the crowded cabin looked as if it would crumple up at any minute. The floor of the kitchen had already caved in." [31]

The committee chose not to view Harlan County's newer, more permanent, model coal camps, such as Closplint or Lynch, the latter alone housing twelve thousand persons, equal to one-third the total population of Bell County.

Here on Straight Creek, the committee discovered Aunt

Molly Jackson, local midwife, coal miner's wife, minstrel of the Kentucky miners' strike, a woman destined to become one of the more famous folksingers of the radical thirties. Aunt Molly's Scotch-Irish great-grandfather had stolen his bride from a Cherokee chief in Oklahoma and brought her to Eastern Kentucky's Clay County. There in the region's preindustrial era, in Aunt Molly's words, "the good old days [before] the coal operators began to swindle and cheat," her mother's family—the Robinsons—and her father's family—the Garlands—dwelt for seven generations. Life dealt harshly with this coal miner's daughter, born Mary Magdalene Garland in 1880. When she was three, her father moved the family to Laurel County to open a store. Because he sold groceries to miners on credit, the store failed after only two years, and he was forced into the coal mines, working six days per week and preaching once on Saturday and twice on Sunday. When Molly was six, her mother died of tuberculosis. Her father remarried and fathered eleven additional children, a total of fifteen. At fourteen, Molly married Jim Stewart and quickly bore two children. After nursing in a Clay County hospital for a decade, in 1908 she moved to Harlan County, where, acting as a midwife, she eventually delivered 884 babies. In 1917, her husband was killed by a slate fall in the mine, and she married another miner, Bill Jackson. Meanwhile, mining accidents blinded her father and a brother and killed another brother and one of her sons.[32]

In only three months during the fall of 1931, thirty-seven Straight Creek children died in the old midwife's arms. Diseases of poverty—tuberculosis, pellagra, and bloody flux—took their lives. "I still hear hungry children cry," she recalled more than twenty years later. "I saw my own sister's little fourteen-month-old baby girl starve to death for milk while the coal operators was riding around in fine cars with their wives and children all dressed up in diamonds and silks, paid for by the blood and sweat of the coal miners."[33] The old lady, who had sung and put together songs since childhood, set her feelings to verse in "I Am a Union Woman" in 1931. "The bosses ride fine horses / While we walk in the mud," she protested. "Their banner is the dollar sign / While ours is striped with blood."[34]

Her miseries, most of them directly attributable to the dangers and inequities of coal mining, radicalized Aunt Molly. "I've been . . . accused of being a Red," she later complained. "I never heard tell of a Communist until after I left Kentucky [1932]—then I had passed fifty—but they called me a Red. I got all of my progressive ideas from my hard tough struggles, and nowhere else." [35]

Her miner father, who had always preached unionism along with the gospel, had taught her to act on her beliefs. Since age five, she had attended union meetings, picketed, sung, and organized. In 1931 her younger half-brother Jim Garland, convinced that the United Mine Workers had betrayed the miners' cause, sheltered the popular young Communist youth organizer Harry Simms and became district organizer for the NMU; and Aunt Molly joined the radical union. She was jailed in Clay County, and her husband was forced to divorce her to keep his mining job. Impressed with her during their November visit, the Dreiser Committee took her out of the Cumberlands to solicit funds in thirty-eight states for the striking miners. Twenty-one thousand people heard her and Jim Garland perform at New York's Coliseum and contributed $900 to the miners' cause. Badly crippled in a bus accident while touring Ohio and rejected by the left-wing Workers Music League, which at the time saw no use for her militant mountain songs beyond the immediate campaign, she returned to the Cumberlands. [36]

By the last half of the thirties, however, New York's radical left had discovered the uses of such ballads as significant propaganda tools. In 1935 and 1936, part of the Garland clan— Aunt Molly Jackson, Jim Garland, and Molly's half-sister Sarah Ogan—moved to New York City to join with Woody Guthrie, Earl Robinson, Will Geer, Harvard-educated Pete Seeger, and others to forge "folksongs into weapons of subversion." Professor Charles Seeger watched her within a few months "convert herself, when expedient, from a traditional singer, who seemed never to have given any particular thought to whether anyone liked or disliked her singing, into a shrewd observer of audience reaction, fixing individual listeners one after another with her gaze, smiling ingratiatingly, gesturing, dramatizing her performance." [37] Also, in New York, she "learned from more sophisticated people the universality of the truths she had discovered in her own experiences, and these became the themes of her best songs." [38]

When the Dreiser Committee encountered Aunt Molly on Straight Creek in late 1931, her songs were not yet affected by the later revolutionary ideology. Her unadorned composition "Kentucky Miners' Wives Ragged Hungry Blues" simply expressed the desperate plight in which the blacklisted Harlan refugees found themselves:

> No food, no clothes for our children, I'm sure this ain't no lie,
> No food, no clothes for our children, I'm sure this ain't no lie,
> If we can't git more for our labor, we will starve to death and
> die. . . .
>
> This mining town I live in is a sad and lonely place,
> This mining town I live in is a sad and lonely place,
> Where pity and starvation is pictured on every face.[39]

After their encounter with Aunt Molly, the Dreiser Committee and the local NMU held a twilight rally in a tiny Baptist church on Straight Creek to test the local state of civil liberties. After the editor of the *Daily Worker* praised the Soviet Union for escaping unemployment, a miner shouted from the audience, "If they won't let us march under the American flag, we'll march under the red flag." ILD representative George Maurer urged miners to join the NMU and strike. He promised that the Workers International Relief would furnish strike relief, the Federated Press would publicize their cause, and the ILD and American Civil Liberties Union would fight their legal battles. At a Sunday afternoon rally in the high school auditorium at Wallins Creek, Finley Donaldson, local NMU chairman, Holiness preacher, and coal miner for thirty-three years until a mine accident disabled him, stole the spotlight. Stalking up and down the platform and pounding his great fist on the table, Donaldson denounced the UMW for its betrayal of the Harlan miners and pleaded with those present to join the NMU. Roaring that "there is no place for a capitalist sympathizer but Hell," he urged miners to use force to obtain their demands. He himself threatened "to kill, murder, rob for my children because I won't let my children starve." [40]

A week after the committee departed, on the basis of evidence gathered at these meetings, a Bell County grand jury indicted each member for criminal syndicalism, a felony and an extraditable offense carrying a maximum penalty of twenty-one years' imprisonment and a $10,000 fine. The same jury indicted Dresiser and Marie Pergain for adultery. When Dreiser had retired Saturday night, Miss Pergain had joined him in his room. Four local busybodies propped toothpicks against his door, and when the toothpicks remained undisturbed next morning, the four concluded that the young lady had spent the night there for immoral purposes.[41]

Dreiser explained to the press that he was impotent, but neither the press nor his close friends believed his disclaimer. The adultery indictment commanded national headlines and, while some committee members were incensed because Dreiser's personal misconduct detracted from the seriousness of their purpose, the sex scandal attracted more national attention to coal-field conditions than they would otherwise have received. Bell County officials agreed not to serve the warrants or seek extradition on the criminal syndicalism charge if the NCDPP ceased its agitation in Kentucky. Dreiser apparently decided he could best serve the radical cause elsewhere and refused to return for trial. John Dos Passos, whom Communist leaders asked to return to Kentucky, also refused. A year and a half later, after labor troubles had subsided, both the criminal syndicalism and the adultery charges were dismissed.[42]

In February, 1932, after an NMU strike had already failed, the NCDPP published its propagandistic report and selected testimony as *Harlan Miners Speak: A Report on Terriorism in the Kentucky Coal Fields*. The title was a misnomer. The only on-site investigation was conducted in another and older coal field, the Jellico field, and in another county, Bell. Few Harlan miners "spoke"; the book was dominated by the observations of Dreiser, Dos Passos, Walker, Levy, and Israel, writers who had visited there, along with Sherwood Anderson and Mary Heaton Vorse, who had not. The committee reported a widespread "reign of terror," which did exist but was largely confined to a few dozen native and outside radicals. Whereas the Dreiser Committee estimated three thousand miners suffering destitution, one week later the Statewide Welfare Relief Committee's investigation disclosed only one-third that number facing actual starvation. In total, *Harlan Miners Speak* distorted and misrepresented local conditions in order to discredit county officials and the UMW, to promote the cause of the NMU in Kentucky and elsewhere, and to instigate a congressional investigation of local conditions.

Although *Harlan Miners Speak* appeared too late to aid the cause, the national attention that attached to the Dreiser Committee's November visit boosted the NMU's immediate fortune. Miners, heretofore unacquainted with Dreiser or his work, were encouraged by the attention of so prominent a national figure and by the committee's promise of strike relief and legal aid if they would join the radical union and strike. Though Harlan miners remained passive, hundreds of Straight Creek and Brush Creek miners enrolled. Thus, the writers' visit gave an impetus to a futile strike that ultimately resulted in even greater unemployment and destitution among the miners.[43]

The investigation did, however, provoke some interest in alleviating the miners' distress. On November 13, Governor Sampson dispatched Harry E. Bullock, a Lexington coal operator and chairman of the Statewide Welfare Relief Committee, to investigate and report on the extent of destitution in Bell and Harlan counties. Assisted by two local members of the state relief committee and by southeastern Kentucky's Red Cross director, Bullock produced an impartial and sophisticated report. Although employed miners were earning only two dollars to four dollars per day, the coal operators, by providing four to six days' weekly employment and by advancing thousands of dollars in credit, much of which could never be repaid, were assuring working miners a reasonable living standard. On the other hand, about one thousand miners and their families, who had been discharged, evicted, and blacklisted because they had participated in the earlier UMW strike or the present radical agitation, were experiencing severe hardship: "They are not Reds, Communists, or trouble makers, but are classed as such by mine operators. . . . These men and their families are in want and will continue to be so long as they are living in the county. . . . These people are all known to mine operators and will not be employed." The Red Cross had refused to aid disputants in an industrial conflict, and the coal operators had refused to contribute to any private or public agency that would assist this group. Only the NMU had attempted to assist them. This in large part explained the radical union's growth in the region. Bullock pleaded with coal operators, local courts, welfare agencies, and the Red Cross to cooperate in feeding and providing jobs for these destitute families, the best cure for social unrest.[44]

Bullock's intelligent recommendations were favorably received in some Harlan County quarters. Editor James Alverson, who in August had advocated the "iron heel," now argued for a helping hand and a full stomach as the best method to assure that "the seed of discontent, Communism, and anarchy will have no place to grow." [45] As firmly committed to philanthropy as to antiunionism, the editor generously supported his new editorial policy with his pocketbook.

Only four days after the writers' committee departed, twenty-eight local charitable groups combined to launch the Harlan County Relief Association. The group raised $5,000 locally, half of it contributed by the Harlan Kiwanis Club and another $500 by the Harlan Fiscal Court. To this, the Red Cross added $38,393 worth of food and garden seeds to provide a total budget of $43,893. Within the next six months, the association distributed food and garden seeds to more than 7,000 persons and eleven thousand sacks of flour to 12,500 persons, and furnished thirty-three thousand hours of work relief to 308 men. In the summer of 1932, on land furnished and plowed by the coal operators and with seeds provided by the Red Cross, Harlan miners planted three thousand new acres in vegetable gardens. The addition of fresh vegetables to the normally drab and starchy miners' diet alleviated some of the dietary deficiencies of 1930–31.

Although the relief association continued to encourage an exodus of blacklisted miners and their families, it sought to relocate them on farms or with employed relatives rather than to drive them forth by starvation and repression. The Harlan County Coal Operators' Association, which refused to assist the relief association's other programs, contributed one-fifth of the funds for its special Rehabilitation Committee that relocated forty-five families, 225 persons, over a two-month period.

At Governor Sampson's invitation, on November 18 the American Friends Service Committee began feeding 45 percent of the children enrolled in fifteen county schools. During the school year 1931–32, the Friends, to whom coal operators did not object because they did not feed starving parents and because they maintained strict neutrality in the industrial conflict, fed 1,405 schoolchildren, 263 preschoolers, and 69 expectant or nursing mothers. Had it not been for the Friends' feeding program, many more children would have perished from malnutrition. The infusion of relief and goodwill by the Friends and the Harlan County Relief Association that winter played an important role in pacifying miners' discontent and siphoning off radical support.

Nine days after the Dreiser Committee's visit, Montgomery County Circuit Court convened to try Bill Burnett for the April slaying of Deputy Sheriff Jesse Pace and to try William B. Jones, William Hightower, and eight other defendants for the Evarts murders of Jim Daniels, Howard Jones, and Otto Lee. The Industrial Workers of the World's General Defense Committee assisted the miners' defense, and, had the trials gone favorably for the miners, the radical union movement might have profited from them. Burnett was tried first and acquitted on a plea of self-defense, but then the tide turned.[46] Either because of Burnett's acquittal or because of the difficulty in establishing Jones's or Hightower's presence at the scene of the ambush, the regular murder indictments against the ten Evarts defendants were replaced by indictments charging conspiracy to murder, an allegation far easier to prove. In addition, each defendant was named in three separate indictments, which meant that if he were acquitted of one charge, he could be tried on a second and even a third. Judge Henry Prewitt refused to grant the defense attorneys additional time to prepare a defense against the new charges and ordered immediate trial of William B. Jones.

The prosecution sought to prove that at the theater meeting on the eve of the Battle of Evarts union miners conspired to murder the three deputies, that Jones was the archconspirator, and that he was present at the scene of battle either deploying his assassins or actually participating in the shooting.

Fred, John, and Hugh Lester testified that they attended the theater meeting and heard Jones urge the miners to arm themselves with rifles, shotguns, pistols, rocks, or red flags and gather by the Evarts-Harlan highway next morning to lie in wait for the Black Mountain deputies who would pass through en route to Harlan to testify at the arraignment of Bill Burnett. The three brothers told the jury that Hightower conducted an affirmative vote on the proposal, told the miners to feign ignorance of the plot, and selected two committees to procure additional arms and ammunition in Bell County and a third to lure Sheriff Blair into their trap.

The defense denied that the Lester brothers had attended the theater meeting and attacked their credibility as witnesses. Roger Vanover testified that on his way to the meeting he met John and Hugh Lester and Charlie Middleton going toward their homes, and Middleton testified that he walked home with the Lesters, who told him they were not going to attend the meeting.[47] John and Hugh Lester, both indicted for participating in the Evarts ambush, were already under indictment for the December, 1930, murder of Lonnie Prince. Fred Jones, brother of the commissary clerk slain at Evarts, represented the Lester brothers in the Prince murder case. Simultaneously, Black Mountain Coal Corporation retained Jones to assist the state in prosecuting the Evarts murder cases in which John and Hugh Lester were defendants. After the two brothers turned state's evidence, both the Prince and Evarts murder indictments against them were dismissed, and both were employed by Black Mountain Coal Corporation.[48] Numerous witnesses impugned the three Lester brothers' reputation for truthfulness and general morality and testified that earlier that year Fred Lester had been dismissed as Verda postmaster for "lack of veracity."[49]

William B. Jones, testifying in his own defense, and numerous defense witnesses gave the jury an opposite account of what transpired at the theater meeting. They contended that the group elected two committees to procure relief supplies in Bell County and distribute them in Evarts and Verda. After a five-minute discussion of the mine guards' abuse of miners and their families, the meeting elected a third committee to seek redress from Sheriff Blair and, if necessary, the governor. They denied the existence of any conspiracy to murder the deputies.[50]

An Evarts coal operator, two Black Mountain mine guards, and an Evarts policeman testified that they saw Jones, carrying a rifle, cross the Clover Fork bridge toward the scene of battle shortly before the shooting began. A Black Mountain miner and his family who lived near the site of the ambush testified that they saw Jones on a neighbor's porch just minutes before the battle.[51]

Jones told the jurors that he was at home before and during the battle. He worked on a union report and wrote letters until 7:00 A.M., when a three-member housing committee arrived. Just as the committee was departing, the shooting erupted, and the four men stood listening on Jones's porch. When the shooting died out, they walked downtown to learn what had happened. The three committee members and numerous other witnesses who had passed Jones's house and seen them talking confirmed his account.[52] A prosecution witness, who had worked on the Clover Fork bridge all morning except for thirty minutes when he was inside mixing paint, saw several armed men cross the bridge but denied seeing Jones, whom he knew.[53]

The employment of Ben Golden, a highly respected Pineville attorney, by the IWW to assist the defense may have prejudiced Jones's case.[54] Although no testimony linked Jones to the IWW or the NMU, in his closing argument, Commonwealth's Attorney W. C. Hamilton asserted that Jones was affiliated with the radical unions and warned jurors of the effect acquittal might have throughout southeastern Kentucky and the world. He charged that Jones had joined the IWW, which advocated the "banishment of God." Hamilton cautioned the jury that, during the spring recruiting marches in Harlan, Jones "carried an American flag in his hand but the red flag of the I.W.W. was in his heart." He warned that the Soviet Union was observing

Jones's fate; and if he were acquitted ,"in Moscow the red flag will be raised higher." If Jones were freed, that very weekend "in Pineville or Harlan there will be celebrations of reds, and property will have no more value than human life is regarded there now." [55] In addition to striking a blow against radicalism, many Bluegrass jurors probably envisioned themselves as helping to restore law and order to violence-prone eastern Kentucky. On December 10, the jury of nine farmers and three businessmen found Jones guilty and sentenced him to life imprisonment. [56]

The Evarts labor trials dragged on for fourteen months, continually reigniting old tensions and reminding miners of the futility of union effort in Harlan County. Immediately following the Jones trial, the local union's president, William Hightower, who had been talking with Sheriff Blair while the battle raged, was convicted of conspiracy to murder and sentenced to life imprisonment. On a defense motion for a change of venue, the remaining murder cases were remanded from Montgomery and Clark counties for trial in Harlan County Circuit Court. There, E. "Big Cigar" Phillips, Chester Poore, Bill Hudson, Jim Reynolds, Al Benson, and F. M. Bratcher were convicted of conspiracy to murder and given lifetime prison sentences. [57]

Satisfied that the ringleaders had been punished and wishing to avoid the expense of further prosecutions, the court, beginning on September 23, 1932, entertained pleas of guilt to lesser charges. Pleas Thomas, Charles Shadrick, Doyle Assad, and Granville Vaughn pleaded guilty to two counts of voluntary manslaughter and received four-year prison terms. Gaines Eubanks, Otto Mills, and Floyd Murphy were sentenced to from two to three years' imprisonment on a plea of guilty to one charge of manslaughter, and a black miner, known as "Dryankle," received one year on a charge of robbery. Garrison Mills, who failed to appear for trial, forfeited a $15,000 bond. The three murder indictments against district union president William Turnblazer were filed subject to reinstatement if he reentered Harlan County, and hundreds of felony indictments were dismissed. [58]

On December 10, 1931, probably hoping to capitalize on resentment aroused by William B. Jones's conviction and wishing to anticipate any wave of apathy that further convictions might evoke, the NMU called a district convention to lay plans for a strike to begin on New Year's Day. Since 125 delegates from southeastern Kentucky, Tennessee, and Virginia had attended a conference in Lexington, Kentucky, on September 14, as high as 70 to 80 percent of NMU members in the region had been pressing New York headquarters for a statewide strike; but because of lack of local organization and a dearth of strike relief reaching Kentucky from the outside, national union leaders procrastinated. Dan Brooks was recalled because he favored an immediate strike, and James S. Allen, editor of *Southern Worker* and advisor on Harlan strike strategy, cautioned that "under no circumstances would we enter blindly into such a venture—because venture it surely would be." [59] On October 31, however, a local organizer warned headquarters: "Center will have to make immediate *decision*. This is a situation certainly new in our history where workers demand a mass strike and we hold them back for weeks waiting for center to take action." She went on to warn that without a strike the miners would lose confidence in the union. [60] Finally, headquarters directed those closest to the Kentucky situation to make the final strike decision, but only after holding a "truly representative" conference in the strike zone. [61] On December 13, 250 local NMU delegates gathered at Pineville to call and plan the strike.

Knowing that their membership consisted almost wholly of unemployed, blacklisted miners incapable of putting pressure on the coal operators, the leadership hesitated to strike. But when delegates assured them that, once the walkout was on, working miners would turn out, a strike was set for January 1, 1932. [62] Frank Borich, the NMU's national secretary, promised strike relief and legal assistance and instructed the miners to ignore court injunctions, organize mass "self-defense" picket squadrons, and march en masse on the county seats to demand relief. Miners' wives and children were urged to join their husbands and fathers on the picket lines. [63]

The NMU made traditional trade-union strike demands that, in light of the depressed and competitive state of the coal industry, were more rash than radical. At a time when Harlan's unskilled miners were earning $2.00 per day and loaders 30¢

per ton, the NMU demanded $4.80 per day for skilled workers, $3.60 to $4.60 for unskilled, and 50¢ per ton for loaders. Its scale represented an approximate return to pre-Depression levels, about twice the existing scale. The union also demanded an eight-hour day; pay for dead work; elimination of coal bucking, which forced loaders to handle coal twice while being paid for a single handling; freedom to trade at independent stores; payment of wages in cash rather than scrip; election of checkweighmen; reemployment of all miners previously discharged for joining the UMW, IWW, or NMU; dismissal of all privately paid mine guards; release of all miners or union leaders jailed for strike activity; freedom to picket, strike, and join the NMU; and recognition of the NMU.[64]

Strike preparations provided the setting for Harlan County's eighth labor-related fatality of the year. On Christmas night, NMU organizer Harry Hirsh, alias Harry Simms, hired Virgil Hutton, an unemployed miner who had not joined the union, to distribute strike-call leaflets at Blue Diamond's camp at Chevrolet. When the company superintendent learned that Hutton and a friend, Kyke Hall, were circulating union handbills, he ordered two mine guards, Owen Sizemore and Dixon, to eject them from company property. The deputies confronted Hutton and Hall on their way home. Deputy Sizemore shined his flashlight in Hutton's eyes and asked to inspect his literature. According to Deputy Dixon, Hutton withdrew leaflets from his pocket and handed them to Sizemore; then, reaching into his pocket a second time, Hutton drew a pistol, shot Sizemore in the back of head, and fled. Dixon fired at the fugitive, grazing his scalp with a bullet. Hutton contended that, when he passed the leaflets to Sizemore, the deputy seized his arm, twisted it behind his back, and began battering his head with a revolver butt. Hutton drew his gun and, firing over his left shoulder, shot the deputy, who had not yet identified himself as a law officer. Hutton exhibited his head wound as proof of the pistol-whipping. Unfortunately for Hutton, his victim was a brother-in-law of Commonwealth's Attorney W. A. Brock and State Senator Hiram Brock. Harlan County Circuit Court convicted the assailant of murder and sentenced him to five years' imprisonment.[65]

The strike was doomed from the beginning. Little more than

1 percent of the Harlan miners responded to the strike call. On New Year's Day, only thirty-one county miners struck two mines on troubled Wallins Creek, and deputies dispersed 150 miners and wives who attempted to hold a rally in the city of Harlan. On Monday, January 4, the Harlan strike peaked with eighty-three miners out. The next day, the strikers' ranks began to thin, and within the week, nearly all Harlan strikers either had returned to work or had been replaced.[66]

In Bell and Knox counties, the NMU enjoyed slightly more success. In Bell County, three hundred, about 10 percent of the county's miners, struck, closing four mines. Many owners welcomed an opportunity to close mines that had not shown a profit for three years. With one-third of the county's miners unemployed and the remainder working two days a week, strikers were easily replaced. Within a week, more than half of the strikers returned. Armed with a sweeping federal court injunction that endorsed eviction of nine strikers from company housing and that prohibited mass picketing, circulating strike literature, uttering any inducement to strike, or entering company property, operators reopened their four closed mines within a month.[67]

The Brush Creek section of Knox County was most seriously affected. Six hundred miners struck, closing four of the county's largest mines for six weeks, but even there, only slightly more than 10 percent of the miners went out.[68] Throughout the entire southeastern Kentucky coal field the strike failed for lack of either outside or local leadership, because the NMU could not deliver sufficient strike relief, and because the NMU attracted mainly unemployed, blacklisted members devoid of bargaining power rather than working miners who might have insured some measure of success.

On New Year's Eve, the national NMU dispatched a task force to Pineville to command the strike. Workers International Relief sent Clarina Michaelson and Norma Martin, who opened a WIR relief warehouse and supervised distribution of strike relief. International Labor Defense sent Dorothy Ross Weber and, later, Allan Taub to handle legal complications. The *Daily Worker* sent Vern Smith to report the strike for the radical press. Margaret Fontaine and Julia Parker, who, under the alias Celia Kuhn, had earlier accompanied the Dreiser Committee, went to perform clerical duties. The group opened a central strike headquarters above a drugstore across from the Pineville courthouse.

Led by young, self-assured, vociferous Bell County attorney Walter Boone Smith, county authorities struck at the Communist leadership. On Monday morning, January 4, deputies raided strike headquarters and arrested six strike leaders: Vern Smith, Norma Martin, Julia Parker, Margaret Fontaine, John Harvey, and Ann Barton. Later the same day, a second raid on a Pineville hotel netted three more, Vincent Kemenovich, Dorothy Weber, and Clarina Michaelson. Two days later, when ILD attorney Allan Taub arrived to defend the nine, he, too, was incarcerated. On Saturday, deputies raided the WIR relief warehouse. On January 14, Allan Taub was released on his promise to leave the state, but six leaders were held until late March and two until mid-April.[69]

In early February, Harry Simms was killed on Brush Creek. Born Harry Hirsh, of a Jewish working-class family in Springfield, Massachusetts, Simms was a veteran of unemployment demonstrations in Waterbury, Connecticut, and Communist youth work in Chattanooga, Tennessee. He had gone to southeastern Kentucky in 1931 at age nineteen to organize for the Young Communist League and the NMU. There he won the respect of NMU miners and their families for his kindness and courage. On the morning of February 10, Simms and Green Lawson were walking up the railroad right-of-way to lead NMU miners to Pineville to greet the visiting committee headed by Waldo Frank. They met two deputy sheriffs riding a handcar. One of them, Arlan Miller, a mine guard at Kentucky Jellico, a Brush Creek mine owned by Brian Whitfield of Harlan County, shot Simms in the abdomen. After bleeding beside the tracks for hours, he died next day in a Barbourville hospital. Barbourville authorities deputized a large force of deputies and prohibited all demonstrations. The body was finally released to a three-man escort that placed it aboard a train bound for New York City, where, draped in a red flag, Simms lay in state at Communist headquarters. Benjamin Gitlow recalled that Communists, young and old, filed past the

bier and vowed to "take revenge against the Hoover terror." [70]
Jim Garland, who had worked with Simms in Bell and Knox
counties, eulogized his fallen comrade at the funeral and,
later, in "The Ballad of Harry Simms," which recaptured the
courage and purpose of the boy's life:

> Harry Simms was a pal of mine.
> We labored side by side,
> Expecting to be shot on sight
> Or taken for a ride,
> By them dirty coal operator gun thugs
> Who rode from town to town,
> Ashooting down the union men
> Where'er they may be found. . . .
>
> Harry Simms was killed on Brush Creek
> In 1932
> He died for the union
> Also for me and you.[71]

On the day Simms was shot, local NMU leaders, just returned from Communist training sessions in eastern cities, dealt
the local movement a fatal blow. There, they had heard Communists praise the Soviet Union and talk of banishing "God
from the skies." They taught that there was no God, no Jesus,
no resurrection of the dead. "All there is for anybody is what
they get in this world." They had heard Communists declare
that "they just as leave their girls to marry a negro as a white
man, let their girls be pleased." Leaders such as Willard Rose,
Henry Collett, Logan Doan, and Holiness preacher Finley
Donaldson issued public statements declaring their firm belief
"in God and the United States," denouncing the NMU for misleading them and their friends, and urging their followers to
withdraw from a union bent on the destruction of government,
religion, and family life.[72] Donaldson boasted that his statement alone persuaded a thousand miners to desert the NMU.
Homer Morris thought the leaders' statements dealt the NMU
a "death blow" and were "far more effective in smashing the
union than the National Guard ever could have been." [73]

Just as the UMW strike before it, the NMU's strike foundered
for lack of adequate strike relief. The feeding stations, accord-

ing to Harry Bullock's report, had been crucial to the recruit-
ment of unemployed, blacklisted miners, and lack of strike
relief cost the union the working miners' support. When the
strike began, Frank Borich reported, "Hundreds of committees
came in from various mines asking if there was enough relief,
and if the Union was able to give enough relief, the mines were
able to come out on strike, but, if not, they stated they would
wait until relief came in." At one mine, 450 miners "came out
when we sent relief but went back when we could not give
relief." [74] The legal seizure of the WIR's Pineville relief headquarters on the strike's ninth day dealt the Communists a
harsh blow.

On February 10, the same day that Harry Simms was slain
and local leaders disavowed the NMU, the Independent
Miners' Relief Committee, a Communist-front group composed
of twelve writers and radicals, arrived in Pineville to reopen
outside relief supply lines into the area, distribute four truck-
loads of food and clothing to striking miners, and test the rights
of free speech and assembly. [75]

Waldo Frank, a novelist and literary critic, headed the ex-
pedition. Enamored of the collectivist spirit of ancient Latin
American Indian and modern Soviet culture, he thought American capitalist culture was sterile and cruelly individualistic.
Frank hoped that intellectuals could use the worker as a revolutionary instrument to forge a new society in the United
States. He journeyed to the Kentucky strike zone to renew his
grasp of American reality. Two years after his visit, in a novel,
The Death and Birth of David Markand, he drew upon the
Kentucky experience to demonstrate how the intellectual's
alliance with workers could restore meaning to a futile, middle-
class existence. [76]

A second committee member, Edmund Wilson, possessed the
aristocrat's sense of noblesse oblige and distaste for American
economic anarchy, nowhere better exemplified than in the
highly competitive coal industry. Wilson viewed capitalism as
an "exploded myth" that had culminated finally in moral and
economic collapse. Seeking an alternative to capitalism, in
1931–32 he observed two coal strikes, one led by socialist Frank
Keeney's West Virginia Mine Workers Union and one by the
Communists in Kentucky. Repulsed by apparent Communist

party attempts to exploit his reputation to further their cause, Wilson concluded that a homegrown variety of communism akin to Keeney's movement in West Virginia held the answer to the United States' social and economic problems.[77]

Still a third member of the group, Malcolm Cowley, editor of *New Republic,* had been observing the Soviet experiment with interest since 1927, but until his Pineville visit, he had never seriously considered revolution. Thereafter, contrasting the solemn, troubled visages of the Kentucky miners with the strong, smiling faces portrayed in Soviet propaganda, and perceiving the Soviet Union as the only effective deterrent to world fascism, he continued as a fellow traveler, though not a member, of the Communist party until the Nazi-Soviet Pact of 1939.[78]

The day before the Frank Committee reached Pineville, it visited nearby La Follette, Tennessee, where the writers distributed milk to lure a crowd while an organizer, Doris Parks, urged the miners to join the NMU and strike. Parks, who had been smuggling relief supplies into Kentucky from Knoxville, and Allan Taub, only recently released from the Pineville jail on his pledge to leave the state, accompanied the committee to Pineville.[79] Having thus allied itself with the NMU, the group was entering enemy country.

Deputies met the writers and four relief trucks at the city limits and escorted the trucks beyond the corporate limit. One truck, laden with clothing, was driven off and overturned. County Attorney Smith and Mayor Brooks informed the committee that their food could be distributed only at the closed mines on Straight Creek and that public meetings were prohibited anywhere in the county. Doris Parks and New York playwright Harold Hickerson, who were meanwhile addressing a crowd of a hundred miners and townspeople gathered around the trucks, were arrested for criminal syndicalism; and deputies distributed their food.

Amid rumors that armed miners were marching on the town to free the eleven NMU jailed leaders, deputies arrested the committee members, shortly after they retired, for disorderly conduct and creating a public nuisance. After a police judge dismissed charges, the mayor, city policemen, and a mob of townspeople escorted them to their hotel and ordered them out of the county immediately. A caravan of fifteen automobiles drove the group to Cumberland Gap, parked, and switched off their headlights. In the darkness, Waldo Frank and Allan Taub were beaten, and the committee members were put out to seek shelter in Virginia.[80] The committee then journeyed to Washington, where they asked Senators Costigan, Cutting, and Logan to investigate "a reign of terror which had abridged all constitutional rights" in southeastern Kentucky. On February 12, New York Congressman Black introduced a resolution calling for a House investigation, and on March 4, Senator Costigan introduced a similar resolution in the Senate. Although the Frank Committee may have helped instigate a later Senate investigation, it failed in its immediate goal of refurbishing the now-dead Kentucky strike.

Because the NMU recruited mostly unemployed miners and so few working miners, the strike never commanded any economic power and was always more a political demonstration of starving, blacklisted miners than a strike. Frank Borich estimated that ten thousand miners, of whom approximately four thousand were unemployed, participated.[81] Local estimates indicate that about eighty-three Harlan miners, three hundred Bell miners, and six hundred Knox miners, a total of fewer than a thousand working miners, as opposed to Borich's estimate of six thousand, struck; and probably far fewer than ten thousand participated in any way. Jack Stachel, Trade Union Unity League official, admitted that within the first few days it became evident that it was "in reality no strike except for the unemployed blacklisted miners." [82] The NMU was, indeed, a union of the damned.

Lacking power to combat the operators economically, the NMU resorted to mass political demonstrations where numbers counted. In this manner, the Communists turned the mass arrests of January 4 to good account; on five separate occasions between January 5 and 12, more than fifteen hundred miners, wives, and children, many of them armed, paraded Pineville's streets demanding the release of strike leaders and the restoration of relief supply lines into the area. The second demonstration nearly resulted in tragedy. Rumors that the mob intended to forcibly release prisoners caused authorities to summon two carloads of Harlan County deputies armed with automatic rifles. The marchers filed past the jail and gathered for speeches and singing on the courthouse lawn. Leaving two deputies to guard their weapons in cars parked across the street, the Harlan deputies went to lunch. A speaker urged the miners to cross the street, disarm the two remaining deputies, and seize their weapons. Alerted, the other deputies rushed out, grabbed their guns, and took cover behind the brick railing on the hotel porch. As the two armed forces confronted each other, Pineville's police chief walked between them and ordered the deputies back to their lunch and the miners back to their meeting. Both sides backed off, and moments later rain dispersed the crowd. Although the demonstrations forced five postponements of preliminary hearings for the nine arrested Communist leaders, each day numbers dwindled. On January 13, with only two hundred demonstrators in town, the leaders were arraigned. The NMU movement in southeastern Kentucky was nearly dead.[83]

After only four and a half years of life, and one furious year of conducting futile strikes amid depressed conditions, the National Miners' Union died, too. After the Harlan strike, the NMU "seemed exhausted" and, "for all practical purposes, finished." By midsummer, 1932, the NMU possessed fewer than five hundred dues-paying members, most of them unemployed and blacklisted, and was unable to pay its eighteen full-time officials. One hundred thousand miners were on strike, all led by the rival UMW that the NMU had been created to destroy. In October, 1933, Frank Borich was deported; and after the dramatic resurgence of the UMW after passage of the National Recovery Act, the NMU disbanded and threw its support to "one militant united miners' union." [84]

The Communists did manage to generate publicity in Kentucky. During the UMW phase of the strike, January 1 to May 15, 1931, when 8,000 or 9,000 miners struck and five men were killed, the *New York Times* carried 6 Harlan County news items; by contrast, during the Communist phase, when 943 miners struck and four men were killed, the same newspaper carried 119 stories from the Kentucky strike zone.[85] Also, during the latter Communist phase, beginning with the Dreiser Committee's investigation in November, 1931, and culminating with a United States Senate investigation in May, 1932, southeastern Kentucky was subjected to ten successive investigations. Lawrence Grauman, Jr., contends that in 1931–32 the Harlan and Bell County strikes attracted more sustained literary attention than had the famed Sacco-Vanzetti case in the previous decade.[86]

The expulsion of the Waldo Frank Committee on February 10 provoked successive waves of journalistic outrage and liberal investigations of the state of civil liberties in Kentucky. Searching diligently, Bell County authorities managed to connect, however tenuously, each group of investigators with either the Communist movement or religious modernism and, thereby, to fan the flames of provincial patriotism and antiradicalism and to either discredit locally the groups' findings or expel them from Kentucky.

On March 25–26, another newly formed Communist auxiliary, the National Student League, sponsored an expedition of two hundred students from five eastern colleges to conduct sociological research in Bell County. Local officials discovered that the NSL occupied a suite of rooms adjoining the offices of the Young Communist League in New York, that Waldo Frank and Allan Taub had coached the students, that in a letter sent from her jail cell Clarina Michaelson had referred to the visitors as the "rah-rah element of Communism," and that some students viewed the assignment as a protest against terror in the coal fields. Two hundred deputies and private citizens halted the first bus in Cumberland Gap and escorted it to the Middlesboro courthouse, where the students were given an alternative of posting individual $1,000 peace bonds or going to jail. When most students chose jail, they were escorted across the state line and ordered back to Knoxville. The students also went to Washington to request a United States Senate investigation.[87]

Two weeks later, a five-member delegation from Marxist-oriented Commonwealth Labor Training Institute, Mena, Arkansas, visited Pineville bearing relief for hungry miners and copies of the Bill of Rights for the Bell and Harlan County sheriffs. The city's police chief met them at the city limits and ordered them out of town. A Bell County citizen drove them to the Bell–Harlan County border, where Harlan men took over and drove to the summit of Black Mountain. The vigilantes took the two instructors and three students into the woods one at a time and whipped them with switches. When the group identified Deputy Sheriff Lee Fleenor as one of their assailants, he denied the allegation, adding, however, that he sympathized with the assailants. That same evening, James Price, an attorney retained by the IWW's General Defense Committee in the Evarts murder cases, was abducted on a Pineville street and driven into Harlan County, where he was beaten with fists and switches and threatened with death should he return to the area. Price did return to Pineville to identify three of his assailants, but local officials refused to press charges.[88]

Twenty-one liberal ministers who petitioned the United States Senate for an investigation were invited to visit the area. On May 4 and 5, Reinhold Niebuhr, William B. Spofford, C. Rankin Barnes, and Cameron P. Hall inspected a Harlan County mine and interviewed Bell County officials, social workers, UMW leaders, ministers, and miners. The group concluded that amid anti-Communist sentiment of hysterical proportions and with the tacit approval of county officials, civil liberties had been grossly abridged. Local citizens also had been extremely careless in distinguishing between shades and degrees of radicalism. When the group again urged a congressional investigation that might curb official sanction of lawlessness, local ministers and officials proclaimed them guilty of religious modernism.[89]

When Bell County attorney Walter Boone Smith learned that an American Civil Liberties Union delegation was contemplating an investigation, he warned the group's president, Arthur Garfield Hays, that just as Bell County citizens would suppress a "mad dog, we will also suppress this un-American Union" and publicly labeled the ACLU as "the constitutional representative of the Soviet Union . . . in the United States," the financier and supporter of "all the intruders that have terrorized our public all along."[90] In light of Smith's opposition, the ACLU applied in United States District Court, London, Kentucky, for an injunction to prohibit local officials from obstructing its investigation, but Judge Cochran denied the injunction because no person had a right to enter a community to make speeches "reasonably calculated to disturb the peace." On May 14, when the delegation attempted to enter Bell County without an injunction, county officials and private citizens blocked them at the border.[91] The ACLU then added its voice to the call for a congressional investigation.

Finally, in May, a subcommittee of the United States Senate Committee on Manufactures, composed of Senators Costigan, Cutting, and Henry Hatfield, conducted a preliminary hearing in Washington to determine whether the situation merited a full-scale Senate investigation. The subcommittee was instructed to ascertain the causes of existing conditions, whether there had been unlawful obstruction of interstate commerce, and whether citizens had been arrested, tried, or convicted in violation of the Constitution or laws of the United States. The subcommittee heard testimony from Howard N. Eavenson, the owner of Clover Splint Coal Company, who candidly and ably represented the Harlan County Coal Operators' Association; two Kentucky National Guard officers; Jim Garland, Jim Grace, and Allan Taub, representing the NMU; Waldo Frank, representing the Independent Miners' Relief Committee; Rob Hall, representing the National Student League; Reinhold Niebuhr, representing the ministers; and Arthur Garfield Hays, representing the ACLU. Most witnesses favored a full investigation, and although some fear was expressed that a probe might lead to another infestation of radicalism, no one strenuously objected. Senators Costigan and Cutting, who discerned evidence of "fascism" and numerous violations of civil liberties, favored a full investigation. Senator Hatfield of West Virginia, who had been highly impressed by the coal operator's testimony, feared further growth of radicalism, and thought most witnesses were either outsiders or "more or less Communists, or so inclined," was opposed. Polled in July on the advisability of a full investigation, a majority of members on the Committee on Manufactures decided against it.[92]

The committee was undoubtedly impressed by the fact that

Harlan County had been free of significant labor trouble for more than ten months and Bell County for four. After February, Bell County's agitation had focused upon civil liberties rather than labor strife. The coal industry was enduring its worst season of the Depression, and wages, employment, and working conditions were at their nadir. Short of the return of general prosperity or governmental stabilization of the nation's coal industry, the coal operators, the union, or Congress could do little to improve conditions. The Senate committee decided to leave well enough alone and thereby avoid possibly provoking further disturbances that might produce further unemployment and misery. The committee's majority either failed to discern or chose to ignore the important connection between civil liberties and labor organization. And their response indicated no awareness that Harlan and Bell County miners were revolting as much against authoritarianism as against economic deprivation.

In their effort to purge the area of radical unionism, Bell and Harlan officials had condoned and encouraged deputy sheriffs and private citizens to take the law into their own hands. Vigilantism, once unleashed, was not easily checked. The following year, when traditional trade unionism reentered Harlan County, public officials, deputies, and private persons responded again with similar ferocious hostility to the UMW. Again, public officials would plead inability to curb popular sentiment and would sanction antiunion terrorism. Their antisocial behavior would be curbed only in 1937, when the La Follette Civil Liberties Committee conducted an investigation specifically on behalf of the civil liberties of labor.

NOTES

1. Theodore Draper, "Communists and Miners 1928–1933," *Dissent,* 19 (Spring, 1972), 391. This is the first scholarly study of the National Miners Union, and the analysis of the NMU's Harlan strike (pp. 380–89) is the best published account. I am indebted to Draper's work for the broader perspective on the NMU and, especially, for the Harlan strike material contained in the Harry M. Wicks Papers, and to my colleague, Professor Donald Sofchalk of Mankato State University, for calling the article to my attention.

2. Ibid., 377–80; William Z. Foster, *Pages from a Worker's Life* (New York, 1939), p. 182.

3. Draper, "Communists and Miners," pp. 382–84.

4. Ibid., p. 381; *Conditions in Coal Fields*, pp. 11, 46–47, 123–25; *Harlan Miners Speak*, pp. 34, 45–47, 239.

5. *Daily Worker*, July 17, 1931, quoted in Draper, "Communists and Miners," p. 381.

6. Anonymous letter, July 20, 1931, NA, RG/280, "Coal Miners (Southeastern Ky.)," Box 294.

7. *Harlan (Ky.) Daily Enterprise*, Sept. 11, 1931.

8. Editorial, ibid., Aug. 9, 1931 (italics are the editor's); editorial, *Pineville (Ky.) Sun*, Aug. 13, 1931.

9. *Harlan Daily Enterprise*, July 28, Aug. 18, 1931; *Harlan Miners Speak*, pp. 81–82; testimony of Henry M. Lewis, LFCH, pt. 11, p. 4009.

10. *Harlan Daily Enterprise*, Aug. 26, 27, 1931.

11. John A. Dotson, "Socio-Economic Background and Changing Education in Harlan County, Kentucky" (Ph.D. diss., George Peabody College for Teachers, 1943), p. 47; *Knoxville (Tenn.) News-Sentinel*, Dec. 17, 1931.

12. *Harlan Daily Enterprise*, Aug. 23, 1931.

13. Ibid., Aug. 6, 25, Sept. 13, 1931; *Pineville Sun*, Aug. 13, 1931; editorial, ibid., Sept. 24, 1931; *Harlan Miners Speak*, pp. 46, 71–73, 92–96.

14. Draper, "Communists and Miners," pp. 386–87; *Harlan Daily Enterprise*, Aug. 11, 31, Sept. 29, 1931, Aug. 29, 1932; *Harlan Miners Speak*, pp. 47, 97–100, 121.

15. "Which Side Are You On? An Interview with Florence Reece," *Mountain Life & Work*, 48 (Mar., 1972), 23–24. Mrs. Reece confused the year of the NMU campaign; it was 1931, not 1930.

16. Ibid., p. 23.

17. S. Bowen [Clara Holden], Oct. 28, 1931, Harry M. Wicks Papers, quoted in Draper, "Communists and Miners," p. 383.

18. Anonymous [Clara Holden?], Sept. 18, 1931, Wicks Papers, quoted ibid., pp. 382–83.

19. *Harlan Daily Enterprise*, Aug. 13, 14, 16, 1931; Don Whitehead, "Take It or Leave It," *Harlan Daily Enterprise*, Aug. 17, 1931; U.S. conciliation commissioner to Hugh L. Kerwin, Aug. 20, 1931, NA, RG/280, "Coal Miners (Southeastern Ky.)," Box 294.

20. Quoted by Margaret Lane, "Noted Woman Writer Tells the Story of Terrible Conditions Existing in Harlan County Field," *United Mine Workers Journal*, Dec. 15, 1931, p. 12.

21. Editorial, *Pineville Sun*, Sept. 3, 1931; Malcolm Ross, *Machine Age in the Hills* (New York, 1933), p. 174.

22. Lawrence Grauman, Jr., "'That Little Ugly Running Sore': Some Observations on the Participation of American Writers in the Investigations of Conditions in the Harlan and Bell County, Kentucky, Coal Fields, 1931–32," *Filson Club History Quarterly*, 36 (Oct., 1962), 348; *Harlan Miners Speak*, pp. 4, 7.

23. Testimony of Major George M. Chescheir, *Conditions in Coal Fields*, p. 146.

24. Ross, *Machine Age in the Hills*, p. 171.

25. Walter Wilson to Theodore Dreiser, July 12, 1931, Theodore Dreiser Papers, University of Pennsylvania; "President Green Hauls Theodore Dreiser over the Coals for His Vicious Attack on the Union," *United Mine Workers Journal*, July 15, 1931, pp. 8–9; W. A. Swanberg, *Dreiser* (New York, 1965), p. 381.

26. Swanberg, *Dreiser*, p. 391.

27. Ross, *Machine Age in the Hills*, pp. 170–71.

28. Daniel Aaron, *Writers on the Left: Episodes in American Literary Communism* (New York, 1961), p. 178; Swanberg, *Dreiser*, p. 389.

29. John Dos Passos, *The Theme Is Freedom* (New York, 1956), p. 87; Robert H. Footman, "John Dos Passos," *Sewanee Review*, 47 (July–Sept., 1939), 371.

30. Testimony of Chescheir, *Conditions in Coal Fields*, pp. 138–40, 145–46, 149, 151; Herndon J. Evans, "Kentucky Hits Communism," *Kentucky Progress Magazine*, 4 (Apr., 1932), 28.

31. *Harlan Miners Speak*, pp. 278, 286.

32. John Greenway, *American Folksongs of Protest* (Philadelphia, 1953), pp. 252–55, 257–59.

33. Ibid., pp. 258, 274.

34. Ibid., pp. 253–54; "I Am a Union Woman" is quoted by R. Serge Denisoff in *Great Day Coming: Folk Music and the American Left* (Urbana, Ill., 1971), p. 25.

35. Greenway, *American Folksongs of Protest*, pp. 261–62.

36. Ibid., pp. 253–54, 258–60, 265, 271; Denisoff, *Great Day Coming*, pp. 46–47.

37. Greenway, *American Folksongs of Protest*, p. 260; Denisoff, *Great Day Coming*, pp. 47, 68–70, 73, 134–35.

38. John Greenway, quoted in Denisoff, *Great Day Coming*, p. 135.

39. Aunt Molly Jackson, "Kentucky Miners' Wives Ragged Hungry Blues," in *Harlan Miners Speak*, pp. v–vii.

40. *Harlan Miners Speak*, pp. 292–96; *Pineville Sun*, Nov. 12, 1931; testimony of Chescheir, *Conditions in Coal Fields*, pp. 140–41.

41. *Pineville Sun*, Nov. 12, 19, 26, 1931.

42. Ibid., Mar. 2, 1933; Swanberg, *Dreiser*, pp. 384, 387–89; Dos Passos, *Theme Is Freedom*, pp. 86–87; Jessie Wakefield to Dreiser, Nov. 23, 1931; Sprad to Dreiser, n.d. [shortly before Aug. 20, 1931]; telegram, Dreiser to Edward B. Smith, Nov. 18, 1931; telegram, William D. Cameron to Dreiser, Nov. 20, 1931; telegram, Dreiser to Cameron, Nov. 20, 1931; Dreiser to Cameron, Nov. 23, 1931, Dreiser Papers.

43. Minutes of a Dreiser Committee meeting, Nov. 13, 1931; Melvin P. Levy to Dreiser, Jan. 28, 1932, Dreiser Papers; testimony of Chescheir, *Conditions in Coal Fields*, p. 151; Bullock Report, *Harlan Daily Enterprise*, Nov. 19, 1931; Ross, *Machine Age in the Hills*, pp. 170–71, 174.

44. Bullock Report, *Harlan Daily Enterprise*, Nov. 19, 1931.

45. Editorial, ibid., Dec. 24, 1931.

46. Nearly a year later, Burnett was convicted of "shooting with intent to kill" at Deputy Frank White (ibid., Nov. 22, 1931, Sept. 25, 1932).

47. Testimony of Vanover and Middleton, *Commonwealth* v. *Jones,* vol. 8, pp. 1188, 1228, vol. 11, pp. 1690–92.

48. Testimony of John and Hugh Lester, ibid., vol. 2, pp. 306, 325–28, 330, vol. 3, pp. 391, 407–8, 411–12; *Harlan Miners Speak,* p. 64; *Harlan Daily Enterprise,* May 21, 1931.

49. Testimony of M. Hatmaker, Lige Fields, George Ellis, Walter Snow, J. H. Young, and G. G. Rawlings, *Commonwealth* v. *Jones,* vol. 11, pp. 1645–48, 1657, 1664–65, 1680, 1684–85, vol. 14, pp. 2143–46, vol. 15, pp. 2190–91.

50. Testimony of W. B. Jones and Vanover, ibid., vol. 7, pp. 1002–12, vol. 8, pp. 1188–90.

51. Testimony of John T. Hickey, Frank Ingle, Mary Ingle, Sol Smith, Roscoe Hickey, Chester Ingle, Ed Ingle, and Mose King, ibid., vol. 1, p. 46, vol. 3, pp. 438–40, 444–49, 450–55, 468–70, vol. 4, pp. 520, 528, 534, 541, 644–45.

52. Testimony of W. B. Jones, George Payne, Robert Posey, Charlie Nuckols, Lester Partin, Chester Jones, J. W. Dickey, ibid., vol. 7, pp. 1019–24, 1030, vol. 8, pp. 1157–58, 1166–69, 1235–37, vol. 12, p. 1781, vol. 14, 2032–34, 2119–20.

53. Testimony of R. B. Davis, ibid., vol. 4, pp. 627–29, 632.

54. *Harlan Daily Enterprise,* Aug. 20, 24, 1931.

55. W. C. Hamilton, quoted by John T. Moutoux in *Knoxville News-Sentinel,* Dec. 10, 1931.

56. *Harlan Daily Enterprise,* Nov. 27, Dec. 10, 1931; testimony of Daniel Boone Smith, LFCH, pt. 12, p. 4318. In 1933, the Kentucky Court of Appeals upheld Jones's conviction. In December, 1940, Acting Governor Myers commuted Jones's sentence to twenty-one years, making him eligible for parole, and on Christmas Eve, 1941, he was pardoned. See *Harlan Daily Enterprise,* Apr. 21, 1933; *United Mine Workers Journal,* Feb. 1, 1941, p. 9.

57. *Harlan Daily Enterprise,* Jan. 14, June 12, July 29, Aug. 4, Sept. 23, 1932, Jan. 9, Feb. 16, 1933. F. M. Bratcher's case was an example of the great disadvantage at which triple conspiracy indictments placed the defendants. After two mistrials and one acquittal on the charge of conspiring to murder Jim Daniels and an acquittal on the charge of conspiring to murder Otto Lee, Bratcher was convicted in a fifth trial on the charge of conspiring to murder Howard Jones.

58. Ibid., Sept. 23, Dec. 21, 22, 1932, Jan. 4, 15, 16, 1933.

59. Anonymous [Jim Allen?], Oct. 28, 1931, Harry M. Wicks Papers, quoted in Draper, "Communists and Miners," p. 383.

60. S. Bowen [Clara Holden], Oct. 31, 1931, Wicks Papers, quoted ibid., p. 383.

61. T. J. [Tom Johnson?] to Harry Jackson, Jim Allen, Dan Slinger, Clara Holden, Nov. 5, 1931, Wicks Papers, quoted ibid., p. 383.

62. Draper, "Communists and Miners," p. 384.

63. *Pineville Sun,* Dec. 17, 1931; *Knoxville News-Sentinel,* Dec. 14, 1931; Harry Gannes, *Kentucky Miners Fight* (n.p., 1932), p. 29.

64. *Pineville Sun,* Dec. 17, 1931; Wilmer G. Mason, *Cincinnati Enquirer,* Apr. 8, 1932; *Conditions in Coal Fields,* pp. 67–68.

65. *Harlan Daily Enterprise,* Dec. 27, 29, 1931, Nov. 18, 1932. Hutton's story is told fully in "Rebuttal memos prepared by Dept. of

Justice Attorneys, London, Ky., July 14, 1938. Re: Mary Helen Coal Corporation, *et al.*; Civil Rights and Domestic Violence," NA, RG/60, Classified Subject Files, Enclosures, Box 3647.

66. *Harlan Daily Enterprise,* Jan. 1, 4, 5, 1932; *Pineville Sun,* Jan. 7, 1932; editorial, *Pineville Sun,* Jan. 14, 1932.

67. *Harlan Daily Enterprise,* Jan. 3, 1932; *Pineville Sun,* Jan. 7, 28, 1932; editorial, ibid., Jan. 14, 1932; Evans, "Kentucky Hits Communism," p. 29; Ross, *Machine Age in the Hills,* p. 176; *Conditions in Coal Fields,* p. 76.

68. *Harlan Daily Enterprise,* Jan. 3, 1932; *Pineville Sun,* Feb. 4, 25, 1932; editorial, ibid., Jan. 14, 1932; "Kentucky Strike Call Meets Little Response; Smokeless Wages Cut," *Coal Age,* 38 (Jan., 1932), 35.

69. *Pineville Sun,* Jan. 7, 14, 21, Feb. 11, 18, Mar. 3, 31, Apr. 21, 1932; *Harlan Daily Enterprise,* Jan. 8, Feb. 11, 1932; Wilmer Mason, *Cincinnati Enquirer,* Apr. 8, 1932; testimony of James C. Garland and Vern Smith, *Conditions in Coal Fields,* pp. 12–13, 76–79; Gannes, *Kentucky Miners Fight,* p. 3.

70. Preval Glusman, "Harry Simms—A Young Revolutionist," *Daily Worker,* May 8, 1934; Mary Elizabeth Barnicle, "Harry Simms: The Story behind This American Ballad," in brochure accompanying Folkways FH 5233, *Songs of Struggle & Protest: 1930–1950,* pp. 3–4; Benjamin Gitlow, *The Whole of Their Lives* (New York, 1948), p. 222; *Harlan Daily Enterprise,* Feb. 10, 12, 1932; *Pineville Sun,* Feb. 25, 1932.

71. Jim Garland, "Harry Simms," in brochure accompanying Folkways FH 5233, *Songs of Struggle & Protest,* p. 7.

72. *Pineville Sun,* Feb. 11, 18, 1932; *Harlan Daily Enterprise,* Mar. 7, 1932; Homer Lawrence Morris, *Plight of the Bituminous Coal Miner* (Philadelphia, 1934), pp. 135–37.

73. Morris, *Plight of the Bituminous Coal Miner,* p. 137.

74. Frank Borich's report to the Politburo, Jan. 28, 1932, quoted in Draper, "Communists and Miners," p. 384.

75. Aaron, *Writers on the Left,* p. 182; Grauman, " 'That Little Ugly Running Sore,' " p. 349; Malcolm Cowley, "Kentucky Coal Town," *New Republic,* Mar. 2, 1932, p. 67. The committee's membership was Waldo Frank, Edmund Wilson, Cowley, Mary Heaton Vorse, Polly Boyden, Benjamin Lieder, Elsie Reed Mitchell, John Henry Hammond, Jr., Liston M. Oak, Quincy Howe, A. M. Max, Harold Hickerson, and Allan Taub.

76. Aaron, *Writers on the Left,* pp. 192–93; Waldo Frank, *The Death and Birth of David Markand: An American Story* (New York, 1934). For the influence of the Pineville trip, see pp. 472–542.

77. Aaron, *Writers on the Left,* pp. 179–82, 184.

78. Ibid., pp. 335–36.

79. *Pineville Sun,* Feb. 18, 1932.

80. Ibid., Feb. 11, 18, 1932; *Harlan Daily Enterprise,* Feb. 11, 1932.

81. Draper, "Communists and Miners," p. 384.

82. Jack Stachel, "Lessons of Two Recent Strikes," *Communist,* June, 1932, pp. 528–32.

83. Evans, "Kentucky Hits Communism," p. 29; Wilmer G. Mason, *Cincinnati Enquirer,* Apr. 8, 1932; *Pineville Sun,* Jan. 7, 14, 1932;

Harlan Daily Enterprise, Jan. 6, 7, 1932; *Conditions in Coal Fields,* pp. 78–79.

84. Draper, "Communists and Miners," pp. 389–91.

85. Ibid., p. 389, n. 81.

86. Grauman, " 'That Little Ugly Running Sore,' " p. 340.

87. Ibid., p. 349; *Harlan Daily Enterprise,* Mar. 16, 22, 23, 27, 28, 29, 1932; *Pineville Sun,* Mar. 31, 1932.

88. *Harlan Daily Enterprise,* Apr. 1, 11, 12, 1932; C. Robert Kay, *Harlan Daily Enterprise,* Apr. 11, 1932; testimony of Reinhold Niebuhr, *Conditions in Coal Fields,* p. 86.

89. *Harlan Daily Enterprise,* May 8, 1932; testimony of Niebuhr, *Conditions in Coal Fields,* pp. 85–88, 95.

90. Walter B. Smith to Arthur Garfield Hays, n.d., quoted in *Pineville Sun,* Apr. 21, 1932; Walter Boone Smith, "Public Forum," *Harlan Daily Enterprise,* April 15, 1932.

91. *Harlan Daily Enterprise,* May 15, 1932; Arthur Garfield Hays, *Trial by Prejudice* (New York, 1933), pp. 334–37.

92. *Harlan Daily Enterprise,* July 11, 19, 1932. The best discussion of Senator Hatfield's motives for opposing an investigation is George J. Titler, *Hell in Harlan* (Beckley, W.Va., n.d.), p. 40.

Chapter 5

Failure of Reform

1933 - 35

In June, 1933, the National Industrial Recovery Act, Section 7(a), which guaranteed employees the right to join a union of their choice and to bargain collectively, seemed to place the federal government squarely on the side of organized labor. Intensified employer opposition, the spread of company unionism, and inadequate enforcement of the legislation, however, allowed most large industries, among them automobiles, steel, rubber, and textiles, to escape genuine unionization. Nevertheless, active unionists in a few industries, notably coal and garments, were able to achieve effective organization. For alert labor leaders, such as John L. Lewis, Sidney Hillman, and David Dubinsky, the National Recovery Act truly proved to be labor's Magna Carta.

The rebuilding of the United Mine Workers of America was the greatest success story of NRA's brief two-year history. During the summer of 1933, the nation's coal camps were the scene of one of the most spectacular dramas in American labor history, directed by a brilliant dramatist, John L. Lewis. On the eve of NRA's passage, Lewis borrowed money, summoned organizers from all the nation's coal fields, and bade them act quickly "before the employers woke up to the fact that there were ways of getting around the law." [1] The coal operators, stunned by extensive financial losses and demoralized by the utter collapse of the wage, price, and market structure of their industry, were unable to mount an effective opposition.[2] Organizers fully exploited the hope and confidence aroused by President Roosevelt and their union chief's influence with the New Deal administration. Everywhere in the coal camps, organizers assured miners by posters, billboards, and union sound trucks that "the president wants you to join the union" and circulated rumors that "John L. Lewis was having beer and sauerkraut with President Roosevelt every night, and to hell with the company guards."[3]

The effect of the legislation and the campaign among miners was electric. A Pennsylvania organizer "noticed a different feeling among the Miners every where they seem to feel that they are once more free men. . . . A new day for the miners is at hand."[4] The miners spontaneously organized themselves, and organizers did little more than assist in establishing new local unions. In only seventeen days, one organizer created forty-two locals. At one meeting at Williamson, West Virginia, forty-two hundred miners from "Bloody" Mingo County, a notorious antiunion stronghold, joined the UMW. Within weeks after NRA's enactment, the UMW had boosted its membership from fewer than one hundred thousand to five hundred thousand and had organized 92 percent of the country's coal miners. Only a few scattered areas—the Uniontown, Pennsylvania, coke field; U.S. Steel Corporation's empire in Gary, West Virginia; and scattered mines in western Kentucky and Harlan County—escaped solid organization.[5]

Perhaps just as significant, the UMW, so plagued by internecine quarrels and rival unionism since 1926 that it had been unable to oppose the operators, once again became the home of all coal miners except in Illinois, where the Progressive Mine Workers continued its feud for a time. In the fall of 1933, NMU followers rejoined the union they had hoped to destroy. Lewis's personal foes were quick to acknowledge his triumph. Lewis's old enemy, Oscar Ameringer, reluctantly admitted that "John turned out to be the only archangel among the angels with fallen arches of the A. F. of L. crowd. . . . Some of my old friends may not like this tribute to John L. . . . But dang it all, he earned it." Two other opponents, John Brophy and

Powers Hapgood, praised Lewis as *"the man of the hour in the labor world."* [6]

After three months of hard bargaining, in September, 1933, operator and union representatives agreed upon a Bituminous Coal Code for their chaotic industry. The code set minimum sale prices for all mines and established district code authorities to enforce compliance. The code also established minimum wages and maximum hours and created district labor boards to enforce its provisions.[7] The Bituminous Coal Labor Board, Division no. 1—South, with headquarters at Cincinnati, Ohio, was granted jurisdiction over southern West Virginia, Virginia, eastern Kentucky, northern Tennessee, and North Carolina. Presidential appointee Charles B. Barnes chaired the southern board; Edward C. Mahan, president of Southern Coal and Coke Company, which had mines in Harlan County, and the largest coal operator south of the Ohio River, served as the operators' representative; and Van A. Bittner, the president of the UMW's District 17, in southern West Virginia, who had helped organize Harlan miners during World War I, represented labor.

At mines under union contract original jurisdiction in a labor dispute lay with the local grievance machinery. In Harlan County, for example, the local mine committee first attempted to negotiate a settlement with the local operator. Failing agreement, either disputant could appeal the case to the Harlan County Arbitration Board, composed of union and operator representatives and an impartial referee. Unable to reach agreement at the intermediate level, either the operator or the district union president could refer the case to the Cincinnati labor board for final determination. At nonunion mines, complaints were filed directly with the Cincinnati board, which attempted to adjust the complaint through direct correspondence with the affected operator. Failing settlement, the board held hearings, to which both operators and union officials were invited with witnesses, and rendered decisions. The NRA's Compliance Division was then charged with enforcing compliance with the board's decisions.[8]

On September 21, 1933, operator and union representatives also signed a historic union agreement covering 340,000 miners in the Central Appalachian Region. The standard contract specified a maximum eight-hour day and and forty-hour week, a basic daily wage of $4.20 in the South, and a grievance procedure consisting of local mine committees and a field-wide arbitration board. On March 30, 1934, a second Appalachian agreement provided for a seven-hour day, a thirty-five-hour week, and a basic southern daily wage of $4.60. When the second contract expired on March 31, 1935, labor-management relations in the coal fields temporarily lapsed into pre-1933 chaos. The coal code was breaking down, and indeed, on May 27, 1935, the Supreme Court invalidated the entire National Industrial Recovery Act. Throughout the southern coal fields the minimum sale price and the wages and hour provisions were being violated with impunity, and southern operators balked at renewing their agreement with the UMW.[9] Only after months of contract extensions, strikes, and federal intervention did most Central Appalachian operators finally sign a third agreement. In the interim, the national government renewed its commitment to collective bargaining in the coal fields by passing the National Labor Relations Act of 1935 (the Wagner Act) and the Guffey Coal Stabilization Act. Signed in September, 1935, the new contract retained the seven-hour day and thirty-five-hour week and increased the southern basic daily wage to $5.10.

Thus, with few exceptions, most notably Harlan County, collective bargaining had been firmly established throughout the nation's coal fields. Harlan, although it produced only 1 percent of the nation's coal, posed a serious threat to the continued success of coal-field labor-management relations. So long as the Harlan field persisted in nonunion operation, so long would its competitors in surrounding fields—Virginia, Tennessee, eastern Kentucky, and Alabama—threaten, as they did in both 1934 and 1935, to terminate their union contracts. Should these southern fields revert to open-shop operation, the northern fields would also be compelled, as they had been in 1927, to break with the union. Consequently, the United Mine Workers, now much stronger and fairly secure, was forced by competitive conditions to continue its unrelenting effort to organize the renegade Harlan field.

In Harlan County, in the summer of 1933, the UMW gathered great momentum as miners in all the surrounding counties of eastern Kentucky, Tennessee, Virginia, and West Virginia joined the union. The union solidly organized neighboring Bell County, which then served as a beachhead from which to launch an invasion of Harlan. Although the Harlan mine owners, unlike most of their competitors, continued adamantly to resist unionization, the passage of NRA and the fresh UMW organizing drive caught them with their guard down. A year earlier, in a fit of pique because most county operators had refused to support his campaign for Republican county chairman, Sheriff Blair had fired half of his 170 deputies—the mine guards who had hitherto excluded organizers from the county and its coal camps.[10]

On March 26, 1932, the same weekend that Bell County citizens were expelling the eastern college students, Harlan County Republicans were preoccupied with selecting a county chairman. John Henry Blair, twice sheriff and once county chairman, supported J. B. Carter for chairman and attempted to purge the county party of Democratic influence. Judge D. C. Jones supported J. Ray Rice, a Harlan businessman. A week before the county convention, when precinct committeemen were chosen, twenty-six precincts supported Carter, six supported Rice, and twenty-nine selected unpledged committeemen. In an effort at compromise, Carter and Rice withdrew from the race, and Judge Jones threw his support to George S. Ward, secretary of the operators' association. Sheriff Blair refused to compromise, however, and personally entered the race against Ward. Judge Jones rallied the coal operators against the sheriff, promising, according to Blair, to dismiss charges against certain defendants in the Evarts murder cases in return for their families' support. In the many company-controlled precincts, Sheriff Blair threatened to discharge mine guards at every mine where the operator instructed his precinct's committeemen to oppose the sheriff. In the convention, only two company-controlled precincts voted for Blair, two abstained, and the remainder supported George Ward, who won by a vote of eighty-eight to forty-four.[11]

Sheriff Blair retaliated by immediately discharging eighty-six deputies at more than thirty coal camps where the operators had refused to support him. Among those dismissed were Ben Unthank, Lee Fleenor, Frank White, and George Lee—men who had previously formed Harlan County's antiunion vanguard. He also sought a murder indictment against Deputy Sheriff Fleenor, who had not as yet been charged with the six-month-old slaying of Baldwin and Moore at the Clovertown soup kitchen.[12] "I intend to protect myself politically," the irate sheriff explained to a reporter. "I did all in my power to aid the operators and they, in turn, have slapped me in the face. I hate to do this, but I warned them before the election that I would do it."[13] While the selection of the operators' association's secretary as county chairman was ultimately a severe blow to the union's political fortunes, the immediate effect was to lower the bars for the union. Within the week, the UMW announced its reentry into southeastern Kentucky.[14] While its progress was glacial until the spring of 1933, the lowering of the guard facilitated the union's initial success under the NRA.

Although the term of the stubborn sheriff expired December 31, 1933, the political outlook for the union beyond that date appeared still more promising. In the autumn of 1933, a slate of reform candidates, Theodore Roosevelt Middleton for sheriff, Morris Saylor for county judge, Elmon Middleton for county attorney, James M. Gilbert for circuit court judge, and Daniel Boone Smith for commonwealth's attorney, entered the Republican primary pledged to a New Deal for Harlan County. They promised to reduce the county's homicide rate, to reform the privately paid deputy system, and to provide equal protection under the law for union members and organizers. The candidates for sheriff and county judge, whose duty it was to appoint and confirm the commissions of deputies, specifically pledged not to reappoint deputies like Unthank, Fleenor, White, and Lee, whom the union found objectionable. As police chief of the city of Harlan, all during the summer of 1933 Theodore Middleton had roped off city streets for union parades and rallies and protected the participants. Smith had aggressively and successfully defended a number of the Evarts murder defendants. The UMW endorsed the entire slate of Republican reformers, who won both the primary and the general elections.[15] At last, it appeared that the miners had triumphed politically over the operator-controlled Republican machine, and probably at no time since the Harlan field was opened had the prospect looked brighter for successful organization.

In the summer of 1933, national representative Lawrence Dwyer and local union field representative Milt Harbin launched an organizing drive in Harlan. In short order, they established locals at eighteen, about half, of the county's mines; some five thousand miners joined the UMW.[16]

On October 27, after a three-week strike at half the county's mines, the Harlan County Coal Operators' Association signed a union contract retroactive to October 2, the date on which the Central Appalachian Agreement took effect. The Harlan Agreement's wage and hour provisions were identical to the Central Appalachian contract: a $4.20 basic daily wage for the South, an eight-hour day, and a forty-hour week. On March 13, 1934, the Harlan operators' association was reluctant to renew its agreement, but largely through the intercession of Mahan, the association signed a second contract containing the standard Appalachian provisions on wages and hours: a $4.60 daily wage, seven-hour day, and thirty-five-hour week. During the long, confused summer of strikes and contract extensions of 1935 that culminated in a new Central Appalachian Agreement, the Harlan operators' association rejected a third contract but agreed to pay the standard Appalachian southern scale of $5.10.[17] Unlike the standard Central Appalachian Agreement, however, the Harlan contract did not recognize the UMW, and its provisions applied only at mines employing one or more members of the UMW. Consequently, from October 27, 1933, until March 31, 1935, only half the county's major mines considered themselves in any way bound by the agreement.[18]

Union and nonunion mines were interspersed throughout the county. In the county's Poor Fork section, Harlan Central was under union contract, but U.S. Coal & Coke and Wisconsin Steel were not. In the Clover Fork section, Black Mountain, Clover Splint, Cornett-Lewis, Berger, High Splint, Darby, Perkins-Harlan, Harlan-Crown, Harlan Ridgeway, and Elkhorn Piney accepted the union agreement; Harlan-Wallins, Clover

Fork, Harlan Collieries, and Benito maintained nonunion operation. On Martin's Fork, Three Point, Black Star, R. W. Creech, Blue Diamond, Mahan-Ellison, Southern Harlan, and Kentucky King were under contract, while Harlan Fuel, Crummies Creek, Mary Helen, Tway, and Bardo were not.[19] The coexistence of union and nonunion mines persisted throughout the NRA years, and the UMW was unable to consolidate the gains so quickly won in the halcyon days of 1933.

The Harlan operators had too much at stake to give up the struggle so easily. No sooner had the union gained a tenuous foothold than the mine owners launched a counterattack that essentially expelled it from the county by mid-1935. Why did the vast majority of Harlan's operators resist unionization more intensely than did their competitors?

Philip Taft and Philip Ross have posited a thesis that might help to explain Harlan mine owners' rigid antiunionism. They suggest that family-owned enterprises, such as Kohler and Perfect Circle, whose managers approached labor-management relations from a more personal, often principled point of view, have been more typically antiunion than large corporations whose managers took a less personal, less principled, businesslike approach to labor relations. Consequently, they argue, resistance to unionism has diminished over the years as more and more firms have passed into corporate hands.[20] Harlan County, with its vivid antiunion history and its mixture of both corporate- and family-owned firms, offers an excellent opportunity to test their thesis. Of thirteen family-owned Harlan mines, 60 per cent were antiunion, but of seven local corporate managements, 86 percent were antiunion. That is, while both types of local management were overwhelmingly antiunion, the corporate professionals were even more hostile than family managers.

Many contemporaries attributed the county's virulent antiunionism to its high degree of absentee ownership. Of eleven absentee firms, 64 percent opposed the union, and of nine locally owned companies, 89 percent were antiunion. While again both absentee- and home-owned firms predominately opposed unionism, the local firms were more hostile than the absentee companies.

In the case of firms that owned mines both inside and be-

yond Harlan's borders, the company's union policy at its outside mines significantly affected its local labor policy. All five
firms (100 percent) that ran nonunion outside mines ran nonunion shops in Harlan. Three (75 percent) of four firms with
organized outside mines ran union mines locally. Of fourteen
firms that owned no outside mines, 86 percent were antiunion.
That is, firms that operated nonunion mines outside Harlan
most resisted local organizations, and firms with outside union
mines offered the best prospects for local unionization.

At first glance, it seems that a mining company's status as an
independent or a captive mine had no effect on its local labor
policy. Of twenty-four independent and captive local mines, 79
percent were antiunion. Of the nineteen independents, 79 percent were antiunion, and of five captive mines, 80 percent were
antiunion. These nearly identical statistics are misleading, however; in practice, the parent firm's union policy nearly always
determined its subsidiary's local policy. For example, Black
Mountain Coal Corporation, whose parent firm, Peabody Coal
Corporation, maintained union relations at its Illinois mines,
retained the only continuing union contract in Harlan after
1933. U.S. Coal & Coke Corporation, like its parent firm, U.S.
Steel Corporation, remained nonunion until 1937, but when
Big Steel signed a union agreement, so did its subsidiary.

While an individual Harlan mine's labor policy might be
affected by its link to a larger firm or its status as a captive
mine, the county's disadvantageous competitive position held
the key to field-wide labor relations. Harlan firms always had
to concern themselves with their operating costs vis-à-vis
northern competitors who enjoyed favorable freight rates. Suffering a thirty-five-cents-per-ton shipping differential, local coal
men sought to shave labor costs either by paying lower wages
or by requiring employees to perform more work for the same
wage via such tactics as the cleanup system, coal bucking, no
pay for dead work, or short weight. Unionism, by requiring
pay for dead work and employment of checkweighmen and
by abolishing coal bucking and the cleanup system, threatened
to end such competitive advantages. Between 1927 and 1933,
when unionism almost disappeared from competing fields,
Harlan operators' nonunion advantage all but evaporated, and
ultimately the Harlan field suffered severe depression. During

the NRA years, however, when most competitors were saddled with code- and union-imposed wage and hour regulation, non-unionism was once again advantageous and profitable. As previously noted, during the NRA period Harlan operators matched the code and union southern wage scale, but, at the same time, they continued to reduce labor costs by exceeding code hours, by enforcing the cleanup system, and, in some cases, by short-weighing their employees. They were thus able to market their coal profitably below both competitive and minimum code prices and capture additional sales contracts. Consequently, with half the county's operators enjoying non-union operation and the other half paying scant attention to union work rules, Harlan's coal production mounted from 1932's 6,888,875 tons to a new high of 15,097,932 tons in 1936. Therein lies most of the explanation for Harlan's vehement antiunionism. The nonunion shop was productive and, for the operators, profitable.

Harlan's nonunion firms profited not only at the expense of outside competitors but at the expense of unionized local firms as well. Thus, in the summer of 1935, when all but three Harlan firms had reverted to nonunion operation, previously organized Clover Splint and Black Star were forced to terminate their union contracts against their will, leaving Black Mountain, a captive mine less subject to competitive pressure, as the county's only union company.[21] In 1935 an attempt was made to dynamite the Black Mountain superintendent's home, and in 1938 arsonists burned the company's tipple. Superintendent E. J. Asbury suspected that some of his nonunion fellow operators instigated both acts to force his company to break with the union.[22] Thus, by sharp competitive practices, and possibly less professional methods, the county's nonunion majority managed to force prounion dissenters into line.

Whereas the competitive situation explains the Harlan operators' almost unique resistance to collective bargaining in coal, the county's privately paid deputy system accounts for their ability to translate their ideas into action. Both West Virginia and Pennsylvania had abolished the private mine guard prior to NRA's passage, leaving only Kentucky's mine owners in possession of a private army with which to wage war against the union.

Because the Harlan operators lacked the sheriff's cooperation in barring union organizers from the county in 1933, they at first resorted to other methods of thwarting the UMW. On May 17, about three weeks before the National Recovery Act's passage, the operators' association met to discuss adoption of a uniform, higher wage scale. Appalachian Coals, a southern voluntary regulatory association with which the Harlan association was affiliated, had recommended a 10 percent wage increase, and the superintendent of Blue Diamond, a firm with mines in both the Harlan and the Hazard, Kentucky, fields, urged adoption of a uniform wage scale to forestall labor agitation similar to that recently produced by wage disparities in the adjoining field. Two weeks later, on the eve of NRA's enactment, the Harlan association adopted a uniform field-wide scale and raised wages 10 percent. Only the Whitfield family's two mines, Clover Fork and Harlan Collieries, rejected the new scale, which otherwise applied to twenty-eight of thirty association mines and to eight thousand miners.[23] Then, after the Harlan association signed a union agreement on October 27, 1933, it matched the union pay scale. Thus, the local mine owners deprived the UMW of the issue of a higher wage scale as an organizing incentive.

The county's largest producer, U.S. Coal & Coke Corporation, which employed thirty-two hundred miners and was considered by union officials the key to successful organization of the county, instituted a company union to forestall UMW organization. On June 3, 1933, in line with U.S. Steel Corporation's national labor policy, the subsidiary launched the Union of Lynch Employees, which the *Harlan Daily Enterprise* candidly appraised as a substitute for the UMW, an organization "charged with harboring radicals and Communists." [24] Until 1938, when U.S. Coal & Coke followed its parent firm in adopting a collective bargaining agreement, the ULE successfully frustrated UMW organization at Lynch; but not until 1937 did other Harlan operators, who feared that company unionism might be transformed into the genuine article, resort to the technique.

In addition to wage increases and company unionism, the Harlan operators soon resumed violent opposition to the union.

By January 1, 1934, the mine owners had regained political control of the county. Thereafter, until 1937, privately paid deputy sheriffs barred union organizers from entering the county; within Harlan, they spied on them, intimidated them, assaulted them, and denied them access to company property. The deputies disrupted union rallies and denied local miners freedom of speech and assembly. The Bituminous Coal Labor Board was powerless to interfere with the county's political machine or its privately paid deputy system; hence, the NRA was doomed to failure in Harlan County.

Even before the political climate worsened, during the summer and fall of 1933 private vigilantes harassed union organizers. As soon as the union's organizational campaign got under way, District 19 president Turnblazer received an ominous warning. "Yours for a one-way ride, Three of Us" invited Turnblazer to "a little party" after the union's next Pineville rally and announced their intention "to put you and Milt Harbin about 6 feet under ground in a pine box." While Turnblazer could avoid the county, Milt Harbin, the union's local field representative who lived at Wallins Creek, could not. On June 1, an unsuccessful attempt was made to bomb his home.[25]

B. H. Moses, a Holiness minister and former Clover Splint miner, organized a local union at Closplint and conducted local union meetings in the church where he and his family lived. During the summer of 1933, two attempts to dynamite the church failed, but a second church where he conducted union meetings was destroyed. A deputy sheriff twice warned him that his union activity endangered his life.[26]

Lawrence "Peggy" Dwyer, the sixty-nine-year-old national union representative who headed the union's campaign in Bell and Harlan, bore the brunt of such attacks. One afternoon in June, 1933, as Dwyer and three assistants were returning to Pineville from a union meeting at Black Star, a deputy sheriff fired a signal shot as their car passed. Two hundred feet beyond, concealed snipers riddled the vehicle with bullets, but the occupants escaped injury. Again on October 11, as Dwyer and three organizers were returning from a union rally at Liggett, ambushers fired on them. One bullet narrowly missed Dwyer's head, and a second wounded Jim Bates in the thigh. When

Dwyer looked back after the attack, he saw two deputy sheriffs jumping into their cars.[27]

On September 10, and again on November 25, Dwyer's Pineville apartment was dynamited. The first blast destroyed a concrete garage near Dwyer's bedroom. The second bomb exploded directly beneath his bedroom window, threw him against the ceiling, and severely damaged the apartment building, but the union veteran escaped with only minor cuts and bruises. Chris Patterson was convicted and imprisoned for the crime, but four indicted Harlan County accomplices were never brought to trial.[28]

When a federal labor conciliator visited Harlan in October, 1933, deputy sheriffs kept him under constant surveillance; miners warned him not to venture out into the county lest he be ambushed. He left convinced that any union organizer who entered Harlan County was placing his life in jeopardy.[29] As 1933 closed, a wave of violence was already mounting against active unionists, but most miners were not yet intimidated and continued to join the union. The UMW looked forward to the new year when the union's friends, Sheriff Theodore Middleton and County Judge Morris Saylor, would at last open the county to successful organization.

On January 1, 1934, the new Republican county officials assumed office, but only County Attorney Elmon Middleton and Circuit Judge James M. Gilbert honored their campaign promises. Immediately, Sheriff Middleton and Judge Saylor reappointed Sheriff Blair's antiunion deputies plus a number of the new sheriff's relatives, who were of no higher character and no less partisan. The sheriff confided to Lawrence Dwyer that he "was forced to do it on obligations I entered into during the primary." A year later, the sheriff told Charles Barnes, chairman of the Bituminous Coal Labor Board, that because the county's operators opposed unionism he intended to use all the power of his office to prevent organization.[30]

Although the sheriff's annual salary was constitutionally limited to $5,000, during the next three years Middleton accumulated $92,000 and emerged as a major county coal operator. He acquired Green-Silvers Coal Company, of which he became president, 230 shares of common stock in Crummies Creek Coal Company, a half-interest in a Rockcastle County wagon mine, and a one-fifth interest in a Tennessee coal company. Jointly with Judge Saylor and Pearl Bassham, superintendent and vice-president of Harlan-Wallins Coal Corporation, the sheriff acquired a one-fourth interest in Verda Supply Company, a privately owned commissary at Harlan-Wallins's largest mine, which earned a 178 percent annual profit during the Depression years, and a one-third interest in a six-hundred-acre tract of coal land that was profitably leased to Bassham's firm.[31] Regardless of how the new sheriff and judge acquired their new-found wealth, their business interests gave both of them a personal stake in the mining industry and made them business partners with the county's most intensely antiunion operator. The same was true of Commonwealth's Attorney Daniel Boone Smith, whom three antiunion coal firms, Harlan-Wallins, Mary Helen, and R. C. Tway, placed on a $2,100 annual retainer.[32]

Fifteen major coal operators, the secretary of the operators' association, and the antiunion editor of the *Harlan Daily Enterprise* signed the sheriff's official bonds, an act that saved him considerable bonding costs and constituted one of his obligations. Several signers, among them Pearl Bassham of Harlan-Wallins, R. C. Tway of R. C. Tway Coal Company, A. F. Whitfield, Jr., of Clover Fork, Bryan Whitfield of Harlan Collieries, C. V. Bennett of Harlan Central, and George Ward, were notorious union-haters; only one, Elmer Hall of Three Point, considered unionism acceptable.[33]

Ben F. Unthank, the operators' association's chief detective and a deputy sheriff under both Blair and Middleton, played a central role in preventing the county's organization. Unthank's primary duty was to spy on union organizers and union meetings and report his findings to George S. Ward. Unthank employed some fifteen assistants, many of them furnished by a Cincinnati detective agency and known to him only by number. Both Unthank and Ward admitted under oath that the agents' chief purpose was to prevent organization of the county's mines. During three major organizing campaigns in

1933, 1935, and 1937, the association doubled the financial assessment on its membership and used a major portion of the additional funds to combat the union.[34]

The new county administration quickly made its position clear. After reappointing union opponents as deputies, early in February the sheriff and county judge locked unionists out of a scheduled courthouse rally. Judge Saylor warned Dwyer that the county citizens' hostility to unionism had grown so intense that, if union organizers entered Harlan, "murder will be committed." [35] A week later, on February 10, a third attempt was made on Dwyer's life. R. C. Tway, one of the best-informed association members, attributed that attack to George Lee, a deputy sheriff seeking revenge for the death of his son, Otto, in the Battle of Evarts. The operators bitterly opposed Dwyer, whom they accused of initiating earlier union violence in West Virginia, Illinois, and Colorado.[36] Dwyer's life was so threatened in Harlan that District 19 president Turnblazer was forced to reassign him to other duties.

When the Harlan agreement was up for renewal in the spring of 1934, antiunion violence intensified, particularly in the vicinity of Harlan-Wallins's Verda mine. In early May, snipers hidden on the mountainside fired on a Verda miners' rally at the Evarts ball park, forcing the meeting to reconvene on railroad property at Ages.[37]

The union scheduled a rally at Verda for Sunday afternoon, May 20. On Friday, Sheriff Middleton announced that he intended to take "drastic action" to rid the county of "roving bands of trouble makers" who were using "mob violence" to intimidate and coerce the coal operators into signing a contract. On Sunday morning, the editor of the *Harlan Daily Enterprise* urged county citizens to support their sheriff, who was "acting to save the homes of this county from these lawless bands" of union pickets, "idle men without jobs" and "men who want no jobs and would not work if they had them." Editor Alverson warned his readers against the union's

> menacing hand that threatens to dip its slimy tenacles [sic] into the peace and quietude of our laboring men—a hand that has appeared before, only to leave misery, despair and destruction among them.

> God pity the men of Harlan County, and God pity their
> families, if this octopus of distrust and this attempted lawless-
> ness succeeds in entwining its ungodly arms around the hearts
> of the working man. The brightness of the future that lies be-
> fore us will be dimmed by this monster, and Harlan County
> will lose more than it can ever regain.

Meanwhile, the sheriff was acting. On Saturday, six deputy
sheriffs, among them Ben Unthank, George Lee, and Frank
White, arrested Marshall Musick, a Baptist preacher who
served as checkweighman and strike leader at Cornett-Lewis,
on a charge of criminal syndicalism. Musick was confined in
the county jail for nine hours and finally released on bond. On
Monday, after Cornett-Lewis signed the Harlan contract,
charges against him were dismissed without a hearing. Very
early Sunday morning, one truckload of union miners from
Liggett gained access to the Verda rally. Soon, sheriff's deputies
arrived, ordered the visiting miners to return to their homes,
and blockaded all highways to prevent other miners from
attending the rally.[38]

On a Sunday afternoon in June, the union scheduled a rally
at Shields. Marshall Musick attempted to lead a group of thirty-
five Cornett-Lewis miners down the railroad tracks to the rally.
At a highway crossing near High Splint, seventeen armed
deputies led by Merle Middleton and George Lee turned them
back. When Musick lagged behind the group, George Lee
jabbed him with an automatic rifle, temporarily paralyzing his
hip and leg. When Musick fell, Merle Middleton, the sheriff's
cousin, kicked him across three railroad tracks. The deputies
pistol-whipped a second miner until he bled profusely, and
several others were threatened and abused.[39]

The Reverend Carl E. Vogel, pastor of Harlan's prestigious
Cornett Memorial Methodist Church, whom the coal operators
had trusted to chair the crucial county relief committee in 1931,
witnessed the High Splint incident and concluded that officers
sworn to execute the laws had become "the greatest violators
of those laws." In addition to preaching reform to his elitist
congregation, he and reform-minded County Attorney Elmon
Middleton conferred several times over the course of the following year on a plan of action. But in September, 1935, after

launching a vigorous prosecution of the county's gambling interests, Middleton was assassinated by a dynamite bomb attached to his automobile. Later, the same month, after receiving numerous complaints from coal operators and businessmen in the Cornett Memorial congregation, the Methodist bishop transferred the Reverend Mr. Vogel to Ashland.[40] Thus, the only hope for internal county reform was removed from the scene.

In June, 1934, District 19 officials appointed Marshall Musick field representative for seventeen local unions in the Clover Fork section. Constantly shadowed by deputies, Musick frequently eluded them by removing his false teeth, wearing an overall jacket and a miner's cap, and blackening his face with coal dust. Musick requested protection from county officials, but Sheriff Middleton informed him that as long as he remained active in "the racketeering labor organization" neither he nor his family could expect assistance from the sheriff's office.[41]

Union officials appointed William Clontz, a Methodist minister and former assistant foreman at the R. W. Creech Coal Company, union field representative for the southern section of the county. In the spring of 1934, an anonymous writer warned Clontz: "If you don't quit giving Trouble you will be took out of hear and you want return any moore don't let this slip your mind." That summer, Clontz's dog dragged an exploded dynamite bomb from under his house, and that fall, ten shots were fired from a passing car into his house. Four bullets penetrated his son's bedroom and narrowly missed the sleeping boy. A reluctant investigation by sheriff's deputies produced no evidence, the grand jury issued no indictments, and Sheriff Middleton advised Clontz to flee the county.[42] In a letter to NRA administrator Hugh S. Johnson, the harried minister confided that constant surveillance by strangers, anonymous threats, and county authorities' refusal to protect him had made him "afraid to lie down in my own home, or go anywhere alone." [43]

On November 30, 1934, the president and secretary of the Kentucky State Federation of Labor led fifteen UMW organizers into Harlan to launch an organizing campaign. The proprietor of the New Harlan Hotel refused to rent them rooms because he feared reprisal by "the biggest gang of dynamiters on earth." Carl Williams, whose suspected participation in the Battle of Evarts had made him persona non grata in Harlan County, was among the group. Deputies Ben Unthank, George Lee, and Frank White entered the hotel lobby and arrested Williams for carrying a concealed weapon. Williams denied the charge, but when he made a threatening move toward his pocket, George Lee beat him on the head and lodged him in the county jail over the weekend. The other organizers fled the county, and the campaign was abandoned.[44]

On Saturday, a week later, when Turnblazer and ten organizers, under orders of the Bituminous Coal Labor Board to inspect Harlan-Wallins's books, registered at the Lewallen Hotel, fifteen deputy sheriffs and mine guards, acting under Sheriff Middleton's orders, took adjoining rooms. The union party was afraid either to continue their mission to Harlan-Wallins or to leave the county, and Governor Laffoon was forced to activate the Harlan National Guard unit to patrol the hotel corridors throughout the night and escort the union men out of the county the next morning.[45]

That Sunday morning, Adjutant General Henry H. Denhardt conferred with George Ward, seven prominent county operators, all county officials, and the mayor of Harlan. Although Circuit Judge Gilbert attributed the trouble to local politics and the undesirable character of some deputy sheriffs, the operators blamed "outside agitators" and assured Denhardt that if organizers were barred from the county the disturbances would cease. Denhardt warned the operators and county officials that if they continued to violate organizers' and miners' rights of free speech and assembly, the governor would be forced to declare martial law in the county. Returning to Frankfort, the adjutant general recommended that Governor Laffoon order Sheriff Middleton to reform his deputy force under penalty of removal from office.[46]

During the NRA years, the *Harlan Daily Enterprise* rarely mentioned labor-management relations. But the hostile public reaction to the Lewallen Hotel incident forced the local editor to speak out lest the coal operators' "very silence had been mistaken for the answer of guilty men." Forced to admit the operators' and sheriff's responsibility for recent disturbances, he defended their motives: "The operators have appealed for protection only to their sheriff, who is pledged to protect property rights. They have tried to keep out these foreign radicals to protect their property and the work it gives to thousands. They have fought for the peace and protection of their employees who would suffer most through a closed industry. . . . If there has been any madness in Harlan County, there has been a reason behind it. Remove the irritation and the sore will heal itself." Editor Alverson, while conceding that "Sheriff Middleton has possibly made mistakes in the selection of his deputies," asserted that no sheriff had been more willing to rectify mistakes once they were brought to his attention.[47] The last statement was totally in error. That very spring a county grand jury had reported that "in practically every homicide which has occurred in Harlan County since the first of the year officers figured prominently" and recommended the dismissal of eight particularly offensive deputies. Sheriff Middleton later confessed to the La Follette Civil Liberties Committee that he had removed none of them and denied having seen the report.[48]

On December 29, 1934, a special convention of union delegates from Districts 19 and 30, state government officials, and interested civic leaders met to organize a new campaign to organize Harlan County. The convention discussed the private deputy system at length and adopted a resolution urging Congress to investigate the county's lack of compliance with national labor law. On January 29, 1935, Kentucky Congressman A. J. May, from solidly organized District 30, introduced a resolution calling for a House investigation of Harlan conditions. Speaking on behalf of his resolution, May charged that Sheriff Middleton was conspiring with county operators to thwart enforcement of the National Recovery Act and was using deputies with extensive criminal records to prevent free speech, peaceful assembly, and collective bargaining. The resolution, however, died in the Rules Committee.[49]

In February, 1935, several UMW organizers attempted to organize the two huge captive mines on Poor Fork, U.S. Coal & Coke Corporation and Wisconsin Steel Corporation. Poor

Fork, in the county's northwest corner, adjoined thoroughly organized UMW District 30. When Samuel Caddy, president of District 30, asked his miners to contribute $10,000 to finance a drive to organize Harlan, they responded with $25,000, and jurisdiction over the two mines was temporarily transferred to Caddy's district. He assigned twelve organizers, working out of Whitesburg, Letcher County, to join with twenty-seven Harlan organizers in organizing the two mines. The local union established a headquarters in the nearby incorporated town of Cumberland.[50]

U.S. Coal & Coke was well prepared for the campaign. Lynch's police chief, Joseph R. Menefee, and six of the company's regular thirteen-man police force had formerly served as mine guards at H. C. Frick Coal & Coke Company mines, U.S. Steel's Pennsylvania mining subsidiary. An eighth officer had previously served as a Pennsylvania state policeman. During the summer of 1934, five Lynch officers had received training in control of mobs and labor disturbances at a special police school held at an H. C. Frick Coal Company mine in Pennsylvania. During the union drive in January and February, 1935, the company employed seven additional officers and stocked a sizable supply of gas projectiles and ammunition. Although the firm was not a member of the Harlan operators' association, Menefee remained in close touch with its secretary, George Ward, and with Sheriff Middleton.[51]

During the union campaign, Lynch officers barred organizers from company property, maintained surveillance of the state highway that passed through the town, sounded their automobile horns to drown union sound trucks, and followed union members from door to door destroying union literature. When some Cumberland merchants complained that the organizers' presence was disrupting their business, Sheriff Middleton arrested them for creating a public nuisance, held them in the county jail over the weekend, and then released them without hearings.[52] This experience must have inspired the composition of "Harlan County Blues," a song that relates a tale of District 30 unionists who wore their UMW buttons on a visit to Harlan County and discovered that

"You didn't have to be drunk," they said,
"To get throwed in the can;
The only thing you needed be
Was just a union man." [53]

Union membership at Lynch, which had risen from one hundred to seventeen hundred during the brief campaign, quickly receded once the organizers were forced to withdraw.[54]

As a result of the Cumberland arrests, on February 12, 1935, Governor Laffoon appointed a four-member commission headed by Adjutant General Henry H. Denhardt to investigate the Harlan situation. During eight days in March, at Frankfort, the commission heard the testimony of Harlan miners, union officials, coal operators, civic leaders, and county officials. In May, the group briefly visited Harlan County and, for purposes of comparison, unionized Bell and Letcher counties. On June 7, the Denhardt Commission issued its report.

In adjoining Bell and Letcher counties the commission found an excellent labor-management relationship and full observance of civil liberties. By contrast, the commission reported, in Harlan County

> there exists a virtual reign of terror, financed in general by a group of coal mine operators in collusion with certain public officials; the victims of this reign of terror are the coal miners and their families. . . . Free speech and the right of peaceable assemblage is scarcely tolerated. Those who attend meetings or voice any sentiment favorable to organized labor are promptly discharged and evicted from their homes. Many are beaten and mistreated in most unjust and un-American methods by some operators using so-called "peace officers" to carry out their desires.
> *There is no doubt* that Theodore Middleton, sheriff of Harlan County, is in league with the operators and is using many of his deputies to carry out his purposes. . . . These mine guards should not be made use of away from the property of their employers. They should not be gunmen or ex-convicts; they should not be organized into flying squadrons to terrorize and intimidate people anywhere in the county wherever the sheriff may direct. . . .
> The present system of deputized mine guards and one-sided administration of the law must be abolished.

The commission emphasized the difficulty of achieving reform through the regular political processes because the electoral system had been thoroughly corrupted. Finally, the commission recommended that Governor Laffoon remove Sheriff Middleton from office, use state policemen to enforce the law and protect the people, and appoint a standing commission to investigate any future "outrages" that deputy sheriffs might commit.[55]

The editor of the *Harlan Daily Enterprise* asserted that the report was prepared by friends of the Democratic governor who were politically hostile to Republican Harlan County. Alverson charged that the investigation was part of a political deal by which Governor Laffoon would assist the union in organizing Harlan County in return for the UMW's endorsement of Thomas Rhea, the governor's personal choice for Democratic gubernatorial nominee. The editor believed that Governor Laffoon intended to

> sell the men of Harlan County, this time to swap them like filthy lucre between unscrupulous politicians and money-grabbing organizers. Sheriff Middleton has been the barrier between this betrayal of the laboring man, and those at Frankfort know it. It is their idea that with Sheriff Middleton out of the way, the deal between the Administration and the labor leaders can be consumated in the interest of their gubernatorial candidate. . . .
>
> When the Administration attempts to destroy the dikes that have withheld the floods of destroying influences, then it is crucifying the Sheriff of Harlan County upon the altar of duty and honesty well performed, and this paper will stand by him till Hades freezes over.[56]

On July 2, 1935, after Harlan miners and union officials filed affidavits against the sheriff, Governor Laffoon charged Middleton with neglect of official duty and ordered him to appear before the governor to show cause why he should not be removed from office. But because the governor fell ill and because Albert B. Chandler defeated Thomas Rhea, whom both the governor and the UMW had endorsed for the Democratic gubernatorial nomination, Governor Laffoon failed to remove the sheriff. When A. B. Chandler assumed the governor's office on December 10, 1935, Sheriff Middleton and five of his Harlan County deputies served as his official escort in the inaugural parade; and in January, 1937, the new governor proclaimed Middleton a "competent, efficient, and energetic" public official and dismissed all charges against him.[57] Thus ended the UMW's attempt to obtain state assistance in opening Harlan County to union organization.

The Harlan mine owners, whose political control of the sheriff's department had proven impervious to attack by the Bituminous Coal Labor Board and had withstood attempts at both internal and external reform, had once again secured their nonunion shop. As a result of the unrestrained attacks on outside organizers and local miners, by the spring of 1935 miners concluded that "it wasn't safe" to organize and either refused to join or relinquished their membership in the UMW.[58] That spring, a visiting NRA code inspector concluded that the vast majority of Harlan-Wallins's employees wanted to join the union but were prevented from joining by "some restraining influence." [59] By mid-1935, the UMW's 1933 membership of five thousand had dwindled to twelve hundred.[60]

In addition to using private mine guards to strike fear into the hearts of union organizers and members alike, the Harlan operators flagrantly violated NRA's Section 7(a) by purging their labor force of union activists. A local miner who dared to join the union was constantly threatened by economic, as well as physical, insecurity.

During the summer of 1933, the UMW established a local at Harlan Collieries. On October 27, 1933, the day the Harlan agreement was signed, the management reduced its work week from forty-eight to forty hours, ostensibly to comply with the NRA code, and discharged thirty union miners, among them all local union officers. A month later, when a former employee applied for reemployment, a company official rejected him, asserting that the mine was still operating an open shop and was "not paying the price nor working under the Code." [61]

A month after the company union was inaugurated at U.S. Coal & Coke Corporation in 1933, the UMW established Lynch Local 6067, which quickly recruited nine hundred members. Lynch policemen monitored the local's first public meeting, held in nearby Cumberland. The next day, the chief mine inspector summoned newly elected local president James Westmoreland to the company office. "If you are going to sign up with John L. Lewis and William Turnblazer," the inspector warned, "I will fire the last one of you." On May 29, 1934, Westmoreland distributed one-page UMW handbills to the Lynch miners as they boarded the man-trip. Although only the previous day company unionists had circulated ten-page ULE pamphlets in the mine, Westmoreland was summarily dismissed for creating a fire hazard. Only six days earlier, Albert E. Timmins, a local mine committeeman, had been fired for failing to set his safety timbers.[62]

At Harlan Central, a party to the first Harlan contract, the manager warned union activists, "You can't play on both sides of the fence. You must leave union off in the mines." [63] Local unionists were afraid to file an official complaint with the Cincinnati labor board because "if we do we are fire [sic] off of the job." [64] On April 2, 1934, 83 of the firm's 119 employees struck because the company refused to negotiate a new local union contract. The local union president and secretary were arrested and jailed for mounting a United States flag on the tipple; two days later, these two along with the union treasurer, sergeant-at-arms, and five other members were discharged and evicted from their company houses. All nine were immediately replaced by nonunion miners.[65]

By November, 1933, the UMW had solidly organized Charles M. Wright's two mines, Harlan Ridgeway and Harlan Crown, both parties to the Harlan contract. When his employees celebrated Mitchell Day, a national miners' holiday, on April 2, 1934, Wright, asserting that the union was not going to run his mine, discharged twenty-seven miners. After all but ten of his 210 employees struck to force reinstatement of the discharged men, Wright promised "Peggy" Dwyer that he would rehire all but five or six of the men. After Dwyer ordered the strikers back to work, however, Wright reneged on his promise and refused to reemploy ten union miners.[66]

By August 1934, 214 of 374 employees at Cornett-Lewis, a party to both Harlan agreements, had joined the UMW. On October 1, company manager R. E. "Uncle Bob" Lawson ordered all union members to sign their dues check-off slips personally in his office, and within a month, membership had plummeted to ninety-eight. On November 5, the company discontinued its night shift and laid off thirty-three employees, fourteen of them union members, subject to reemployment as soon as feasible. Within two weeks, seven union and nine non-union men were rehired, leaving seven unionists, among them every local union officer, still unemployed. A strike to force their reinstatement was broken within a week; this time, seventeen strikers, including again all local officers, were not rehired. On December 21, Lawson conducted a referendum to determine whether the company should continue under union contract, and his employees, forced to sign their ballots, voted 267 to 5 against union operation.[67]

In May, 1934, at Verda, one of Harlan-Wallins's five local mines, unionists met on the L & N right-of-way, established a local union, and elected officers. Within a week, the company fired seventeen miners who attended the rally, among them every newly elected officer. Harlan-Wallins also carefully screened new employees to exclude union members. One miner who applied for a foreman's job at Verda was presumed to be a union member because he hailed from solidly organized District 30, in eastern Kentucky. Deputy Sheriff Bob Eldridge and his son blackjacked the applicant and marched him at gunpoint to the nearest railroad depot to leave the county. He was warned in no uncertain terms that Harlan-Wallins hired no union miners.[68]

After their dismissal at U.S. Coal & Coke, James Westmoreland and Albert Timmins were refused a hearing by the Union of Lynch Employees' grievance committee. They then carried their cases to the Cincinnati labor board, which on June 8, 1934, held its first hearing on a Harlan case. In 1933, U.S. Steel Corporation had refused to place its mines under either the Bituminous Coal Code or the Central Appalachian union agreement; but the firm had bound itself, by what was known as the Presidential Agreement, to abide by the NRA's maximum hour and minimum wage provisions. Although the National Labor Board advised the Cincinnati board that the Presidential Agreement did not exempt the steel firm's Kentucky mines from its jurisdiction, the coal subsidiary's president, Thomas Moses, contended that it did. Moses submitted affidavits denying that Westmoreland and Timmins had been discharged because of union activity, but denied the labor board's jurisdiction and refused to send witnesses. On June 19, the board ruled that both men had been fired for union activity and ordered their reinstatement. When U.S. Coal & Coke refused them reemployment, the board referred its decision to the NRA's Compliance Division, where it became snarled in red tape and was never enforced. The UMW spared Westmoreland prolonged hardship by appointing him a Harlan County field representative, but Timmins, the father of seven children, was less fortunate.[69] Suspecting the worst, Timmins appealed directly to President Roosevelt because "many men before me have appealed to your agencies without avail. I have failed beforehand if I follow in their footsteps. . . . I ask you to intercede for me in . . . support of your own written promises to labor." [70] Even the president's prodding did not move the Compliance Division.

Having received complaints that Harlan Central had discharged nine unionists, used company guards to intimidate union miners and expel them from its camp, and violated code hours, on May 11, 1934, the Cincinnati labor board summoned the firm to a hearing. Company superintendent C. V. Bennett flippantly wrote Chairman Barnes that the company could not afford to send witnesses to the Queen City and requested either a local hearing or permission to mail affidavits proving the company's innocence. Harlan Central rejected the second Harlan contract, and in August, 1934, District 19 president Turnblazer advised Chairman Barnes to drop the matter because the company's property was so heavily guarded that it was impossible to organize.[71]

On October 17, 1934, in an ex parte hearing, the Bituminous Coal Labor Board found Harlan-Wallins Coal Corporation guilty of exceeding NRA code hours and ordered the firm to pay back wages to affected employees. The board ordered district president Turnblazer and Virginia code inspector E. H. Esser to inspect the company's books to determine the amount of overtime pay due its employees. But on December 8, 1934, as noted earlier, when Turnblazer and ten assistants journeyed to Harlan to join Esser, fifteen deputies and mine guards trapped them overnight in a local hotel, and the National Guard had to escort them safely out of the county.[72]

Because only one Harlan operator had found it convenient to attend a board hearing in Cincinnati and because both union officials and board personnel were afraid to convene in Harlan County, the labor board scheduled hearings on several accumulated complaints against eleven Harlan firms in Pineville, Bell County, on January 12–14, 1935. Of eleven operators asked to attend, only R. W. Creech appeared, and even he refused to comply with the board's order to reinstate an employee who had been fired for union activity.[73] The Pineville sessions symbolized the complete collapse of the coal board's authority in Harlan.

In two years of operation, the Bituminous Coal Labor Board received ninety-one complaints from Harlan County; held seven formal hearings, all but two of them ex parte because the invited operators refused to attend; and issued six decisions. None of the six decisions was voluntarily complied with, and none was enforced.[74] A mine foreman at Clover Fork best summed up most Harlan operators' attitude toward the National Recovery Administration. When nine union employees refused to work beyond code hours, the foreman ordered them to either return to work or get out. "Roosevelt's not running this mine," he bellowed, "and we are not working any 7 hour shifts." [75]

As early as December, 1933, local miners had pretty accurately assessed the labor board's potential impact in Harlan County. "Our faith in the Government must not be shaken," two discharged Lynch miners wrote the president, "but we are really beginning to wonder if the N.R.A. really means anything to us—if it is a guarantted [*sic*] right of the American citizen, then we begin to wonder if this right is not given to us." [76]

Thus, considering the actual course of events in Harlan County, the United States Supreme Court's invalidation of the National Industrial Recovery Act was no loss to unionism there. The Harlan miners' initial enthusiastic response to NRA belied the county operators' contention that the vast majority of their employees had no desire to organize. The extraordinary intensity of the local operators' and county officials' opposition to unionism accounted for the UMW's failure there. The labor board was powerless to dismantle the local operators' political control of the county or the private mine-guard system. The labor board also proved itself incapable of stopping local mine owners from discharging union miners, cheating on weights, exceeding code hours, or underselling code prices. Union representatives, denied free access to the county, were unable to recruit members, form locals, operate the grievance machinery, or service contracts. Individual miners, so long as union membership threatened their job security or their personal safety, either refused to join or dropped out of the union. Consequently, by the summer of 1935 the UMW's eighteen local contracts had dwindled to one—at Black Mountain Coal Corporation—and only twelve hundred members remained, most of them affiliated with the Black Mountain local.[77]

The NRA also failed to stabilize coal prices. In the spring of 1934, eight of Harlan County's nonunion firms contracted one-half million tons of coal to the Louisville & Nashville Railroad at fifteen cents per ton below the code's minimum price. The practice quickly spread beyond Harlan County's borders, and by the end of the year, half of southern production was being sold below code prices. By February, 1935, the national price structure completely collapsed. Van A. Bittner warned a Senate committee that Harlan County's continued violation of both price and labor regulations "is going to have a tremendous effect on breaking down prices and wage standards . . . and the [nonunion] southern territory will keep creeping and creeping on and up." Fear of a return to cutthroat competition and a breakdown of collective bargaining in the national coal industry, rather than the frequently alleged desire for dues payments from nine thousand local miners, accounted for the UMW's unrelenting effort to organize the Harlan County miners.[78]

The National Recovery Administration was not an unqualified failure in Harlan County; it did serve a useful educational function. Some local operators who had never before operated under union conditions, such as E. J. Asbury of Black Mountain, Armstrong Matthews of Clover Splint, Elmer D. Hall of Three Point, Edward C. Mahan of Southern Harlan and Mahan-Ellison, and R. W. Creech of R. W. Creech Coal Company, discovered they could live with the union.

The NRA had a profound impact on Edward Mahan, for example. Serving for twenty-five years on the Southern Appalachian Coal Operators' Association's executive board, he had "spent a considerable portion of that time in resisting Federal legislation to control the industry, and in fighting the United Mine Workers of America." [79] In 1932, he had opposed federal regulation of the coal industry because it would allow the UMW to dominate the industry and because a uniform national wage scale, in combination with a freight-rate differential, would inevitably close a large number of southern mines. He did not think that "the record of the United Mine Workers in the past 20 years . . . has been such as to justify this nation in legislating them into complete domination of the coal industry." [80] In 1933, he had opposed enactment of NRA "especially on account of its labor provision, and only acquiesced in it when we were compelled to do so." But after the act passed, he decided "to make the best of it and gave the measure, including the labor provisions, my full support, principally because the industry was in such a deplorable condition that I felt nothing that was done could make it any worse." During the entire life of the Bituminous Coal Labor Board, Division no. 1—South, Mahan served as the operators' representative, placed both of his Harlan County mines under union contract, and in both 1933 and 1934 was instrumental in persuading other Harlan operators to sign a union agreement. After NRA failed, Mahan supported enactment of the Guffey Coal Stabilization Act, which reenacted both government regulation of the coal industry and a government guarantee of collective bargaining, as the only chance to prevent the industry from "getting back to its former deplorable condition." [81] In only three brief years, Mahan's position had evolved from opposition, through acquiescence, to full support of federal government regulation of the coal industry and collective bargaining.

The presence of such influential operators on its executive board shattered the nonunion solidarity and moderated the policy of the Harlan County Coal Operators' Association. Had their restraining voices been absent from the association's councils, the record of the next two years might have been even more dismal.

NOTES

1. Powers Hapgood, "Radio Address to Miners," *Breeze* (Ill.) *Courier*, Dec. 14, 1935, clipping in John Brophy Papers, Catholic University of America. See also Oscar Ameringer, clipping in Brophy Papers.
2. Testimony of Edward C. Mahan in U.S., Congress, Senate, Committee on Interstate Commerce, *Stabilization of Bituminous Coal Mining Industry. Hearings* on S. 1417, 74 Cong., 1 sess. (1935), p. 523.
3. James A. Wechsler, *Labor Baron: A Portrait of John L. Lewis* (New York, 1944), p. 96.
4. John Ghizzoni to Lewis, June 12, 1933, Brophy Papers. See also W. Jett Lauck, Docket, June 20, 21, 1933, W. Jett Lauck Papers, University of Virginia.
5. Leo Wolman, "Labor under the NRA," in *America's Recovery Program*, ed. Clair Wilcox, Herbert F. Fraser, and Patrick Murphy Malin (New York, 1934), p. 98; *United Mine Workers Journal*, July 1, 1933, pp. 3–4; LFCH, pt. 10, pp. 3444–45.
6. Ameringer, clipping in Brophy Papers; Hapgood, "Radio Address to Miners" (the italics are Hapgood's).
7. For the making of the Bituminous Coal Code see James P. Johnson, "Drafting the NRA Code of Fair Competition for the Bituminous Coal Industry," *Journal of American History*, 53 (Dec., 1966), 521–41.
8. Charles B. Barnes, Report Submitted by Chairman of the Bituminous Coal Labor Board, Division no. 1—South and Division no. 1—North, June 7, 1935, NA, RG/9, NRA, BCLB, Correspondence File.
9. Johnson, "Drafting the NRA Code," p. 538.
10. *Harlan* (Ky.) *Daily Enterprise*, Mar. 27, 31, 1932; *Knoxville* (Tenn.) *News-Sentinel*, Apr. 3, 1932.
11. *Harlan Daily Enterprise*, Mar. 27, 31, 1932; editorial, ibid., Mar. 27, 1932; *Knoxville News-Sentinel*, Mar. 25, 27, 28, 1932; *Courier-Journal* (Louisville, Ky.), Mar. 28, 1932; editorial, ibid., Mar. 29, 1932.
12. *Harlan Daily Enterprise*, Mar. 27, 31, 1932; *Knoxville News-Sentinel*, Apr. 3, 1932.
13. *Courier-Journal*, Mar. 28, 1932.
14. *Pineville* (Ky.) *Sun*, Apr. 7, 1932.
15. Testimony of Lawrence Dwyer, LFCH, pt. 10, pp. 3461–63, 3465–66, pt. 12, pp. 4342–43; testimony of Carl Williams, ibid., pt. 11, pp. 3875–76; testimony of Daniel Boone Smith, ibid., pt. 12, pp. 4309, 4346; *Harlan Daily Enterprise*, Aug. 11, Nov. 17, 1933.
16. Testimony of William Turnblazer, LFCH, pt. 10, p. 3620.
17. *Harlan Daily Enterprise*, Oct. 27, 1933; *United Mine Workers Journal*, Oct. 1, 1933, p. 12, Apr. 15, 1934, pp. 4–5, 9, Oct. 1, 1935, pp. 3–4, 7; *Pineville Sun*, June 20, Oct. 3, 1935.

18. Testimony of Turnblazer, LFCH, pt. 10, p. 3620.

19. Turnblazer to Charles Barnes, Feb. 28, 1935; F. L. Poindexter to W. P. Ellis, Mar. 23, 1934, NA, RG/9, NRA, BCLB, Correspondence File.

20. Philip Taft and Philip Ross, "American Labor Violence: Its Causes, Character, and Outcome," in *The History of Violence in America: Historical and Comparative Perspectives,* ed. Hugh Davis Graham and Ted Robert Gurr (New York, 1969), pp. 385–86.

21. Testimony of Joseph Timko, LFCH, pt. 11, pp. 4013–14, 4021–23, 4026–28; testimony of Armstrong Matthews, ibid., pp. 4052–53; testimony of C. B. Burchfield, ibid., p. 4036.

22. George J. Titler, *Hell in Harlan* (Beckley, W.Va., n.d.), p. 92.

23. Minutes of meetings of the Harlan County Coal Operators' Association, May 17, May 29, 1933, LFCH, pt. 9, pp. 3277–79; *Harlan Daily Enterprise,* May 30, June 1, 1933; *Pineville Sun,* June 1, 1933.

24. Testimony of Howard N. Eavenson in U.S., Congress, Senate, Committe on Mines and Mining, *To Create a Bituminous Coal Commission. Hearings* on S. 2935, 72 Cong., 1 sess. (1932), pp. 497–98; testimony of James Westmoreland, LFCH, pt. 11, pp. 3904–5; affidavit, E. H. Hollingsworth, June 5, 1934, NA, RG/9, NRA, BCLB, Case File, Case no. 442; *Harlan Daily Enterprise,* June 5, 1933.

25. "Three of Us" to Turnblazer, Apr. 29, 1933, quoted in U.S., Congress, Senate, *Congressional Record,* 73 Cong., 1 sess. (1933), vol. 77, p. 4580; *United Mine Workers Journal,* July 15, 1933, p. 2.

26. Testimony of B. H. Moses, LFCH, pt. 10, pp. 3495–99.

27. Testimony of Dwyer, ibid., pp. 3459–60, 3463–65; *Pineville Sun,* Oct. 12, 1933.

28. *Pineville Sun,* Sept. 14, Nov. 30, 1933, Jan. 4, 11, March 15, 1934; testimony of Dwyer, LFCH, pt. 10, pp. 3467–70.

29. U.S. conciliation commissioner to Hugh L. Kerwin, Oct. 13, 1933, NA, RG/280, "Coal Miners, Pineville, Ky.," Box 363.

30. Testimony of Dwyer, LFCH, pt. 10, p. 3470; Barnes, memorandum of testimony before the Denhardt Commission, May 6, 1935, NA, RG/9, NRA, BCLB, Correspondence File.

31. Testimony of Theodore Middleton, LFCH, pt. 12, pp. 4142–49, 4155–56; testimony of Pearl Bassham, ibid., pt. 13, pp. 4514–15.

32. Testimony of Daniel Boone Smith, ibid., pt. 12, pp. 4310–12.

33. Testimony of Conrad Howard, U.S. District Court, Eastern Kentucky, *United States of America* v. *Mary Helen Coal Corporation, et al,* trial transcript (NA, RG/60, Classified Subject Files, Enclosures), vol. 6, pp. 1216, 1220–35 (hereafter cited as *U.S.* v. *Mary Helen*).

34. Testimony of Ben Unthank, National Labor Relations Board, Case no. 9-C-232, "District 19, U.M.W.A. and Clover Fork Coal Company," hearing transcript, Apr. 2, 1937, read into the record, *U.S.* v. *Mary Helen,* vol. 13, pp. 3059–60, 3063, 3067, 3069–73; minutes of executive board meeting of the Harlan County Coal Operators' Association, July 19, 1933, Nov. 20, 1935, Jan. 20, 1937, LFCH, pt. 9, pp. 3280, 3306–7, 3315–16; testimony of George Ward, ibid., pt. 10, pp. 3506–7.

35. Testimony of Dwyer, LFCH, pt. 10, p. 3470.

36. Dwyer to Barnes, Feb. 20, 1934; telegram, Dwyer to Barnes,

Mar. 1, 1934, NA, RG/9, NRA, BCLB, Case Files, Case no. 322; Poindexter to Ellis, Mar. 23, 1934, ibid., Correspondence File.

37. Testimony of Marshall Musick, LFCH, pt. 11, pp. 3813–14.

38. *Harlan Daily Enterprise*, May 18, 20, 1934; testimony of Musick, LFCH, pt. 11, pp. 3813, 3816–19; Bill Jacks, G. E. Tipton, and Roy Hensley to Frances Perkins, May 21, 1934; Barnes to N. W. Roberts, May 25, 1934, NA, RG/9, NRA, BCLB, Case Files, Case no. 322.

39. Testimony of Musick, LFCH, pt. 11, pp. 3809–11; testimony of Carl Vogel, ibid., pt. 10, pp. 3612–13.

40. Testimony of Vogel, ibid., pt. 10, pp. 3611–18; *Harlan Daily Enterprise*, Sept. 4, 5, 1935, Jan. 13, 1936.

41. Testimony of Musick, LFCH, pt. 11, pp. 3811–12, pt. 12, p. 4233.

42. Testimony of William M. Clontz, ibid., pt. 10, pp. 3624–25, 3627–28, 3630–32, 3639; testimony of Middleton, ibid., pt. 13, pp. 4425–26; Barnes to Brown, Feb. 21, 1935, NA, RG/9, NRA, BCLB, Correspondence File.

43. Clontz to Hugh S. Johnson, May 24, 1934, NA, RG/9, NRA, BCLB, Case Files, Case no. 322.

44. Testimony of A. T. Pace, LFCH, pt. 11, pp. 3868–72; testimony of Williams, ibid., pp. 3873–74; testimony of George Lee, ibid., p. 3889; testimony of Frank White, ibid., p. 3894.

45. Testimony of Turnblazer, ibid., pp. 3877–82; testimony of Middleton, ibid., pt. 13, p. 4585; testimony of Bassham, ibid., pp. 4525–33; D. E. Perkins to Henry Denhardt, Dec. 12, 1934, ibid., Exhibit 1316, p. 4630; ibid., Exhibit 1321, p. 4633.

46. *Harlan Daily Enterprise*, Dec. 10, 1934; *Pineville Sun*, Dec. 13, 1934.

47. Editorial, *Harlan Daily Enterprise*, Dec. 13, 1934.

48. Testimony of Middleton, LFCH, pt. 13, pp. 4414–15.

49. *United Mine Workers Journal*, Jan. 15, 1935, pp. 10–12; U.S., Congress, House, *Congressional Record*, 74 Cong., 1 sess. (1935), vol. 79, pp. 1202, 1860, 8987.

50. *United Mine Workers Journal*, Jan. 15, 1935, pp. 10–12; testimony of Dale Stapleton, LFCH, pt. 11, pp. 3912–13.

51. Testimony of Joseph Menefee, LFCH, pt. 11, pp. 3958–61, 3966–68, 3971–75, 3984–85.

52. Testimony of Stapleton, ibid., pp. 3913–20; *Harlan Daily Enterprise*, Feb. 17, 1935; *Pineville Sun*, Feb. 14, 1935.

53. George Davis, "Harlan County Blues," in George Korson, *Coal Dust on the Fiddle: Songs and Stories of the Bituminous Industry* (1943; rpt., Hatboro, Pa., 1965), p. 316. This 1940 field recording may be heard on *Songs and Ballads of the Bituminous Miners*, Library of Congress Archive of Folk Song AFS L60, recorded and edited by George Korson. A more recent recording by Davis of "The Harlan County Blues" appears on *When Kentucky Had No Union Men*, Folkways FTS 31016.

54. Testimony of Stapleton, LFCH, pt. 11, pp. 3915–16, 3921.

55. Denhardt Commission Report, quoted in U.S., Congress, House, *Congressional Record*, 74 Cong., 1 sess. (1935), vol. 79, pp. 8987–88 (italics are the commision's).

56. Editorial, *Harlan Daily Enterprise*, June 7, 1935.

57. Ibid., June 9, July 5, Dec. 10, 1935, Jan. 17, 1937; testimony of Timko, LFCH, pt. 11, pp. 4029–30.

58. Testimony of R. N. McDonough, Bituminous Coal Labor Board, Division no. 1—South, "Re: *District No. 19, U.M.W.A.* v. *Harlan-Wallins Coal Corporation,*" hearing transcript, Pineville, Ky., Jan. 13, 1935, NA, RG/9, NRA, BCLB, Hearings and Decisions, pp. 16, 21. See also Barnes to Brown, Feb. 21, 1935, ibid., Correspondence File.

59. E. H. Esser to Barnes, Oct. 26, 1934, ibid., Case Files, Case no. 585.

60. Testimony of Turnblazer, LFCH, pt. 10, pp. 3620–22.

61. Testimony of Bruce Williamson, *U.S.* v. *Mary Helen,* vol. 30, pp. 6680–94, 6696–97, 6721–23, 6726; Williamson to Franklin Roosevelt, Oct. 3, 1933; Burley Paris to Johnson, Nov. 27, 1933, NA, RG/9, NRA, BCLB, Case Files, Case no. 93.

62. Testimony of Westmoreland, LFCH, pt. 11, 3897, 3901–11; affidavit, G. H. Sambrook, May 29, 1934, NA, RG/9, NRA, BCLB, Case Files, Case no. 442.

63. Millard Smith to Johnson, n.d., NA, RG/9, NRA, BCLB, Case Files, Case no. 332.

64. E. J. Baumgardner to Barnes, Mar. 16, 1934, ibid., Cases no. 163 and 332.

65. Affidavit, B. B. Bloomer et al., Apr. 19, 1934; Baumgardner to Barnes, Apr. 6, 1934; C. V. Bennett to Barnes, Apr. 12, 1934; affidavit, Bill Bennett, Apr. 23, 1934, ibid.

66. Henry Hamblin and Brownlow Estes to Johnson, Nov. 14, 1933, ibid., Case no. 181; telegram, Robert Childers to Barnes, Apr. 2, 1934; Lawrence Dwyer to Barnes, Apr. 13, 1934; Barnes, memorandum of interview with C. M. Wright, Apr. 14, 1934; Dwyer et al. to Barnes, May 5, 1934, ibid., Case no. 388.

67. Testimony of R. E. Lawson, *U.S.* v. *Mary Helen,* vol. 23, pp. 5154–55; testimony of Lawson, LFCH, pt. 11, pp. 3846–47, 3856; ibid., Exhibit 1242, pp. 4064–65; testimony of Westmoreland, ibid., pp. 3825–28, 3833; Poindexter to Isaac Swift, Nov. 21, 1934, NA, RG/9, NRA, BCLB, Case Files, Case no. 514; testimony of Musick, LFCH, pt. 11, pp. 3820–21; *Harlan Daily Enterprise,* Dec. 23, 1934.

68. Testimony of Musick, LFCH, pt. 11, p. 3814; C. W. Pierce to Johnson, Aug. 21, 1934; Pierce to Barnes, Oct. 1, 1934, NA, RG/9, NRA, BCLB, Case Files, Case no. 585.

69. Testimony of Westmoreland, LFCH, pt. 11, pp. 3905, 3908–11; Johnson, "Drafting the NRA Code," pp. 538–39; memorandum of telephone conversation, Barnes to Thomas Moses, June 4, 1934; Barnes to Roberts, June 21, 1934; W. V. Whitman to Barnes, June 5, 1934; Barnes to Roberts, June 29, 1934, NA, RG/9, NRA, BCLB, Case Files, Case no. 442; minutes of meeting of Bituminous Coal Labor Board, Division no. 1—South, Louisville, Ky., Jan. 15, 1934, p. 2; Turnblazer to Barnes, July 6, 1934, ibid., Correspondence File; Bituminous Coal Labor Board, Division no. 1—South, "Re: *James L. Westmoreland* v. *U.S. Coal and Coke Company, Lynch, Kentucky,*" Decision, June 19, 1934, LFCH, pt. 10, Exhibit 1236-A, pp. 3795–98.

70. Albert Timmins to Franklin Roosevelt, May 22, 1934, quoted in *United Mine Workers Journal,* June 1, 1934, p. 5.

71. Telegram, Barnes to Bennett, May 7, 1934; telegram, Bennett to Barnes, May 11, 1934; Bennett to Barnes, May 12, 1934; Turnblazer to Barnes, June 30, 1934; Barnes, memorandum of interview with Turnblazer, Aug. 29, 1934, NA, RG/9, NRA, BCLB, Case Files, Cases no. 163 and 332.

72. Bituminous Coal Labor Board, Division no. 1—South, "Re: *District No. 19, U.M.W.A.* v. *Harlan-Wallins Coal Corporation*," Decision, Oct. 17, 1934, LFCH, pt. 10, Exhibit 1236–C, pp. 3800–3801; testimony of Turnblazer, ibid., pt. 11, pp. 3877–82; Commonwealth of Kentucky, Military Dept., Special Orders, no. 160, Dec. 8, 1934, ibid., Exhibit 1246, p. 4066.

73. Testimony of Turnblazer, LFCH, pt. 10, pp. 3621–22; *Pineville Sun,* Jan. 17, 1935.

74. Barnes to Brown, Feb. 21, 1935; Barnes, Report Submitted by Chairman of the Bituminous Coal Labor Board, Division no. 1—South and Division no. 1—North, June 7, 1935, NA, RG/9, NRA, BCLB, Correspondence File; Barnes to Roberts, July 10, 1934, ibid., Case Files, Case no. 322.

75. Affidavit, George North, Dec. 18, 1934, ibid., Case Files, Case no. 648.

76. F. R. Trusley and W. A. Dove to Roosevelt, Dec. 15, 1933, ibid., Case no. 208.

77. Barnes to Brown, Feb. 21, 1935, ibid., Correspondence File; testimony of Turnblazer, LFCH, pt. 10, pp. 3620–22; testimony of Timko, ibid., pt. 11, pp. 4013–14.

78. *Pineville Sun,* May 17, 1934; Bituminous Coal Labor Board, Division no. 1—South, "Re: *District No. 19, U.M.W.A.* v. *Harlan Ridgeway Mining Company*," hearing transcript, Cincinnati, Ohio, May 10, 1934, NA, RG/9, NRA, BCLB, Case Files, Case no. 388; *United Mine Workers Journal,* Jan. 15, 1935, p. 12; testimony of Mahan, *Stabilization of Bituminous Coal Mining Industry,* pp. 524, 535–36; Barnes to Mahan, May 28, 1935, NA, RG/9, NRA, BCLB, Correspondence File; F. Raymond Daniell, "Behind the Conflict in 'Bloody Harlan,'" *New York Times Magazine,* June 26, 1938, p. 1; testimony of Van Bittner, *Stabilization of Bituminous Coal Mining Industry,* p. 146.

79. Testimony of Mahan, *Stabilization of Bituminous Coal Mining Industry,* pp. 522–23.

80. Testimony of Mahan, *To Create a Bituminous Coal Commission,* pp. 534–35.

81. Testimony of Mahan, *Stabilization of Bituminous Coal Mining Industry,* pp. 523–24; *United Mine Workers Journal,* Oct. 15, 1933, p. 10; Kerwin to Turner Battle, Mar. 5, 1934, NA, RG/174, Perkins File, Box 34; Turnblazer to Barnes, Feb. 28, 1935, NA, RG/9, NRA, BCLB, Correspondence File.

Chapter 6

Operators at the Bar

1935 - 38

Between 1935 and 1938, the national government's new pro-union labor policy and the Committee for Industrial Organization's aggressive organizing activity began the creation of a mass labor movement in the United States.

Faced with the failure and invalidation of the National Industrial Recovery Act, with intensified hostility of the business community, and with a serious political challenge from the Left, the New Deal administration responded with the Wagner Act. The act reiterated Section 7(a) of the NRA's guarantee of collective bargaining rights and outlawed the employers' most potent antiunion weapons: the company union, blacklists, yellow-dog contracts, and discrimination in hiring, firing, or job tenure of employees on the basis of union activity. The act created the National Labor Relations Board to administer and enforce its provisions.

Throughout the twenty-one-month interim between the Wagner Act's passage and its approval by the United States Supreme Court on April 12, 1937, the new national labor policy was widely violated. Assured by Liberty League lawyers that the act would never stand the test of constitutionality, powerful antiunion industrialists yielded little.

During this breach, a subcommittee of the Senate Committee on Labor and Education, known as the La Follette Civil Liberties Committee, manned by Senator Robert M. La Follette, Jr., a Progressive from Wisconsin, and Senator Elbert Thomas, a Democrat from Utah, launched an investigation into violations of labor's civil liberties by employers intent on preventing unionization. Through widely publicized hearings and reports, the committee exposed employers' widespread use of labor espionage and strikebreaking, industrial munitions, manipulation of public opinion and back-to-work movements, and privately employed plant guards to prevent organization and thwart national labor policy. The committee portrayed the open shops of the United States as something less than bastions of individual liberty, and its exposés further diminished the prestige of businessmen already bearing the onus of the Depression. Like most congressional investigations, the La Follette probe did not exhibit much impartiality. In its timing, conduct, and choice of situations to explore and witnesses to be heard, the La Follette Committee coordinated its efforts with the organizational drives of the CIO and orchestrated its spectacular findings to arouse the greatest possible public support for organized labor.[1]

John L. Lewis was just then beginning to split the relatively inert AFL by organizing its more idealistic and ambitious members into an aggressive rival labor federation, the CIO. By 1938, the AFL, challenged by its militant rival's success, also resorted to industrial unionism. Aided by favorable government policy and a sympathetic public opinion, and goaded by each other, the two federations began to build a powerful labor movement.

Harlan County was overtly affected by all this. The La Follette Civil Liberties Committee's most spectacular investigation focused on Harlan. As a result of the Senate probe and local operators' continued opposition to national labor policy, the United States Department of Justice prosecuted sixty-nine county operators and law officers for criminally conspiring to violate the Wagner Act. The National Labor Relations Board conducted six local elections, held five hearings, and issued four decisions. During the 1939 Harlan coal strike, the Works Progress Administration pursued its highly controversial policy of providing strike relief in an industrial dispute. The AFL encouraged its rival mine union, the Progressive Mine Workers of America, to challenge UMW-CIO dominance of local collective bargaining, and it succeeded in organizing, at the Wisconsin Steel Corporation at Benham, the only successful PMW local outside the state of Illinois. Harlan County operators also allied themselves with the national conservative opposition to Roosevelt. Two Liberty League attorneys, Charles I. Dawson, the anti–New Deal, former judge of the federal district court at Louisville, and Forney Johnston, an Alabama attorney who attained national prominence by opposing the National Recovery Act and the Tennessee Valley Authority, represented the Harlan County Coal Operators' Association in both the La Follette hearings and the Mary Helen conspiracy case.[2] Harlan County, from 1935 through 1939, provides an excellent case study of the entire range of New Deal labor policies in practice.

When the Wagner Act was enacted, the Harlan miners stood completely defeated in their efforts to organize. The NRA had failed to halt discharges of union miners or to eliminate short-weighing, the cleanup system, and coal bucking; nor had it stabilized coal prices. Union organizers still could not enter the county to recruit members or to service union contracts. Nor had NRA made it safe for local miners to join the union or to attend its rallies. The UMW's sizable 1933 membership had dwindled to twelve hundred, and only Black Mountain Coal Corporation was still operating under union contract. Sheriff Middleton and County Judge Saylor, who had promised a "new deal" for the union in Harlan County, had reversed their position and now posed a more formidable opposition to the union than had their predecessors. In the Denhardt Commission's report, the Laffoon administration had put its finger on the key to Harlan County's antiunionism but had failed to remedy the situation. The newly elected governor, Chandler, staunchly supported the antiunion sheriff, and the United States House of Representatives had declined to investigate Harlan's noncompliance with the National Recovery Act.

It quickly became apparent that the Wagner Act had changed nothing in Harlan County. On Sunday afternoon, July 7, 1935, union miners gathered at Evarts to celebrate the law's enactment and to lay plans for reorganizing the county. Ben

Unthank and other deputies guarded the Pineville-Harlan highway to prevent union leaders from reaching Evarts. A score of deputy sheriffs, among them Merle and Mose Middleton, drove past the rally and blew their car horns to drown the voices of union speakers. George Lee, Frank White, and John Hickey were sent by Sheriff Middleton to preserve order at the rally. As the trio stepped out of their car, John Anglian shouted, "Here comes one of King Middleton's gun thugs." John Hickey handed his guns to Frank White and attacked Anglian. Enraged by the sight of a union celebration near the scene of his son's death in 1931, George Lee jerked the sixty-six-year-old speaker, "Rockhouse" Munhollen, from the platform and beat him. The crowd quickly dispersed. A celebration of "labor's Magna Carta" had turned into what came to be known as the Second Battle of Evarts. Although Judge Saylor issued warrants for the arrests of deputies Lee and Hickey and of Munhollen and two other miners, the grand jury failed to indict.[3]

Persisting in their campaign, UMW organizers in two weeks doubled the county's union membership, to twenty-five hundred. But on July 20, when union leaders attempted to enter the county to open a union headquarters, Ben Unthank, George Lee, Frank White, and three other deputies blocked them at the county line. Ten state patrolmen whom Governor Laffoon had dispatched to protect the organizers were overawed by the deputies, and the union had to abandon its drive. Shortly thereafter, George Ward assured Methodist minister Carl Vogel that the coal operators would not permit the Wagner Act to interrupt the nonunion operation of their mines.[4] Union organizers shunned the county until early 1937.

The union's failure in Harlan threatened to disrupt collective bargaining throughout the southern coal fields. On September 22, 1935, after several contract extensions and prolonged negotiations failed to produce a new national agreement, the UMW called a nationwide walkout. Although ten thousand other District 19 miners struck, most Harlan miners remained on the job. On the first day of the strike, Sheriff Middleton dispatched Ben Unthank and a squad of deputies to crush incipient strike action at Clover Splint and Kentucky Cardinal. After a four-day strike, a national agreement was signed providing for a $5.10 southern basic daily wage and a seven-hour day. Black Mountain immediately signed a union contract, but Clover Splint and Black Star, although reluctant to break with the union, refused to place themselves at a competitive disadvantage. On October 1, other members of the operators' association matched the union wage scale but refused to participate in contract negotiations. Because Harlan produced nearly one-half of District 19's tonnage, it required a six-week strike to force competing Tennessee and southeastern Kentucky operators to sign a union agreement.[5]

At this juncture, the UMW turned to political and legal action to gain access to Harlan County's miners. In the Democratic gubernatorial primary, as noted earlier, the union endorsed Thomas Rhea, Governor Laffoon's chosen successor, over Lieutenant Governor Albert B. "Happy" Chandler. Although Laffoon had enacted a highly unpopular sales tax, he had created a state patrol and used it to assist the union in Harlan, exposed the antiunion conduct of Harlan County officials, and filed charges against the sheriff that might result in his removal from office. Should Rhea win election, he was expected to remove the sheriff, abolish the private deputy system, and pardon Jones and Hightower. As acting governor, Chandler had refused to pardon Jones and Hightower. In the campaign, he opposed any deal to free the Evarts defendants, opposed the sales tax, and posed as the true friend of the working man. Harlan County's Democratic boss, Herb Smith, whom Governor Laffoon had made regional highway commissioner and local dispenser of administration patronage as a reward for his support in 1931, adroitly shifted his support to Chandler, thrice engineered heavy majorities for Chandler in Harlan County, and retained his position as local administration man.[6]

On August 3, 1935, to prevent what he called "the most stupendous and well planned election steal ever attempted in Kentucky," Governor Laffoon sent fourteen hundred National Guardsmen to supervise Harlan's gubernatorial primary. The soldiers were deployed in the seventy-one precincts where Chandler's chances were best; for example, one hundred supervised the polls at Harlan-Wallins's camp at Verda. One hundred unionists from the Jellico, Tennessee, headquarters of the UMW's District 19 followed in the troops' wake bearing signs emblazoned "RHEA WILL FREE HARLAN." In a five-way Democratic race, Chandler won a Harlan majority, but Rhea commanded a statewide plurality, thereby necessitating a runoff primary. In September, the troops returned for the runoff election, in which Chandler obtained a sixty-six-hundred vote majority in Harlan and carried the state. At a huge Pikeville UMW rally in October, with the union's preferred candidate out of the running, John L. Lewis belatedly endorsed Chandler for governor. Well aware that union endorsement was unnecessary for his success, Chandler, on November 5, handily defeated his Republican opponent, King Swope. Backlash resulting from six National Guard interventions in the county within a year, Herb Smith's support, and the unpopular sales tax all helped Chandler in Harlan; and for the first time in its history, the county produced a twenty-two-hundred-vote majority for a Democratic gubernatorial candidate. On inauguration day, December 10, 1935, the *Harlan Daily Enterprise*'s editor exulted at Laffoon's departure with the headline "Praise God from Whom All Blessings Flow." [7]

Before Laffoon left office, he pardoned William Hightower, William Hudson, Gaines Eubanks, "Big Cigar" Phillips, and Bill Burnett, but left William B. Jones, Al Benson, Chester Poore, and Jim Reynolds to serve six more years on their sentences. Governor Chandler invited Sheriff Middleton and five Harlan deputies to serve as his personal escort in the inaugural parade and in early 1937, in the midst of the county's most bitter union campaign, dismissed all charges against the sheriff. [8]

Throughout 1936, the UMW worked vigorously to abolish the privately paid deputy system. In January, State Representative Roy Conway of Pikeville introduced an abolition bill in the state legislature. The UMW's national convention endorsed the measure, but the Harlan County Coal Operators' Association and the U.S. Coal & Coke Corporation lobbied against it. In February, the Kentucky House passed the bill (52 to 36), but the Senate killed it in the Rules Committee (16 to 18). [9]

In April, District 19 president William Turnblazer and T. C.

Townsend, the UMW's southern counsel, appeared at a preliminary hearing held by the newly created La Follette Civil Liberties Committee. Their explanation of how private deputies were used to suppress freedom of speech and assembly, freedom of the ballot, and labor's right to organize paved the way for the committee's 1937 investigation of Harlan. That fall, Labor's Non-Partisan League of Kentucky urged Governor Chandler to convene a special session of the legislature to abolish the private mine-guard system. It also scheduled a series of eight radio broadcasts on station WHAS, Louisville, to build public support. When after only three broadcasts a Harlan County grand jury subpoenaed Representative Roy Conway and John Young Brown, attorney for UMW District 30, other scheduled speakers were afraid to appear.[10] The private deputy system would survive until the La Follette exposé aroused Kentucky citizens to demand its abolition.

Meanwhile, the union had brought suit in federal court to gain access to the county. On December 28, 1935, fourteen unionists filed suit in United States District Court, London, Kentucky, for $350,000 in damages against Sheriff Middleton and Circuit Judge James M. Gilbert for false arrest and imprisonment resulting from the sheriff's February raid on Cumberland union headquarters. Filing such a suit in local courts would have been a futile gesture, but James Westmoreland's Virginia residence at the time of the arrest gave the federal court jurisdiction. On December 4, 1936, the court awarded Westmoreland $1,500 damages from Sheriff Middleton.[11]

Believing that the legal victory had opened the county to organization, on January 11, 1937, fifteen UMW recruiters registered at the New Harlan Hotel to launch another major union drive. Five days later, Governor Chandler dismissed charges against Sheriff Middleton, and on January 20, the operators' association again doubled the financial assessment on its members and increased its monthly payments to Ben Unthank from $150 to $1,000, which permitted him to employ fifteen additional detectives.[12] Union organizer L. T. Arnett described the result of the governor's and the association's action: "Immediately after the 16th . . . they began to tighten up awful on us, and it seems to me there were more deputy sheriffs then than there were miners in Harlan County. We saw more of them than we did the miners. They just got thick everywhere." [13]

Early Saturday morning, January 23, three stench bombs, detonated in the hallway of the hotel, drove the organizers and other guests down to the lobby. Moments later, an explosion rocked the town as dynamite bombs destroyed two of the organizers' automobiles parked at the railroad depot. The crime was never solved. A desk clerk had seen two masked men descending the hotel staircase during the gas attack but could not identify them. City policemen salvaged the remnants of the exploded gas canisters, which the La Follette Committee later demonstrated would have retained their identification numbers, and delivered them to the sheriff. The sheriff contended that he had presented the mutilated canisters to a county grand jury, but grand jury officials denied ever receiving them. At any rate, the evidence was lost. The La Follette Committee later proved that Sheriff Middleton had purchased similar gas bombs, but the sheriff insisted that deputies had exploded all of his bombs in practice sessions.[14]

On Sunday afternoon, January 31, snipers fired on local union representative Marshall Musick and his wife as they strolled down the railroad right-of-way after visiting members of his congregation. Bullets splattered on the road all around the couple, and one pierced the preacher's hat.[15]

On Monday, a week later, as six organizers were returning from a Black Mountain union meeting down a winding mountain road between Verda and Ages, they noticed Deputy Frank White sitting in a parked car. Beside the car, brush and debris were strewn across the highway. As they maneuvered their cars through the obstacle course, White blew his horn, and assailants hidden on the hillside fired a volley of shots at the vehicles. An Ohio organizer, Tom Ferguson, suffered a severe shoulder wound.[16]

The next day, February 9, friends warned Musick that his life was in danger. At 7:00 P.M., confident that his family would be safer in his absence, he caught the coal train to union headquarters at Pineville. At 8:30 P.M., three cars halted in front of the Musick home. The occupants fired a volley of bullets through the living room, instantly killing the organizer's teenage son, Bennett.[17]

This time the antiunionists had overstepped the bounds of decency. Even Harlan's citizens, inured to the harrassment, beating, and wounding of union organizers, balked at the cold-blooded murder of an innocent youth. The sheriff's office deputy, Henry Lewis, perhaps suspecting that his fellow deputies were involved, resigned his commission, admitting that "killing the Musick boy . . . was a bad piece of work." [18]

Even in the face of this atrocity, however, the Harlan elite managed to keep the lid on locally. Both a regular and a special grand jury, one headed by a deputy and the other by an operator's brother, investigated the New Harlan Hotel gassing, the Ferguson wounding, and the Musick murder and adjourned without returning indictments.[19]

The Musick murder was, however, more than the nation could stomach. The incident provoked the La Follette Committee's investigation and proved to be the turning point in the ongoing struggle to free the miners of Harlan County.

Union officials, temporarily suspending their campaign, rushed to Washington, D.C., armed with affidavits and photographs to urge the La Follette Committee to investigate the terrorist campaign against the union in Harlan County. The committee staff quickly began serving subpoenas. On March 22, the committee held a preliminary session and on April 14, two days after the Supreme Court upheld the Wagner Act, convened regular sessions.

The Senate hearings dealt with the period 1933–37, thereby focusing on years when the miners' right to organize and bargain collectively had been protected by federal law and avoiding the embarrassing union violence of 1931. The committee sought to show that the Harlan County Coal Operators' Association was continuing to finance and direct a widespread conspiracy to control county politics and to use the sheriff and his deputies to prevent unionization of the county's mines, thereby violating national labor law.

The committee exhibited an association by-law that pledged all members to oppose the closed shop to indicate that one of the group's main purposes was to wage a concerted fight against the effective organization of member mines. The Reverend Carl Vogel testified that George Ward had assured him, even after the Wagner Act's passage, that the association would not permit the union to organize its mines. Association minutes proved that during each of the union's major campaigns in 1933, 1935, and 1937, the organization had doubled its financial assessments on member firms. Secretary George Ward, confessing that he had destroyed the association's financial records in anticipation of just such a congressional investigation, admitted that the additional monies had been mainly used to enable the association's chief field detective, Deputy Sheriff Ben Unthank, to employ extra agents to oppose unionization. Ward admitted that Unthank maintained constant surveillance of union activity and regularly reported to him, but professed ignorance of any other actions taken by Unthank or his agents. Many union witnesses linked Unthank directly to numerous antiunion acts.[20] Unthank fled the county before subpoenas were served and returned only after the hearings recessed, thus avoiding the senators' questions.

The committee also exposed the direct link between the operators' association and key county political officials. George Ward testified that, since 1932, he had chaired the county's dominant Republican party and that, since 1936, when the Democratic party had emerged as a viable contender for public offices, association president S. J. Dickenson had chaired the opposition party. Witnesses proved that Theodore Middleton, Morris Saylor, and Daniel Boone Smith had campaigned for the respective offices of sheriff, county judge, and prosecuting attorney in 1933 mainly on promises to reform the deputy sheriff system and to guarantee union organizers and members equal protection under the law. County records proved that George Ward and fifteen coal operators signed the new sheriff's bonds. Sheriff Middleton admitted that since taking office, on a salary constitutionally limited to $5,000 per annum, he had increased his personal fortune by at least $92,000, acquired an interest in five coal mines, joined the operators' association, and engaged in two profitable joint business ventures with Pearl Bassham, the county's most antiunion operator and the association's largest financial contributor. Judge Saylor shared in the two joint business ventures with Middleton and Bassham. Three coal companies placed Commonwealth's Attorney Smith, who had previously done little legal work for county operators, on an annual retainer.[21] Even if one discounts the implication that the coal operators bought control of the three county officials, all three had acquired a personal stake in barring the union from Harlan County.

Once in office, the sheriff and county judge appointed and commissioned numerous well-known union enemies as deputy sheriffs; and Middleton told Lawrence Dwyer that he did so because of obligations incurred to the mine owners during the campaign. Among their 169 deputy appointees were 64 indicted and 37 convicted felons.[22] The sheriff admitted to the committee that "there has been a lot of violence and crime committed by my deputies"; [23] but when a 1934 grand jury had disclosed that "in practically every homicide which has occurred in Harlan County since the first of the year officers figured prominently" and recommended the dismissal of eight troublesome deputies, the sheriff had ignored its plea.[24]

Numerous witnesses testified that Sheriff Middleton and Deputy Unthank either allowed or ordered deputy sheriffs to exclude union organizers from the county, disperse union rallies, and break strikes. Deputies were implicated in the numerous attacks on "Peggy" Dwyer, the shootings of Jim Bates and Tom Ferguson, the entrapment of Turnblazer and his party in the New Harlan Hotel, and the murder of young Bennett Musick.[25] In the last case, two unreliable witnesses, Lawrence and Martha Howard, testified that on the evening of February 9 they overhead Frank White and other deputies talking about "going to see old man Musick." Kelly Fox, a young mechanic who had been afraid to testify before the county grand jury, told the committee that he had secretly witnessed the murder. He had seen Deputy Frank White, in the glare of the second car's headlights, lean out of the front car's window and fire the fatal shots.[26]

The testimony continued: When union field representatives Marshall Musick and William Clontz, both long-time residents of the county, appealed to their sheriff to protect themselves and their families, Middleton refused and advised them, instead, to leave the county. When the private deputy system came under attack in Kentucky, a county grand jury squelched a series of public radio broadcasts intended to build public support for abolition of the system. And when the state legislature threatened to pass an abolition bill, the operators' association and U.S. Coal & Coke Corporation officials lobbied vigorously to defeat it.[27]

The committee also spotlighted Pearl Bassham, superintendent of Harlan-Wallins Corporation, largest financial contributor to the association and member of its executive board. Bassham, in addition to signing the sheriff's bonds, sharing lucrative business connections with him, and allowing Merle Middleton, the sheriff's cousin and Harlan-Wallins's chief deputy, to use the company's mine guards to harrass the union, had until recently required all company employees to sign yellow-dog contracts, discharged all known union miners, and ordered his mine guards to bar all union organizers and members from company property—all this in callous violation of the Wagner Act. Only after he had been subpoenaed as a witness by the committee and had attended its preliminary session had Bassham undergone a sudden change of heart and discontinued these illegal practices.[28]

Union officials assessed for the committee the effect of the Harlan mine owners' and county officials' antiunion actions. Union membership, which in the early days of the National Recovery Administration had reached five thousand, had since plummeted to twelve hundred, and of eighteen thriving locals only one remained by 1937. This had occurred, union leaders contended, because Sheriff Middleton, Deputy Sheriff Unthank, and their antiunion deputies had made it unsafe for them to enter the county to recruit members or service contracts.[29]

Because the committee's staff could call whatever witnesses it chose and because cross-examination was not permitted, the La Follette Committee tarred the association and county officials with a broad brush. The committee heard much perjured testimony. For example, evidence introduced at the later conspiracy trial proved that on the evening of the Musick slaying Lawrence and Martha Howard had been confined in the county jail and could not have overheard deputies plotting the crime. Former Harlan-Wallins mine guard B. C. "Thug" Johnson seemed to know too much about far too many anti-union incidents to begin with; and when he testified that Harlan-Wallins deputies went "thugging," hunting union organizers, armed with "two 30–30 high-powered pump shotguns," he demonstrated such an incredible ignorance of firearms amid the gun culture of Harlan County as to destroy the credibility of his entire testimony.[30]

Several prounion association members, among them E. J. Asbury, Elmer Hall, and Armstrong Matthews, according to testimony given at the later conspiracy trial, knew nothing of and disapproved of the association's support of Middleton's and Unthank's use of deputies to harass the union. The association was engaged with the sheriff and some of his deputies in an illegal conspiracy to prevent unionization, but it was not an association-wide conspiracy. Only by assuming that membership in and financial contributions to the association, which had many purposes other than opposing unionism, constitute conspiracy could one implicate Asbury, Hall, Matthews, and others in the conspiracy. Under the direction of an inner nucleus of active conspirators, including George Ward, Pearl Bassham, Theodore Middleton, Ben Unthank, and perhaps others, the operators' association had assumed a corporate character alien to the intentions of several of its members. Between these two groups, the active conspirators and the non-conspirators, lay a third group of members, undefinable in numbers, who suspected a conspiracy, knew none of the details and for legal reasons did not want to know, but silently approved the association's antiunion activity. The committee, however, did not call dissenters Asbury and Hall as witnesses and did not ask others, Armstrong Matthews and C. B. Birchfield, the right questions. Consequently, the hearings left the public with the impression that every member of the operators' association had conspired with the sheriff and his deputies to prevent organization of their mines by any necessary means, including murder, and forced Asbury, Hall, Birchfield, Matthews, and Creech to share the odium of Ward, Bassham, Theodore Middleton, Unthank, White, Lee, Fleenor, and Merle

Middleton. Even the sophisticated members of the National Labor Relations Board, in its later Clover Fork Coal Company hearing, concluded from Ward's and Unthank's testimony that the operators' association existed solely to oppose unionization in violation of national law and ordered Clover Fork to withdraw its membership in the association.[31]

The La Follette Committee, as Jerold Auerbach demonstrated in his study of its activities, was little interested in gathering information productive of additional labor legislation and still less in dealing impartially with violators of the Wagner Act. Instead, the partisan senators and their staff sought to discredit antiunion employers and assist the CIO unions in organizing recalcitrant industrialists' shops and mines.[32] The committee's investigation in Harlan turned the tide for the UMW there. Although the exposé did not force local operators to accept a union contract, it resulted in a temporary local political upheaval, permanent abolition of the notorious private mine-guard system, and the nearly solid organization of local mines almost while the committee still sat.

On April 23, 1937, after conferring with Turnblazer and county operators, Governor Chandler dispatched state patrolmen to Harlan County to protect union organizers and, after a second conference on May 14, restricted deputy sheriffs to serving warrants and prohibited them from engaging in any law-enforcement activities that might hamper organization.[33]

Meanwhile, encountering strong public criticism and facing a popular, union-backed Democratic opponent in the 1937 election, County Judge Morris Saylor belatedly jumped aboard the reform bandwagon. On May 10, Saylor issued warrants for the arrest of Deputy Frank White on a charge of murdering Bennett Musick and for the arrest of deputies Unthank and Lee, charged with shooting up Bill Clontz's automobile. On June 22, the judge revoked Lee Fleenor's deputy commission for disturbing the peace; that afternoon, George Lee, Wash Irwin, and Allen Bowlin resigned their deputy commissions in protest. That same evening, Wash Irwin, a witness in the recent Senate probe, drove to the crest of Pine Mountain with his associates to listen to a prize fight on his car radio. Fellow deputies later discovered his lifeless body slumped over the steering wheel; he had been shot three times in the back of the head. The following week, Judge Saylor issued warrants for the arrest of deputies Lee Fleenor, George Lee, Perry Noe, Henry Metcalf, and Allen Bowlin, all charged with Irwin's murder, but none was indicted. Two days after Irwin's death, the judge removed deputies Frank White, Roy Metcalf, Perry Noe, and Leonard Creech; two additional officers, John Hickey and Henry Metcalf, resigned. Saylor replaced the dismissed deputies with six friends of the UMW, one of them, Bill Clontz, a union organizer.[34]

But Judge Saylor's action came too late. Although he defeated a Republican challenger in the primary, he lost the general election by eleven hundred votes to Cam E. Ball, who became Harlan County's first Democratic county judge. The thoroughly discredited Sheriff Middleton dared not run; but his Republican nephew, Herbert Cawood, no friend of the union, succeeded him. After both the Harlan County Circuit Court and the Kentucky Court of Appeals sustained Democratic charges of election irregularities and voided the election of Republicans as sheriff, county attorney, jailor, and coroner, however, Judge Ball, on June 25, 1938, appointed his Democratic running mates, Clinton Ball, L. C. Wall, Clarence Poer, and Gilbert Blanton, to those offices. The county's first county-wide Democratic regime was short-lived, however; that fall, in a special election, county voters returned the Republican candidates to the four contested offices.[35]

On January 4, 1938, Governor Chandler convened a special session of the state legislature to reform the private deputy system. The resultant act, which took effect on May 30, 1938, prohibited appointment of any deputy possessing a criminal record or an undesirable reputation, prohibited any mine or plant guard from acting beyond the company premises, and required that such a guard's wages be paid into and disbursed by the state treasury. Eight years after Pennsylvania and three years after West Virginia, Kentucky became the last state to abolish the infamous private mine-guard system, an archaic institution that for seven years had served as the Harlan operators' greatest bulwark against the union and as the focal point of labor-management violence.[36] The antiunion gun thug, the major factor that had allowed Harlan operators to maintain their nonunion shop for five years after 92 percent of the country's miners organized, was no more.

These impending political changes and the La Follette Committee's watchful protection allowed the UMW to reenter Harlan County on April 24, 1937, and to make its first real gains in four years. Every Sunday between April 25 and June 20, the union held huge rallies protected by the state police. By May 10, seven thousand miners, about half of the county's coal diggers, had joined the union, and the southern end of the county was solidly organized. By August, nine thousand, or 65 percent, of the county's miners had joined the union.[37]

The union's progress in Harlan may have prevented its expulsion from the southern coal fields. On April 2, 1937, the union concluded a two-year national agreement that provided for a $5.60 southern basic daily wage and a seven-hour day; but because Black Mountain was the only Harlan County firm to sign the agreement, other District 19 operators held out for a month. Two important events may have helped persuade the Southern Appalachian operators to relinquish their opposition. The agreement reached between the CIO and U.S. Steel Corporation on March 2 inspired hope for the eventual organization of U.S. Coal & Coke Corporation's three thousand miners at Lynch. The fact that by early May the UMW had recruited five thousand Harlan miners also encouraged the conviction that Harlan County would eventually be unionized. Consequently, on May 2, Tennessee and southeastern Kentucky operators signed a union contract.[38] Had the Harlan field appeared likely to retain its favored nonunion position, the Southern Appalachian Operators' Association would doubtless have proven more recalcitrant.

In mid-May, Governor Chandler began pressing the operators to negotiate a Harlan agreement. The UMW had granted the Tennessee and southeastern Kentucky operators a special dispensation for measuring the height of coal seams, a factor that appreciably affected the tonnage rate for coal loaders. On the other hand, the union had permitted Virginia operators a monthly union-dues assignment rather than the two-year dues checkoff required by the national agreement. The UMW offered the Harlan operators a choice of either of these concessions, but they demanded both, and negotiations for a 1937 Harlan contract collapsed.[39]

As a result of the La Follette exposé, several mines, among them Harlan-Wallins and Clover Splint, withdrew from the Harlan operators' association, leaving that body to represent only the employers of six thousand miners. The union then made significant gains among nonmember firms. In the six months following June 21, 1937, the union signed contracts covering 1,500 employees at Harlan-Wallins, 400 at Clover Splint, 150 at Harlan Crown, 1,400 at Black Mountain, 3,000 at U.S. Coal & Coke Corporation, 700 at Black Star, and 325 at Berger and Cook & Sharp. Although the U.S. Coal & Coke agreement recognized both the Union of Lynch Employees and the United Mine Workers as bargaining agents for their respective members, the company did withdraw its sole support from the ULE. By the end of 1937, approximately six thousand county miners were covered by some type of UMW agreement.[40]

As for the association members, however, George Titler reported at midyear that the "operators are at present waging the strongest opposition the union has faced in Harlan County."[41] With the county invaded by talented and able union organizers, the operators stigmatized by public opinion and under investigation by the FBI, the sheriff under investigation by Treasury agents, and the companies stripped of private mine guards, association members fell back on the old technique of discharging union employees and initiated a new weapon—company unionism—to defeat organization. At individual mines, a small nucleus of antiunion employees, with the cooperation and encouragement of company officials, organized local company unions. On Poor Fork, the Union of Lynch Employees at U.S. Coal & Coke was joined by the Benham Employees' Association at Wisconsin Steel and the Poor Fork Employees at Harlan Central. On Clover Fork, the Yancey Workmen's Association organized at Harlan Fuel, the Hi-Lo Association at High Splint, and the Wallins Creek Employees' Association at the Good Coal Company. In the otherwise thoroughly organized southern section of the county, the Insull Employees' Association formed at Southern Mining Company.[42]

When the UMW established a local at Clover Fork, the last

county mine to be organized, in June, 1937, the foremen and nonunion employees circulated a petition declaring that they were satisfied with nonunion conditions and refused to work with union men. Superintendent George Whitfield invited his union miners to quit, then discharged several of them. On July 14, nonunion employees struck, demanding the dismissal of twelve union employees. Whitfield discharged the twelve and invited the nonunion men to an all-day beer blast at the company commissary. Afterward, the celebrants reassembled at the mine mouth and purged still more unionists. Having secured the dismissal of a total of sixty union members, the 160 satisfied nonunion workers resumed operation.[43]

When the union mounted its February, 1937, campaign, Good Coal Company superintendent J. L. McIntyre warned his employees not to join the UMW and promised to assist them in chartering a company union. When the UMW's local mine committee notified him on June 5 that they represented a majority of his employees, he threatened to close his mine: "You can look at this Black Mountain union up here. . . . They are all the time raising hell. . . . I don't want no such organization as that in our camp. . . . We only have a few thousand dollars in our company, and before I will recognize the United Mine Workers, I will drag my steel, sell my machinery . . . , close the drift mouth and quit." Later that month, the company organized the Wallins Creek Employees' Association, but all except twenty-four of its 182 employees joined the UMW. The company posted a work order for September 6, to conflict with a UMW Labor Day rally. When only forty miners reported for work, McIntyre fired 115 union members.[44]

Confronted by a cancellation of contract negotiations and by county-wide antiunion actions similar to those at Clover Fork and Good Coal, on July 10, 1937, the UMW filed charges with the NLRB against twenty-seven Harlan firms for promoting company unions and intimidating and discharging miners for union activity. Over the next nine months, the new labor board conducted local hearings on charges filed against Clover Fork, Harlan Fuel, Green-Silvers, Good Coal, and Harlan Central. Between November, 1937, and April, 1939, the NLRB ordered

Clover Fork, Green-Silvers, Harlan Fuel, and Good Coal to reinstate a total of 205 union employees with back wages, to pay back wages to eight union miners who had secured employment elsewhere, and to place nine others on a preferential hiring list. The board's Harlan Fuel decision set an important precedent by declaring exclusion of organizers from company property an unfair labor practice. The United States Circuit Court of Appeals upheld the Clover Fork decision in 1938, thereby strengthening the NLRB's authority.[45] Little by little, the NLRB was whittling away Harlan operators' freedom to conduct their affairs in defiance of national law.

Whereas the UMW benefited from the NLRB's decisions on unfair labor practices, it fared poorly in a series of four 1937 elections to determine the appropriate bargaining agent at county mines. Wisconsin Steel Company employees voted 398 to 225 to authorize the Benham Employees' Association as bargaining agent, U.S. Coal & Coke employees voted 1,880 to 746 to authorize the Union of Lynch Employees, and Southern Mining Company employees voted 126 to 103 to authorize representation by the Insull Employees' Association. Only at Black Star, where no company union existed, did employees vote three-to-one for UMW representation. At Wisconsin Steel, the BEA later obtained a charter from the Progressive Mine Workers of America (AFL) to establish the only enduring PMW local outside Illinois. U.S. Coal & Coke and Southern Mining Company employees later disbanded their company unions and affiliated with the UMW, but the company-union movement demonstrated surprising strength in 1937.[46]

Because the Harlan County Coal Operators' Association still had not signed a union contract, the federal government moved against them on a broader front. As result of the La Follette Committee's disclosures and in response to requests from John L. Lewis, Senator La Follette, and Governor A. B. Chandler, in May, 1937, United States Attorney General Cummings ordered twenty FBI agents to Harlan to seek evidence of a possible conspiracy to violate national labor laws. Within a month, the agents had concluded their investigation and submitted a lengthy report to the Justice Department. On September 27, 1937, at Frankfort, Kentucky, a federal grand jury indicted twenty-two coal companies, twenty-four coal operators, Sheriff Theodore Middleton, and twenty-two of his deputies for conspiring to deprive miners of civil rights accorded them by the Wagner Act. The defendants were charged with violating the Civil Rights Act of 1870, Section 19, Title 18, of the United States Criminal Code, which provided for a maximum penalty of ten years' imprisonment and a $5,000 fine.[47]

Why did the national government divert its prounion effort from the tedious but so far successful NLRB action to a quicker but much more difficult mass prosecution for conspiracy that carried criminal rather than civil penalties? Did the government, with the country in the throes of a second deep recession in 1937–38, actually intend to convict and imprison a sufficient number of coal operators to effectively shut down the Harlan County coal industry?

Two tactical considerations help explain the government's shift in strategy. First, while the NLRB could force individual companies to abandon their support of company unions and to stop discharging and discriminating against union members, it could not compel them to sign a union agreement. Perhaps the government sought not so much to convict the Harlan operators as to force them to sign a union contract. That was, in effect, the result of the conspiracy prosecution. After spending $1 million to defend themselves in 1938, the following year the operators' association signed a union agreement rather than submit to retrial of the conspiracy case.[48] Second, the government may have sought to reform Harlan County politics. The NLRB, like the Bituminous Coal Labor Board before it, could not attack the operators' control of county politics or the private mine-guard system, which had not yet been abolished when the prosecution was launched in 1937. Since state Republican chairman Robert Tway, county Republican chairman George Ward, county Democratic chairman S. J. Dickenson, active local Republican politician Ben Unthank, Sheriff Middleton, and twenty-two of his deputies were among those indicted, political reform may well have been one of the government's objectives.

The case, lasting eleven weeks, from May 16 to August 2,

1938, was tried in United States District Court, London, Kentucky, before a jury composed of eight farmers, two country storekeepers, a bookkeeper, and a carpenter. The government's case contained few surprises; most of the prosecution's witnesses had previously testified before either the La Follette Committee or NLRB examiners.

The government's evidence of an association-wide conspiracy was exceedingly tenuous. The government dismissed charges against E. J. Asbury and his firm, Black Mountain Coal Corporation, before the trial opened, and then called him as a witness. A member of the association's executive board, one of its larger financial supporters, and a regular attendant at its meetings, prounion Asbury was an insider whose testimony could have been extremely damaging to the defendants. Instead, Asbury confirmed the testimony of other operator defendants that no antiunion conspiracy or even an association blacklist existed and that each member firm conducted its own labor policy independently of the association. As proof, Asbury noted that his own firm had, since 1933, retained a continuing union contract while other association firms had not. In fact, Asbury recalled only one occasion when either the association's executive board or general meeting had even considered labor policy. On that occasion, an executive board meeting held shortly after the La Follette hearings, prounion Elmer Hall of Three Point Coal Company had objected to the association's using funds, partially contributed by his firm, to pay Ben Unthank to oppose unionization and had threatened to withdraw his membership in the association. Elmer Hall, testifying for the defense, recalled that he had objected to Unthank's employment and threatened to withdraw his membership, but after George Ward assured him that the association had dismissed Unthank, Hall had retained his membership.[49] Asbury's testimony, crucial to the government's case, proved a liability rather than an asset to the prosecution.

Contrary to government allegations, an association-wide conspiracy probably did not exist. Apparently an antiunion conspiracy was broadly financed by the entire membership, but knowledge and direction of the plot was confined to a tiny, intimate group of association members and law officers. When

FBI agents questioned the operators, Elmer Hall told them that Pearl Bassham and R. C. Tway would be the two men to question concerning Ben Unthank's antiunion activities. E. F. Wright, Jr., superintendent of Southern Mining Company, told an agent that four men were responsible for all of Harlan's labor troubles.[50] A defense objection prevented the agent from naming the four culprits in the courtroom, but any regular attendant at the trial would have guessed George Ward, Ben Unthank, Theodore Middleton, and Pearl Bassham. Unlike most defendants, George Ward and Ben Unthank declined to testify in their own defense, but Judge H. Church Ford permitted a government attorney to read into the record their self-incriminating testimony given during the NLRB's Clover Fork hearing. Both admitted that the association had paid Unthank at least $2,252 during the UMW's organizing drive in January and February, 1937, mainly to spy on union organizers, report to Ward, and prevent organization of the miners.[51] Had the government confined its prosecution to the small nucleus of active conspirators, it probably would have convicted them.

In contrast to the one-sided La Follette hearings, the government's case against the deputy sheriffs was considerably weakened by rebuttal testimony. Lawrence and Martha Howard testified, as they had before the Senate Committee, that they had overheard Frank White and other deputies in a Harlan restaurant plotting the Musick murder, but the defense produced a jail log and several witnesses to prove that on the day of the slaying the Howards were confined in the county jail.[52] Kelly Fox testified again that he had watched Frank White commit the murder, but three girls testified that White had spent the evening drinking and dancing with them.[53] On the evening before Frank White was scheduled to testify in his defense, he was murdered as he sat on the front porch at the tourist camp that housed defense witnesses. Chris Patterson, who had earlier been imprisoned for dynamiting Lawrence Dwyer's apartment, was apprehended nearby reeling drunkenly with a gun in his hand and was charged with the murder. Five months later, Theodore Middleton posted bond for Patterson, and Lee Fleenor drove him back to Harlan County. The following week, Patterson's bullet-riddled body was discovered lying beside a county highway.[54]

C. B. Spicer, a Harlan defense attorney, and Lee Fleenor's uncle, Everett, hired witnesses to testify falsely that union organizers, believing that Marshall Musick had taken his family with him to Pineville, had themselves shot up the minister's house to turn public opinion against the mine owners and deputies. Several defense witnesses implicated Belton Youngblood, an Alabama organizer, and Granville Sargent, a Harlan native, in the murder. Government agents, however, secured an affidavit from a county couple who, on the evening of the Musick murder, had visited the home of a key defense witness and found him completely immobilized with an acute case of gonorrhea. Confronted with the affidavit, the youth's mother convinced her son to retract his testimony and confess to perjury. Other defense witnesses returned to the stand, retracted their perjured testimony, and accused Spicer and Fleenor of subornation of perjury. After the conclusion of the conspiracy trial, a federal grand jury indicted several county residents for perjury and subornation of perjury; and although most charges were dismissed, Judge Ford disbarred attorney Spicer.[55] In the conspiracy trial itself, the jury was left to judge between Kelly Fox's charge that Frank White had committed the murder and the three girls' testimony in White's defense.

Government witnesses offered strong evidence of multitudinous discharges and discrimination for union activity, solid enough to convince NLRB experts that four Harlan firms had violated the Wagner Act, but defense witnesses countered with testimony showing that the same miners had been fired or demoted for loading dirty coal or violating safety regulations. The sheer scope of the case—twelve thousand pages of testimony taken from 569 witnesses—and the subtle and highly technical nature of the evidence overwhelmed and confused the inexpert jurors. Numerous operators contended that their firms acted individually on labor matters, and the government was unable to prove that so elemental a conspiratorial device as an association blacklist linked the discharges together.[56]

The government's case was lost from the moment jury selection was completed. On the first day of the trial, one juror

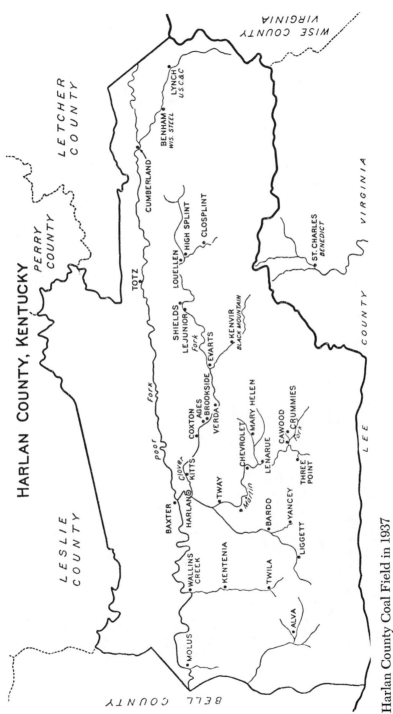

HARLAN COUNTY, KENTUCKY

LETCHER COUNTY

PERRY COUNTY

LESLIE COUNTY

WISE COUNTY VIRGINIA

VIRGINIA

LEE COUNTY

BELL COUNTY

LYNCH
U.S.C.&C.

BENHAM
W/U.S. STEEL

CUMBERLAND

HIGH SPLINT

CLOSPLINT

LOUELLEN

ST. CHARLES
BENEDICT

TOTZ

SHIELDS

LEJUNIOR

KENVIR
BLACK MOUNTAIN

EVARTS

Clover Fork

Poor Fork

BROOKSIDE

AGES

COXTON

VERDA

MARY HELEN

KITTS

CHEVROLET

LENARUE

CAWOOD

CRUMMIES

Martin

Fork

THREE
POINT

BAXTER

HARLAN

TWAY

BARDO

YANCEY

WALLINS
CREEK

KENTENIA

TWILA

LIGGETT

MOLUS

ALVA

Harlan County Coal Field in 1937

Tipple at Crummies Creek Coal Company, 1937. During the 1939 strike Crummies Creek, where working conditions and wages surpassed union standards, had the best production record.

Miner riding on coal car emerging from drift mouth.

vowed to others that "he would rot before he would send a man to the penitentiary to help John L. Lewis, the United Mine Workers or the C.I.O." Until the trial's last week, however, the remaining eleven jurors stood solid for convicting all defendants. Then, a mini-feud erupted among the jurymen when one of them remarked that conditions were just as bad in Clay County where he and five others jurors resided. Perhaps as a result, three Clay County jurors voted for blanket acquittal of all defendants, and two others for a divided verdict. In the final tally, five jurors voted to convict all fifty-five remaining defendants, three voted for blanket acquittal, and four voted to acquit some and convict others. The judge declared a mistrial, and the prosecution requested a retrial.[57] Considering that three-fourths of the jury had voted to convict some of the defendants, retrial continued to pose a serious threat to the mine owners and their political allies.

Even though the government lost its case, the *Nation* interpreted the trial as a "Roosevelt Revolution." Once Harlan citizens had seen their coal barons in the prisoner's dock, the editor thought, the county would never again be the same.[58] Also, the coal operators, having spent an estimated $1 million for direct and indirect defense costs, felt compelled to sign a union contract in the hope of avoiding retrial.

Defense attorney Forney Johnston and the editor of the *Knoxville News-Sentinel* immediately urged the operators and the union to negotiate a settlement. Meeting at Tate Springs, Tennessee, representatives of the UMW, the NLRB, the Harlan operators, and attorneys Johnston and Dawson reached tentative agreement on August 18. After obtaining Lewis's approval, on August 27, in Cincinnati, Turnblazer, Titler, and the twenty-two-member Harlan County Coal Operators' Association signed a contract. The two issues that had prevented agreement in 1937, dues checkoff and coal measurement, were compromised. The union won dues assignment for the life of the contract, and the operators were prohibited from bargaining with a company union unless it had won certification in an NLRB election. The operators were permitted to measure coal in the traditional manner. Clover Fork and Harlan Fuel were to pay $20,000 and $4,000 respectively into a pool to be divided among employees discharged for union activity and to dismiss all house-eviction suits pending against union members. Harlan Central and Green-Silvers were to dismiss all eviction suits and reemploy all miners discharged for union activity. In return for these concessions, the NLRB agreed not to enforce its Clover Fork, Harlan Fuel, and Green-Silvers decisions, not to issue a Harlan Central decision, and to dismiss UMW charges of unfair labor practices against forty other Harlan firms. When this contract expired on March 31, 1939, the operators' association agreed to participate in national contract negotiations.[59]

The coal operators compromised their nonunion principles. The Harlan agreement deleted the Central Appalachian Agreement's standard clause recognizing the UMW as a sole bargaining agent for all company employees, and both sides interpreted the local contract to imply something less than full union recognition. The operators, however, did accept the standard dues checkoff provision. Financially, the operators fared well. Already matching the union's basic daily wage scale, the operators avoided raising coal-loading rates by winning the right to measure coal according to local custom, and they escaped any major monetary penalty for former unfair labor practices. Still unable to secure formal union recognition, the UMW gained a limited degree of union security by obtaining dues assignment for the life of the contract and by placing an obstacle in the way of easy recognition of company and rival unions. The latter was important because repercussions of labor's civil war were being experienced locally; the UMW's rival, the Progressive Mine Workers of America (AFL), had recently issued charters to the former Benham Employees' Association at Wisconsin Steel and the Union of Lynch Employees at U.S. Coal & Coke. Since neither daily wages nor coal-loading rates were increased, rank-and-file miners gained only a slight degree of security for their union.

Already in 1937, Harlan-Wallins, Black Mountain, Clover Splint, Black Star, Berger, Harlan Crown, and Cook & Sharp had signed a UMW contract, and U.S. Coal & Coke had signed a joint agreement with the UMW and the Union of Lynch Employees. The 1938 agreement covered such hardcore anti-union association members as Clover Fork, Harlan Collieries,

Harlan Fuel, Harlan Central, Cornett-Lewis, Mary Helen, Crummies Creek, High Splint, R. C. Tway, Blue Diamond, and Bardo, as well as more moderate association members such as Three Point, Mahan-Ellison, and Southern Harlan. In October, PV & K Coal Company, Elcomb, R. W. Creech, and Green-Silvers signed the Harlan agreement, and the Progressive Mine Workers local at U.S. Coal & Coke dissolved itself and affiliated with the UMW. After the UMW won NLRB elections at Perkins-Harlan and Kentucky Cardinal in December, they, too, signed the Harlan contract. By the close of 1938, well over twelve thousand county miners were under UMW contract, and only Southern Mining Company, Good Coal Company, and Wisconsin Steel remained outside the UMW's grasp.[60] In September, 1938, the successful organizer of Harlan County, George J. Titler, confidently informed the United States attorney general's office that "every Operator in Harlan County is doing their utmost to keep the faith and it is my opinion this matter is working out as well as can be expected." [61]

The Roosevelt administration's action and its effect in 1937 and 1938 revealed the meaning of the New Deal for Harlan County. Through the La Follette investigation, the conspiracy prosecution, and the National Labor Relations Board's enforcement of the Wagner Act, the New Deal extended a new dimension of liberty to the Harlan miner. New Deal actions resulted in abolition of the private deputy system and gave union officials free access to the county and to company property. Union men, who in the spring of 1937 could not safely travel the county or occupy a hotel room in the county seat, by 1938 roamed the county soliciting union membership at will and maintained a headquarters in Harlan. Miners who wished to affiliate with the union could assemble and join without fear of physical reprisal, discharge, eviction, or job discrimination. Violence in labor-management relations was already yielding to the civilized tactics of mediation and negotiation.

While political change fell short of a partisan revolution, thousands of former Republican miners had been encouraged by the New Deal's solicitude for labor to switch their allegiance to the Democratic party and to create a new political equilibrium. During the course of the 1930s, the county had cast its first Democratic vote for president, governor, county judge, and jailor. Although the United Mine Workers was not yet secure, it was free to exert its strength in 1939 to achieve a new balance of economic power between operators and miners. The New Deal did not transfer economic, political, or social power from one class to another; it was no Roosevelt Revolution. A drastic reform, the creation of a new balance of economic, political, and social power, was Harlan's New Deal.

NOTES

1. Jerold S. Auerbach, *Labor and Liberty: The La Follette Committee and the New Deal* (Indianapolis and New York, 1966), pp. 173–75.

2. George Wolfskill, *Revolt of the Conservatives: A History of the American Liberty League, 1934–1940* (Boston, 1962), pp. 71, 78, 151; "Kentucky Feudalism," *Time*, May 3, 1937, pp. 13–14; Rodney Dutcher, *Knoxville* (Tenn.) *News-Sentinel*, Apr. 29, 1937.

3. Testimony of George Gray, *U.S.* v. *Mary Helen*, vol. 13, pp. 3163–66, 3173, 3175, 3177; Edward B. Smith, *Knoxville News-Sentinel*, May 27, 1938; Wilmer G. Mason, *Cincinnati Enquirer*, July 1, 1938; *Cincinnati Enquirer*, July 14, 20, 1938; *Pineville* (Ky.) *Sun*, July 11, 1935.

4. Testimony of Joseph Timko, LFCH, pt. 11, pp. 4014–17; testimony of George Lee, ibid., pp. 4058–59; testimony of Carl Vogel, *U.S.* v. *Mary Helen*, vol. 14, 3351–54.

5. *Coal Age*, 40 (Oct., 1935), 434; *Pineville Sun*, Sept. 26, 1935; testimony of Armstrong Matthews, LFCH, pt. 11, pp. 4053–56; U.S., National Labor Relations Board, "In the Matter of Clover Fork Coal Company and District 19, United Mine Workers of America," *Decisions and Orders*, vol. 4, p. 206 (hereafter cited as 4 NLRB; other NLRB decisions and orders will be similarly cited); *United Mine Workers Journal*, Nov. 15, 1935, p. 7.

6. Testimony of William Turnblazer, U.S., Congress, Senate, Committee on Education and Labor, *Violations of Free Speech and Assembly and Interference with Rights of Labor, Hearings* on S.R. 266, 74 Cong., 2 sess. (1936), p. 142; *Harlan* (Ky.) *Daily Enterprise*, July 1, 5, 9, 1935; *Pineville Sun*, June 13, 27, July 11, 1935; *United Mine Workers Journal*, July 1, 1935, p. 5; John H. Fenton, *Politics in the Border States* (New Orleans, 1957), pp. 24–25.

7. *Harlan Daily Enterprise*, Aug. 4, 6, 13, Sept. 10, Nov. 7, Dec. 10, 1935; *United Mine Workers Journal*, Nov. 15, 1935, p. 6.

8. *Harlan Daily Enterprise*, Dec. 10, 1935, Jan. 17, 1937; testimony of Timko, LFCH, pt. 11, pp. 4029–30; LFCH, pt. 12, Exhibit 1286, pp. 4181–82.

9. *Harlan Daily Enterprise*, Feb. 11, 1936; *United Mine Workers Journal*, Feb. 15, 1936, p. 17; testimony of George Ward, LFCH, pt. 10, p. 3519; testimony of Joseph Menefee, ibid., pt. 11, p. 3983.

10. Testimony of T. C. Townsend and Turnblazer, *Violations of Free*

Speech and Assembly, pp. 125–42; *United Mine Workers Journal,* Sept. 15, 1936, p. 7; testimony of John Young Brown, LFCH, pt. 12, pp. 4178–80.

11. *Harlan Daily Enterprise,* Dec. 29, 1935; *United Mine Workers Journal,* Jan. 1, 1936, p. 11, Jan. 15, 1936, p. 11, Dec. 15, 1936, p. 3; testimony of James Westmoreland, LFCH, pt. 11, pp. 3934–35.

12. LFCH, pt. 12, Exhibit 1286, pp. 4181–82; *Harlan Daily Enterprise,* Jan. 17, 1937; minutes of executive board meeting of the Harlan County Coal Operators' Association, Jan. 20, 1937, ibid., pt. 9, pp. 3315–16; testimony of Ward, "Clover Fork Coal Company and District 19, United Mine Workers of America," NLRB hearing, Aug. 12, 1937, read into the record, *U.S.* v. *Mary Helen,* vol. 13, pp. 3079–80; testimony of Ben Unthank, "Clover Fork Coal Company and District 19, United Mine Workers of America," NLRB hearing, Aug. 2, 1937, read into the record, ibid., pp. 3059–60, 3063, 3067–73.

13. Testimony of L. T. Arnett, LFCH, pt. 12, p. 4188.

14. Ibid., pp. 4190–93; testimony of Matt Bunch, *U.S.* v. *Mary Helen,* vol. 13, pp. 3283–84; testimony of Theodore Middleton, LFCH, pt. 10, p. 3439, pt. 12, pp. 4206–9; testimony of George Jenkins, ibid., pt. 12, pp. 4350–52.

15. Testimony of Marshall Musick, LFCH, pt. 12, pp. 4230–33.

16. Testimony of Tom Ferguson, ibid., pp. 4216–19; testimony of Arnett, ibid., pp. 4194–95.

17. Testimony of Marshall Musick, ibid., pp. 4233–36; testimony of Mrs. Mallie Musick, ibid., pp. 4237–39; testimony of Kelly Fox, ibid., pt. 13, pp. 4431–34.

18. Testimony of Henry M. Lewis, ibid., pt. 11, p. 4009.

19. Testimony of Daniel Boone Smith, ibid., pt. 12, pp. 4332–34; George J. Titler, *Hell in Harlan* (Beckley, W.Va., n.d.), pp. 123–24.

20. LFCH, pt. 9, Exhibit 1100, p. 3269; testimony of Vogel, *U.S.* v. *Mary Helen,* vol. 14, pp. 3351–54; minutes of executive board meetings of the Harlan County Coal Operators' Association, July 19, 1933, Nov. 20, 1935, Jan. 20, 1937, LFCH, pt. 9, pp. 3280, 3306–7, 3315–16; testimony of Ward, ibid., pt. 10, pp. 3506–7; testimony of Timko, ibid., pt. 11, pp. 4015–17; testimony of Lee, ibid., pp. 4058–59.

21. Testimony of Ward, LFCH, pt. 10, p. 3525; testimony of Lawrence Dwyer, ibid., pp. 3461–63, 3465–66; testimony of Middleton, ibid., pt. 12, pp. 4142–49, 4155–57; testimony of Pearl Bassham, ibid., pt. 13, pp. 4514–15; testimony of Smith, ibid., pt. 12, pp. 4310–12.

22. Testimony of Dwyer, ibid., pt. 10, p. 3470; Auerbach, *Labor and Liberty,* pp. 117–18.

23. Testimony of Middleton, LFCH, pt. 13, p. 4416.

24. Ibid., pp. 4414–15; Final Report of the Harlan County Grand Jury, May 5, 1934, ibid., pt. 10, Exhibit 1214, p. 3730.

25. Testimony of Dwyer, ibid., pt. 10, pp. 3459–60, 3463–65; testimony of William Hall, ibid., pt. 12, p. 4223; testimony of Turnblazer, ibid., pt. 11, pp. 3877–82; testimony of Middleton, ibid., pt. 13, p. 4585; testimony of Kelly Fox, ibid., p. 4434.

26. Testimony of Lawrence and Martha Howard, ibid., pt. 12, p.

4249; Wilmer G. Mason, *Cincinnati Enquirer,* July 1, 1938; testimony of Fox, LFCH, pt. 13, pp. 4431–34.

27. Testimony of Musick, LFCH, pt. 12, p. 4233; testimony of William M. Clontz, ibid., pt. 10, p. 3639; testimony of Middleton, ibid., pt. 13, pp. 4425–26; testimony of Brown, ibid., pt. 12, pp. 4178–80; testimony of Ward, ibid., pt. 10, p. 3519; testimony of Menefee, ibid., pt. 11, p. 3983.

28. Testimony of Bassham, ibid., pt. 10, pp. 3579–81, pt. 13, pp. 4521–23, 4542; testimony of Robert Eldridge, ibid., pt. 12, p. 4291.

29. Testimony of Turnblazer, ibid., pt. 10, pp. 3620–22.

30. Wilmer G. Mason, *Cincinnati Enquirer,* July 1, 1938; testimony of Bill C. "Thug" Johnson, LFCH, pt. 12, pp. 4357, 4359.

31. Testimony of Elmer Hall, *U.S.* v. *Mary Helen,* vol. 22, pp. 4968–69; 4 NLRB 207.

32. Auerbach, *Labor and Liberty,* pp. 173–75.

33. *Harlan Daily Enterprise,* Apr. 27, May 10, 14, 17, July 7, 16, 1937; *Knoxville News-Sentinel,* May 16, 1937; *Pineville Sun,* May 20, 1937.

34. *Harlan Daily Enterprise,* May 11, June 4, 22, 23, 24, 28, 1937; *New York Times,* May 11, June 27, 1937.

35. *Harlan Daily Enterprise,* July 14, Nov. 7, 1937, June 24, 26, 1938.

36. Ibid., Jan. 4, 25, May 15, 1938.

37. Ibid., Apr. 25, 26, May 3, 10, 17, 30, 31, June 5, 6, 7, 10, 14, 20, Aug. 4, 1937; *Knoxville News-Sentinel,* Apr. 25, May 17, 1937.

38. *United Mine Workers Journal,* Apr. 15, 1937, pp. 3–4; *Harlan Daily Enterprise,* Apr. 8, 1937; *Knoxville News-Sentinel,* Mar. 3, Apr. 2, 6, May 4, 1937; *New York Times,* May 3, 1937.

39. *Knoxville News-Sentinel,* May 16, 1937; *Harlan Daily Enterprise,* May 21, June 16, 23, July 11, 1937; statement by Charles I. Dawson, *U.S.* v. *Mary Helen,* vol. 4, pp. 1121–29.

40. *Harlan Daily Enterprise,* June 6, 22, 23, July 2, 4, 27, Aug. 26, 29, Sept. 2, 19, 23, 24, Dec. 3, 21, 1937; *Knoxville News-Sentinel,* Apr. 25, 1937.

41. George Titler, quoted in *Harlan Daily Enterprise,* July 21, 1937.

42. Ibid., Apr. 2, 27, 1938; *Knoxville News-Sentinel,* May 23, 1937; 8 NLRB 36, 63; Wilmer G. Mason, *Cincinnati Enquirer,* July 12, 1938; 12 NLRB 154; *United Mine Workers Journal,* Sept. 15, 1939, p. 14.

43. 4 NLRB 213–14; *Harlan Daily Enterprise,* July 14, 15, 1937.

44. 12 NLRB 139–47, 150.

45. *Harlan Daily Enterprise,* June 30, July 11, Oct. 22, 24, 25, 26, Dec. 21, 1937, Apr. 21, 22, 25, 26, May 1, 3, 4, 8, 1938; *United Mine Workers Journal,* July 1, 1938, p. 6; 4 NLRB 203, 211, 240–41; 8 NLRB 27, 31–32, 63–65; 12 NLRB 137, 154–57.

46. *Harlan Daily Enterprise,* Aug. 3, Nov. 11, 22, Dec. 19, 1937; *United Mine Workers Journal,* Sept. 15, 1939, p. 14.

47. Memorandum, Brien McMahon for J. Edgar Hoover, May 11, 1937; press release, U.S., Dept. of Justice, May 19, 1937, NA, RG/60, Correspondence, Box 17063; *Harlan Daily Enterprise,* May 20, June 1, 23, Sept. 28, 1937; *New York Times,* Sept. 22, 28, 1937; *United Mine Workers Journal,* May 1, 1938, p. 9.

48. George J. Titler, who conducted the UMW's 1937–39 organization campaign in Harlan, agrees that the government sought to force the operators to accept a contract. See Titler, *Hell in Harlan*, pp. 181–82; *Knoxville News-Sentinel*, Aug. 2, 1938; Louis Hofferbert, *Knoxville News-Sentinel*, Aug. 28, 1938; Wilmer G. Mason, *Cincinnati Enquirer*, Oct. 3, 1939.

49. Testimony of E. J. Asbury, *U.S.* v. *Mary Helen*, vol. 4, pp. 1184, 1199, 1206–7; testimony of Elmer Hall, ibid., vol. 22, pp. 4968–69.

50. Testimony of R. E. Peterson, ibid., vol. 5, pp. 1410–11; testimony of T. M. O'Leary, ibid., p. 1471.

51. Testimony of Ben Unthank and George Ward, "Clover Fork Coal Company and District 19, United Mine Workers of America," NLRB hearing, Aug. 2, 1937, read into the record, ibid., vol. 13, pp. 3059–60, 3063, 3067, 3069–73, 3079–80.

52. Wilmer G. Mason, *Cincinnati Enquirer*, July 1, 1938.

53. Ken White, *Harlan Daily Enterprise*, June 10, 1938; *Harlan Daily Enterprise*, July 18, 19, 1938; *Cincinnati Enquirer*, July 19, 1938.

54. *Harlan Daily Enterprise*, July 7, Dec. 11, 1938; W. M. Jones to Obrien [*sic*] McMahon, Dec. 10, 1938; John T. Metcalf to McMahon, Dec. 10, 1938, NA, RG/60, Correspondence, Box 17063.

55. Testimony of Birley Watts, *U.S.* v. *Mary Helen*, vol. 32, pp. 7412–19; testimony of Murphy Kelly, ibid., pp. 7362–69; testimony of Albert Hoskins, ibid., vol. 45, pp. 11,369–79; testimony of Mrs. Lela Bartley, ibid., pp. 11,425–32; testimony of Mrs. Easter Farley, ibid., pp. 11,443, 11,456; testimony of John Barnes, ibid., pp. 11,402–10; "Rebuttal memos prepared by Dept. of Justice Attorneys, London, Ky., July 13, 1938, Re: Mary Helen Coal Corporation, *et al.*, Civil Rights and Domestic Violence," NA, RG/60, Enclosures, Box 3647; U.S. District Court, London, Kentucky, "In Re: C. B. Spicer, Attorney, Dec. 5, 1938," ibid., Correspondence, Box 17063.

56. *Cincinnati Enquirer*, July 26, 1938; *Harlan Daily Enterprise*, May 20, 1938; editorial, *New York Times*, July 29, 1938; Louis Hofferbert, *Knoxville News-Sentinel*, July 26, 1938.

57. F. Raymond Daniell, *New York Times*, Aug. 2, 1938; *Knoxville News-Sentinel*, Aug. 2, 1938; *Cincinnati Enquirer*, Aug. 2, 1938.

58. "Bloody Harlan Reforms," *Nation*, Aug. 6, 1938, p. 121.

59. *Knoxville News-Sentinel*, Aug. 2, 1938; editorial, ibid., Aug. 3, 1938; Louis Hofferbert, ibid., Aug. 28, 1938; *Harlan Daily Enterprise*, Aug. 28, 1938; *Cincinnati Enquirer*, Aug. 28, 29, 1938; Titler, *Hell in Harlan*, p. 182.

60. *Harlan Daily Enterprise*, Aug. 28, 30, 1938; Louis Hofferbert, *Knoxville News-Sentinel*, Aug. 28, 1938; *United Mine Workers Journal*, Oct. 15, 1938, p. 14, Nov. 1, 1938, p. 4, Jan. 1, 1939, p. 7; "Two More Harlan Operators Sign Union Contracts," *Coal Age*, 43 (Nov., 1938), 78; *Pineville Sun*, Sept. 1, 1938; Titler, *Hell in Harlan*, p. 182.

61. Titler to McMahon, Sept. 19, 1938, NA, RG/60, Correspondence, Box 17063.

Chapter **7**

Striking a New Balance of Power

1939

In spite of the progress made toward successful unionization and the establishment of collective bargaining, Harlan County's turbulent decade climaxed in another costly and violent strike. It began as part of the UMW's six-week national shutdown of the bituminous coal industry to obtain a union shop. In Harlan, the union-shop issue resulted in a fifteen-week strike that pitted the twenty-four-member operators' association, backed by Governor Chandler, against the county's nine thousand union miners, supported by the powerful United Mine Workers of America, the federal government, and the bulk of the nation's public and editorial opinion.

On March 14, 1939, the Joint Appalachian Conference convened in New York City to renew the national contract that would expire at the end of the month. The coal operators sought an eight-hour day and a fifty-cent-per-day wage reduction; union representatives demanded a six-hour day and a fifty-cent-per-day wage increase. The conferees quickly agreed to continue the wages and hours provisions of the 1937 agreement, a seven-hour day and a basic daily wage of $6.00 in the North and $5.60 south of the Ohio. Lewis, who feared that the UMW was seriously threatened by the rival Progressive Mine Workers chartered by the AFL in 1938, demanded jurisdictional protection for his union. He proposed either a union-shop clause, which would require all employed miners to join the UMW, or elimination of the traditional penalty clause, which prohibited strikes during the life of the contract. In the absence of a penalty clause, the UMW would be free to strike any mine owner who hired rival union or nonunion miners.

Unable to reach agreement on a union security provision, Appalachian miners struck for forty-three days. On May 13, a vast majority of the nation's operators signed a union-shop agreement. Seven southern associations, the Kanawha group in West Virginia, the Virginia and Southwestern Virginia associations, the Southern Appalachian Association in Tennessee and southeastern Kentucky, the Big Sandy-Elkhorn, Hazard, and Harlan associations in eastern Kentucky, rejected the contract and left the conference. Although the seven associations employed only 45,000 of the 338,000 Appalachian miners, their concerted opposition seriously jeopardized the conference's future stability. Within five days, however, six of the rebel associations signed the standard union-shop agreement and left Harlan standing alone as the bulwark of the open shop.

When the national strike began on April 3, for the first time in Harlan's history every county mine closed. Daily rail shipments of fifteen hundred cars abruptly fell to one hundred cars that had collected on county sidings before the strike began.[1]

During the strike's second week, the county's most relentless union opponents, the Whitfields, attempted to reopen their Clover Fork mine. Between three and five hundred union pickets swarmed onto company property, blocked the highway, the railroad tracks, and the drift mouth, and surrounded the company commissary and office building, Clover Fork canceled its work order, again idling all the county's forty-three mines.[2]

The third and most of the fourth week passed without incident. Then on April 27, when Kentucky Cardinal showed signs of reopening, more than a thousand pickets converged on the mine, damaged the shop, slashed telephone lines, trapped company officials in the commissary, and, according to a mine foreman, threatened to "kill the first man who darkens the drift mouth." George Titler rushed to the scene to disperse the pickets, but the company's superintendent urged Governor Chandler to send observers to "see where the law has broken down."[3]

That weekend, several hundred persons gathered on the riverbank at Evarts to watch union zealots forcibly baptize nine nonunion miners "in the name of the father, the son, and John L. Lewis." The county judge condemned their "sacrilegious" act and placed twenty-one participants under a $500 peace bond. Union officials, clearly recognizing that a repetition of the 1931 violence was the one factor that could destroy their cause, cautioned the strikers to refrain from coercive acts.[4]

Realizing that food, shelter, morale, and patience were the keys to a successful strike, union officials were most solicitous of the strikers' needs. A 50 percent decline in local retail sales indicated a considerable degree of belt-tightening, but the miners were experiencing no severe privation. In a novel display of union-management cooperation, most large firms with a sizable union membership extended a one-dollar daily relief credit to four thousand county miners. The union guaranteed repayment either by returning miners or, if individual strikers did not return, by the union. At camps with negligible union membership the company extended credit to nonunion miners, and the union fed its own. At the few mines that offered no credit, the union supported its membership.

As the strike entered its fifth week several operators discontinued relief credit and prepared to resume operation. On May 1, State Industrial Relations Commissioner William C. Burrows and state police commander Major Joe Burman conferred with county officials, operators, and union leaders and sent twenty-eight state policemen to protect working miners.

When Clover Fork reopened on May 2, no pickets appeared, and the mine ran coal for one day. At three o'clock next morning, however, more than a thousand pickets arrived, planted a solid phalanx of men before the mine entrance, smashed the windows of a car that attempted to crash their line, threw a nonunion miner in the river, and verbally abused others who reported for work. The Whitfields were again forced to close. Observing their failure, other operators canceled their work orders but petitioned Governor Chandler for troop protection.[5]

On May 4, seventeen hundred pickets peacefully shut down Good Coal Company, which had worked the previous day, and marched on to Kitts to thwart Clover Fork's third attempt to operate. Thirty state policemen blocked them at the highway and railroad bridges, but the pickets outflanked the state troopers by scaling the mountainside and planted themselves at the mine entrance and along both sides of the incline. Ed Whitfield announced that the company would forego any attempt to operate until the governor sent adequate troop protection because "someone would get killed if we tried it." For two days small picket squadrons maintained an around-the-clock vigil to hold the company to its word, and the fifth week closed with no mines in operation.[6]

During the strike's sixth week, Harlan operators announced that no mines would reopen until they could act in concert with adequate troop protection. A delegation of Bell and Harlan county officials called on the governor to request National Guard intervention and assured him that, if protection were adequate, 75 percent of the miners would return to work. County Judge Cam Ball, for example, assured the govenor that three-fourths of the county's miners were "facing starvation and want to return to work." On May 10, Governor Chandler announced publicly that the key issue in dispute was a closed-shop demand that he opposed, and that if no agreement had been reached by Monday, May 15, he would dispatch the National Guard to permit county mines to resume open-shop operation.[7]

Only three days later, most Appalachian operators signed a union-shop contract, and within a week, all national operators' associations except Harlan's had followed suit. Had Governor Chandler deferred his troop commitment for a week, perhaps even three days, he might not have sent troops. By his hasty promise, the governor encouraged Harlan operators to hold out. On Monday, May 15, while 86 percent of Appalachian miners returned to the pits, seven hundred guardsmen occupied Harlan County; and the local operators attempted to reopen without a contract.

The press roundly condemned the governor's intervention. In a Sunday editorial, the *Courier-Journal* asserted that in light of the national coal settlement there was no threat of a coal shortage and that the Harlan miners were in no danger of starvation. Neither the local operators' desire for uninterrupted profits nor John L. Lewis's wish to protect himself from the incursion of a rival union justified this "risk of almost certain bloodshed." The editor believed that the fundamental issue in Harlan was preservation of order and the protection of life, neither of which had been seriously threatened, and that "the threat to human life will come when passions are stirred by the entrance of troops into the Harlan field." Influential national commentator Heywood Broun accused the governor of playing the "role of a Hill-Billy Hitler or a Mountaineer Mussolini" and warned that the American people were in no mood to "permit troops to bayonet miners back into the pits and turn blue grass to purple." The *Louisville Times* denounced the Harlan operators "who fondly imagine that they can stem the tide of collective bargaining" and who had rejected a reasonable compromise between an open shop and a closed shop.[8]

On Saturday, before the troops arrived, George Ward announced that the operators were "unalterably" opposed to the national contract because its closed-shop demand encroached on managerial prerogatives and its wage scale placed an intolerable financial burden on county operators. Yet county operators were sharply divided. As a result of the La Follette and Mary Helen exposés, several major firms had deserted the operators' association, which now spoke for only twenty-four employers of 4,800 of the county's 13,900 miners. When Ward announced that thirty-seven of the county's forty-two mines planned to reopen when troops arrived, six large mines—U.S. Coal & Coke, Wisconsin Steel, Black Mountain, Clover Splint, Creech, and Black Star—simultaneously declared their intention to remain closed. Of the six dissenters, only Creech was an association member. On the first day of military occupation, the breech widened further when officials at Black Mountain and Harlan-Wallins, which together employed 2,600 miners, announced that they intended to sign the union-shop agreement.[9]

The UMW faced the serious challenge of maintaining strike support in a newly organized field. Since the issue was union security, even in victory, the Harlan miners stood to gain no increase in wages or reduction of hours. Recalling how quickly troops had broken the 1931 strike, union leaders doubted that new union members would hold out in a prolonged strike conducted under military occupation. While publicly predicting that 90 percent of the miners would continue their strike, strike leaders privately confided that they would be satisfied if 50 percent stayed out. The union avoided many of 1931's pitfalls. In 1931, district officials had been barred from the county and lost control of the strike; in 1939, George Titler retained complete command. In 1931, the bankrupt UMW had been unable to furnish strike relief and legal assistance; in 1939, with a full treasury and its morale bolstered by a recent strike victory, the union generously sustained the strikers. The union had distributed $30,000 in strike relief before the troops arrived, and thereafter the union's relief was substantially increased and supplemented by Works Progress Administration assistance. The union neutralized the threat of eviction by posting bond for house rental, thereby permitting strikers to maintain occupancy for the strike's duration. After April 20, the constant vigilance of either FBI agents or assistant United States attorney generals lessened the temptation of National Guardsmen or local officials to abridge civil liberties. In addition, union officials could always appeal to a friendly national government to retry the conspiracy case against Harlan operators.[10] The county environment was much more conducive to maintenance of strikers' morale and less productive of violence than in 1931. Moreover, the success of the 1939 strike provides abundant proof that the Harlan miners' movement had a deeper meaning than a simple struggle for improved working conditions. It was a struggle for power within the county, and the strike posed basic issues that all good unionists could support.

The National Guardsmen arrived on May 15. They blockaded the Virginia and Tennessee borders to forestall invasion by pickets from adjoining union districts. They established checkpoints, commanded by machine guns, at all strategic intersections of county highways to control picket movements into any section of the coal field. Soldiers admitted only twenty-five pickets to individual mines and dispersed all mass picket movements. A Knoxville reporter, who spent the day observing troop deployment, concluded that although martial law had not been officially declared, it existed in practice. George Titler protested to the governor that the troops "could not have been used to better advantage if they had been under the command of the coal operators." [11]

Throughout the first week of military occupation Harlan Central at Totz was the site of continuous confrontation between troops and picket squadrons. Because Totz was so close to the huge idled mines of U.S. Coal & Coke and Wisconsin Steel, bands of roving pickets from Lynch and Benham daily attempted to close Harlan Central. Additional troops arrived on Tuesday, and 65 soldiers were stationed at Totz to protect fifty nonunion miners, who loaded only five rail cars. On Wednesday, troop strength reached 1,250. Soldiers closed the entire length of the Clover Fork and Poor Fork highways and blocked two hundred carloads of pickets from Lynch, Benham, and Cumberland from entering Harlan Central. But 150 miners picketed Harlan Central anyway. They reduced the work force from fifty to forty, and on Thursday they closed the mine. [12]

On May 22, the union, anxious to avoid a violent incident that might alienate public opinion, halted picketing and demonstrations, and the National Guard reciprocated by removing all roadblocks. At the close of the strike's eighth week, the *Courier-Journal* editor rejoiced that county residents were "passing through their ordeal with calmness, serenity, and an untarnished good name. Harlan County isn't what it used to be." [13]

Meanwhile, the union was demonstrating remarkable solidarity. On Monday, May 15, six mines reopened, but only 450 of the county's 13,900 miners worked. They loaded 108 rail cars compared to a normal 1,500-car output. Crummies Creek, where working conditions and wages surpassed union standards, made the only respectable showing, with 250 of its 700 employees reporting for work. The back-to-work movement peaked on Wednesday, when 2,500 miners loaded 357 cars at twenty-five mines. Then, although troops could guarantee that miners who wished to work could do so with minimum personal risk, the movement receded. By Friday, 2,300 miners loaded only 204 cars at twenty-three mines. For the entire week, carloadings totaled 1,142, far below normal daily production,

Miners near Harlan listening to UMW speakers on May 14, 1939, after the National Guard had been called out to oversee the reopening of the mines. Harlan operators had refused to sign the union-shop contract accepted by all other national operators' associations.

National Guardsman at Crummies Creek mine as a few miners went back to work on May 15. According to union officials, less than 2 percent of the miners returned to the pits, in spite of the operators' demands and the presence of the troops.   Wide World

Working miners being escorted through picket lines at Totz by National Guardsmen.   Wide World

Picket being taken into custody by National Guardsmen. It was alleged that this man had been with a group of striking miners who had beat up a working miner and tossed him into a nearby river.   Wide World

Miner arguing with his wife and pickets about returning to work. Some miners who went back to work were threatened by pickets.   Wide World

Picket line and troops at Harlan Central mine at Totz, which was being operated by nonstriking miners. The pickets finally forced the mine to close.   Wide World

Nonstriking miners at Totz mine going to work protected by National Guardsmen.   United Press International

fewer than 17 percent of the county's miners worked, and only half of the county's mines reopened. Open-shop operation was dramatically failing.[14]

While continuing negotiations with the operators' association, union officials approached the nineteen independent operators. On May 18, the first breakthrough occurred when U.S. Coal & Coke placed its three thousand employees under the standard captive-mine contract that eliminated the penalty clause and recognized the UMW as sole bargaining agent. Within the next nine days, Harlan-Wallins, Black Mountain, Black Star, Clover Splint, Berger, and Harlan-Perkins signed union-shop agreements, bringing the total number of miners under contract to 7,175.[15]

On May 31, Wisconsin Steel Company, which had remained closed for eight weeks, resumed open-shop operation. The Progressive Mine Workers of America (AFL) claimed majority representation at the mine and demanded sole recognition as bargaining agent, but local UMW members refused to accede to the claim, to consent to an NLRB election, or to return to work. Unable to determine the proper bargaining agent or to sign a contract, the mine reopened under troop protection, and 309 of its 364 employees returned to work. Three months later, the PMW handily defeated the UMW in an NLRB election and signed a local contract.[16]

Meanwhile, operators' association ranks remained firm. On May 23, the *Harlan Daily Enterprise,* now owned by PV & K Coal Company, predicted a break in operator ranks. The next day, when association members met to privately discuss negotiations, dissension was so vigorous that loud and angry voices carried out to the hallway, but no break occurred. Even after June 14, in the strike's eleventh week, when the association discharged its negotiating committee and released member firms to seek their own terms with the union, no immediate break occurred. Creech, which had never opened, and Blue Diamond and Mahan-Ellison, both of which had signed union-shop contracts in other coal fields, were expected to sign contracts, but did not. Blue Diamond reopened with fewer than one-third of its employees working, and Creech, PV & K, and Benito remained closed. Only during the twelfth week did the association's solidarity finally break. Creech, which had never requested troops, had never attempted to reopen, and had continued to grant its 350 employees one dollar daily credit for three months, signed a contract. Union officials expected the Creech defection to pave the way for others, but the remaining association mines maintained the open shop for the full fifteen-week duration of the strike. By June 21, 7,500 of the county's 13,900 miners were working under union conditions, but twenty-two mines were running an open shop. All major mines, except PV & K and Benito, were open, and production was back to normal.[17]

Both the state and national governments were deeply involved in the conflict. For an entire month until negotiations were broken off on June 14, both state and national conciliators participated in the negotiations. After April 20, FBI agents and assistant United States attorney generals constantly monitored the state of civil liberties in the county. Until a contract was finally signed on July 19, United States Attorney General Frank Murphy and his assistants threatened the Harlan operators with retrial of the conspiracy case; and on June 1, Judge Ford docketed the case for trial in October. On May 22, the Works Progress Administration began distributing surplus food to striking miners. It gave each miner and his family a two-week ration of thirty pounds of grapefruit, three pounds of butter, six pounds of dried milk, six pounds of wheat cereal, four pounds of dried beans, and ten pounds of corn meal. As late as mid-July, after most union miners had returned to work, the WPA was still feeding more than two thousand miners' families, or ten thousand persons. Simultaneously, the UMW daily distributed $1,400 worth of meat, flour, sugar, potatoes, coffee, and canned goods. The union and the federal government, acting in concert, assured all strikers of an adequate, balanced diet.[18]

The Roosevelt administration's support of the Harlan strike accounted in large part for the difference between union defeat in 1931 and union victory in 1939. Abolition of the private deputy system, the Justice Department's protection of civil liberties during the strike, and federal strike relief prevented the starvation and abuse of strikers that in 1931 had resulted in

desperation, violence, and defeat. The threat of renewed prosecution for conspiracy helped convince the operators to sign a
contract.

The UMW helped prevent the forcible eviction of strikers
from company houses that in 1931 had bred so much bitterness
and violence. During June and early July, nonunion companies
filed eviction suits against 368 striking employees. The union
posted bond covering twice the house rental and court costs,
pending appeal to a higher court or settlement of the strike.[19]
As a result of all this, the county remained quiet. By June 25,
only three hundred soldiers remained, but a crisis was yet to
occur.

Harlan's June production nearly equaled that of previous
years and exceeded by 24 percent production for June, 1938,
when many mines had been idled by the conspiracy trial.
Production was not being curtailed, and the strike was losing
its effectiveness. Consequently, on July 8, Turnblazer proposed
that if association members would sign a union-shop contract,
the union would not enforce its provisions at individual mines
until their union membership exceeded 60 percent. The association, however, rejected compromise.[20]

In a last-ditch effort to compel nonunion operators to sign
an agreement, at a mass union rally on Sunday, July 9, Turnblazer declared that "the fight is still on" and ordered picketing
to resume at open-shop mines to curtail production during the
peak season. On Monday, George Titler reorganzied the picket
squadrons and ordered them out the next day.[21] The action
unleashed all the pent-up frustration of the fifteen-week-old
strike and resulted in the county's first outbreak of mass
violence since the Battle of Evarts.

At dawn on Wednesday, July 12, acting on Titler's orders,
union miners picketed five mines. At the drift mouth of the
Mahan-Ellison mine, at Stanfill, a bloody clash erupted between
pickets and National Guardsmen. A picket, Dock Caldwell,
jerked the mine motor's trolley pole loose from its wire to
prevent a man-trip of nonunion miners from entering the
mine. According to the guardsmen's account, when Captain
Hanbery interfered, an unidentified picket shot him in the
stomach. As the captain fell to the ground, he pulled his re-

volver and opened fire on the picket line. Then, soldiers and pickets exchanged shots.[22] According to union witnesses, when Caldwell jerked the trolley pole free, Captain Hanbery panicked and shot Caldwell in the chest. Another picket wrested a rifle from Private W. T. Mason, struck Mason in the eye, and shot Hanbery in the abdomen with the military weapon. The pickets asserted that only one shot was fired by a union man and that Mason's rifle was the only weapon in a picket's possession. After Hanbery was wounded, he and other guardsmen fired into the defenseless picket lines.[23] Two union pickets, Dock Caldwell and Daniel Noe, were fatally wounded. Caldwell died within the hour and Noe four days later. Three other pickets, Noble Bowman, John Kennedy, and Frank Laws, were seriously wounded. Two soldiers suffered injuries. Captain Hanbery recovered from his abdominal wound and Private Mason from a minor eye laceration.[24] Judging by the results, the Battle of Stanfill was a largely one-sided affray.

Sometime after the battle, National Guard officers displayed to the press a collection of pistols, blackjacks, knives, brass knuckles, and clubs that they said were confiscated from arrested pickets. Officers explained that seven regulation military sidearms among the collection resembled weapons stolen five years earlier when the Williamsburg, Kentucky, arsenal burned. George Titler contends that the military revolvers belonged to guard officers who arranged the exhibit to forestall public criticism of the soldiers' conduct at Stanfill. Titler asserts that he instructed pickets to carry nothing resembling a weapon, and that "this request was carried out to the letter. . . . When the pickets were searched . . . at Stanfill after the riot, there was not one gun found on a mine worker picket."[25]

On the scene, guardsmen arrested 227 union members, including George Titler and his wife, who drove to Stanfill after the riot, and marched them nine miles to the Harlan County jail. As the march proceeded up Harlan's main street, a miner attempted to seize a rifle from a passing soldier. The guardsman grazed the miner's scalp with a bullet, and when his mother protested, he shot her in the leg. Five hundred guardsmen, including a tank detail, were rushed back to the county, and the jail was placed under heavy guard. Titler and Turnblazer, who was conducting negotiations at Stearns, Kentucky, during the riot, were charged with banding and confederating, sedition, and forcible rebellion. Four pickets were charged with carrying concealed deadly weapons, three with disturbing the peace, and 221 with banding and confederating. County Judge Ball set the prisoners' total bond at over a quarter of a million dollars.[26]

Feeling flared as high outside Harlan as within the county. Governor Chandler blamed Turnblazer's and Titler's "incendiary" speeches at the Sunday rally for inciting the riot. He warned that, while mercy would be extended toward pickets acting under orders, the state would vigorously prosecute their superiors, whose "methods are typical of those of violence advocated by John L. Lewis." On the floor of Congress, Congressman Clare Hoffman, a Republican from Michigan, roared that Dock Caldwell gave his life in a misguided attempt to "follow the decree of John L. Lewis," and he castigated the National Labor Relations Board for conspiring with Lewis and Turnblazer to deprive Harlan miners of their liberty to work without joining the UMW. The *Pineville Sun's* editor declared that "the blood of the dead and dying in Harlan County's latest outbreak is on the hands of William Turnblazer and others who stirred to fighting madness miners in that field." [27]

John L. Lewis replied to Governor Chandler in kind. Lewis charged that Harlan miners "are now being shot, harried and incarcerated by Happy Chandler. He pursues and wounds them with the same ferocity and lack of restraint that characterizes the habits of a Dominican dictator." Lewis asserted that Governor Chandler incited the riot by using the National Guard to break the strike. He urged President Roosevelt to remove the soldiers from Harlan County.

The *Philadelphia Record* blamed the violence on the Harlan operators who had refused to conform to the wishes of a vast majority of the nation's coal operators and who persisted in their defiance of national labor law. The *Record* editor urged the government to retry the conspiracy case immediately while "blood is making fresh stains on Harlan county soil and on the nation's record on civil rights. . . . Let the Government meet lawless force with legal force and put an end to civil rights' public enemy No. 1." [28]

Operator and union representatives immediately agreed to resume contract talks. Whereas previously violence and the use of mine guards and troops had usually redounded to the operators' advantage, they could no longer count on such a result. On July 14, as they were departing for a negotiating session in Knoxville, W. J. Cunningham, president of the operators' association, and Turnblazer received telegrams from Secretary of Labor Frances Perkins urging them to reach immediate settlement. Over the weekend, an impatient national administration dispatched its top industrial troubleshooter, John R. Steelman, to Knoxville. On Monday, with negotiations still deadlocked, Dr. Steelman utilized the ultimate weapon in the conciliator's arsenal. He advanced a formula for settlement. If either or both parties rejected the formula, the conciliator would publicize his recommendation and its rejection so that the offending party bore the brunt of public criticism. Union leaders immediately accepted his recommendation. After two days of procrastination, on July 19, the strike's 109th day, the Harlan operators signed a contract.[29]

The key issue in dispute, union security, was compromised along lines suggested by Lewis before the national strike began. The Harlan contract contained neither a union-shop clause nor a penalty clause. The operators saved face by avoiding a union shop, yet elimination of the penalty clause permitted the union to effectively ward off incursions by rival unionists. Elimination of the penalty clause did not cause an automatic influx of all miners into the union, however, as the union shop would have.

Association members recognized the UMW as sole bargaining agent for all employees at their mines, a very real gain for the union. All eviction suits against striking miners were immediately dismissed. The firms were permitted to retain all non-union miners employed during the strike; but where jobs were available, strikers were to be immediately rehired, and where no employment was available, they were to be placed on a preferential hiring list. Because of the subsequent wartime demand for coal, discharged strikers suffered only temporary unemployment. The agreement, which would expire on March 31, 1941, covered forty-eight hundred employees at twenty-four association mines.[30]

National Guard checkpoint during 1939 Harlan strike.

Troops blockading road near Verda to prevent pickets from disrupting mine operation.

Guardsmen confining strikers arrested shortly after troops had been fired upon by men concealed in hills around Cornett-Lewis Coal Company mines. The guardsmen swept the hills with rifle and machine-gun fire and drove the miners out to the road. Wide World

Truckload of arrested miners arriving at the Harlan County jail.

United Press International

National Guard troops marching miners to jail after the Battle of Stanfill, July 12, 1939. A total of 227 union members were arrested. Bond for the prisoners was set at over a quarter of a million dollars.

Knoxville News-Sentinel

Union and operator representatives signing the Harlan agreement in Knoxville, July, 1939. Seated, left to right, are George S. Ward, R. E. "Uncle Bob" Lawson, Earl Hauck, O. E. Gassaway, Judge Charles I. Dawson, and William J. Turnblazer. Standing, left to right, are George J. Titler, T. C. Townsend, and W. H. Sienknecht.

Knoxville News-Sentinel

The *Courier-Journal* editor most perceptively interpreted the contract's long-range implications. For nine years the key issue in Harlan had been contact between union leaders and miners, and the Knoxville settlement had resolved that issue in the union's favor. Union representatives were now completely free to espouse their cause; recognition had lent the union additional prestige; and henceforth, nonunion families would be forced to live in daily contact with union neighbors. If, by 1941, the UMW had not recruited nearly every county miner, the editor thought it would "have proven itself singularly inept in its own field." [31] Two years later, the Knoxville agreement would be succeeded by a closed-shop contract that also eliminated the North-South wage differential. The 1939 agreement, with an important assist from the subsequent wartime coal boom, culminated a decade-long struggle for a new balance of industrial power in Harlan County.

While operator and union representatives were negotiating a contract, federal and state officials were laying a further basis for enduring local labor-management peace. For four days, Assistant Attorney Generals Hopkins and Schweinhaut conferred with Governor Chandler at the state capital. On July 19, the same day the union and operators reached agreement, Attorney General Frank Murphy invited Chandler to Washington to seek a solution to legal problems that had accumulated over a decade of labor-management warfare. The ensuing discussions dealt with a wide range of legal questions: federal prosecution of Harlan operators and law officers for conspiracy, state prosecutions resulting from the Battle of Stanfill, and pardons for the four union leaders still serving prison sentences for participation in the Battle of Evarts. On July 24, in Washington, Murphy and Chandler discussed the general problems and scheduled an enlarged conference at White Sulphur Springs, West Virginia. [32]

On August 10, Assistant Attorney Generals Welly K. Hopkins and Brien McMahon, representing the Justice Department, Governor Chandler and Lieutenant Governor Keen Johnson, representing the Commonwealth of Kentucky, Charles I. Dawson, representing the conspiracy-case defendants, and attorneys Earl Hauck, T. C. Townsend, Ben Moore, and James Golden, representing the UMW, gathered at the West Virginia resort. The conference aroused much speculation that the participants intended to settle both the Mary Helen and Stanfill prosecutions, but the results remained a carefully guarded secret. Two weeks after the conference, a Harlan County grand jury returned 241 additional indictments in connection with the Stanfill riot, bringing the total number of defendants in the case to 420.[33]

On September 29, a special session of Harlan County Circuit Court convened to try the Stanfill riot cases. Explaining that since the riot occurred the county's labor-management conflict had been settled to the satisfaction of all parties and that Governor Chandler recommended a compromise, Commonwealth's Attorney Daniel Boone Smith moved that all Stanfill indictments be dismissed; and Special Judge J. S. Forester so ordered.[34]

Three days later, at London, Kentucky, the United States District Court convened to retry the Mary Helen conspiracy case. Assistant Attorney General Welly K. Hopkins informed the court that after the case was filed, "an impossible and medieval industrial system" in Harlan County had been abandoned, and "gun thug" rule had been abolished. County mines were open again, the miners employed, and the soldiers withdrawn. The coal operators had recognized the miners' right to organize and bargain collectively and had ceased discriminating against union labor. A labor-management agreement was in force, and a grievance system was functioning. In the government's judgment, the public interest would be best served by dismissing the conspiracy charges. Judge H. Church Ford heartily concurred.[35]

NOTES

1. *Harlan* (Ky.) *Daily Enterprise,* Apr. 3, 9, 1939.
2. Ibid., Apr. 12, 14, 1939.
3. Ibid., Apr. 30, 1939.
4. Ibid., Apr. 30, May 1, 1939.
5. Ibid., May 2, 3, 1939.
6. Ibid., May 4, 1939.
7. Ibid., May 10, 1939; *Courier-Journal* (Louisville, Ky.), May 8, 10, 1939.

8. Editorial, *Courier-Journal,* May 15, 1939; Heywood Broun, *Knoxville* (Tenn.) *News-Sentinel,* May 17, 1939; "Harlan Operators in Error in Refusal to Sign Up for Union Shop" (editorial), *Louisville* (Ky.) *Times,* May 15, 1939, p. 6.

9. *Courier-Journal,* May 14, 1939; J. Howard Henderson, *Courier-Journal,* May 16, 23, 26, 1939; Wilmer G. Mason, *Cincinnati Enquirer,* May 16, 1939.

10. *Harlan Daily Enterprise,* May 15, 1939; Henderson, *Courier-Journal,* May 15, 19, 1939.

11. Louis Hofferbert, *Knoxville News-Sentinel,* May 15, 1939; George Titler, quoted in *Harlan Daily Enterprise,* May 15, 1939.

12. Hofferbert, *Knoxville News-Sentinel,* May 16, 17, 1939; Henderson, *Courier-Journal,* May 18, 19, 21, 1939; Mason, *Cincinnati Enquirer,* May 17, 1939; *Knoxville News-Sentinel,* May 17, 1939; *Harlan Daily Enterprise,* May 17, 1939.

13. Fred W. Perkins, *Knoxville News-Sentinel,* May 22, 1939; Mason, *Cincinnati Enquirer,* May 23, 1939; editorial, *Courier-Journal,* May 26, 1939.

14. Henderson, *Courier-Journal,* May 16, 21, 1939; Hofferbert, *Knoxville News-Sentinel,* May 15, 1939; *Knoxville News-Sentinel,* May 17, 1939; *Harlan Daily Enterprise,* May 17, 19, 1939.

15. *Harlan Daily Enterprise,* May 19, 24, 28, 1939; Henderson, *Courier-Journal,* May 19, 22, 23, 1939; Mason, *Cincinnati Enquirer,* May 20, 1939; Hofferbert, *Knoxville News-Sentinel,* May 24, 1939.

16. *Harlan Daily Enterprise,* May 30, 31, June 4, Sept. 7, 1939; *Knoxville News-Sentinel,* June 1, 1939.

17. *Harlan Daily Enterprise,* May 23, June 6, 7, 12, 15, 16, 21, 1939; Henderson, *Courier-Journal,* May 25, 1939; *Knoxville News-Sentinel,* June 15, 1939.

18. *Harlan Daily Enterprise,* May 18, 19, 1939; Henderson, *Courier-Journal,* May 18, 19, 22, 1939; Mason, *Cincinnati Enquirer,* May 23, 1939; *Cincinnati Enquirer,* July 15, 1939; Perkins, *Knoxville News-Sentinel,* May 17, 1939; George J. Titler, *Hell in Harlan* (Beckley, W.Va., n.d.), pp. 183–84.

19. *Harlan Daily Enterprise,* June 9, 27, 29, July 2, 10, 11, 1939.

20. Ibid., July 5, 1939; *Cincinnati Enquirer,* July 15, 1939.

21. *Harlan Daily Enterprise,* July 10, 1939.

22. Ibid., July 12, 1939.

23. Titler, *Hell in Harlan,* pp. 196–97; *Knoxville News-Sentinel,* July 12, 1939.

24. *Harlan Daily Enterprise,* July 12, 17, 1939.

25. Ibid., July 12, 1939; Titler, *Hell in Harlan,* pp. 196–97.

26. Titler, *Hell in Harlan,* pp. 197–99; *Harlan Daily Enterprise,* July 12, 13, 1939.

27. *Harlan Daily Enterprise,* July 12, 1939; U.S., Congress, House, *Congressional Record,* 76 Cong., 1 sess. (1939), vol. 84, p. 9037; editorial, *Pineville* (Ky.) *Sun,* July 13, 1939.

28. *Harlan Daily Enterprise,* July 13, 1939; editorial, *Philadelphia Record,* July 15, 1939, clipping in NA, RG/60, Correspondence, Box 17063.

29. *Harlan Daily Enterprise,* July 14, 16, 1939; Hofferbert, *Knoxville News-Sentinel,* July 19, 1939.

30. *Harlan Daily Enterprise,* July 19, 1939.

31. Editorial, *Courier-Journal,* July 21, 1939.

32. *Harlan Daily Enterprise,* July 18, 1939; *Cincinnati Enquirer,* July 20, 25, 1939; Mason, ibid., July 23, 1939; O. John Rogge to John T. Metcalf, July 24, 1939; memorandum, Welly K. Hopkins for G. Mennen Williams, Sept. 21, 1939, NA, RG/60, Correspondence, Box 17063.

33. *Harlan Daily Enterprise,* Aug. 10, 24, 1939; *Cincinnati Enquirer,* Aug. 10, 1939.

34. *Harlan Daily Enterprise,* Sept. 29, 1939.

35. Ibid., Oct. 2, 1939.

From Golden Age to Exodus

1939-78

Throughout the 1930s, as we have seen, the Harlan mine owners fought to retain economic, political, and social control of the county. Their inferior competitive position within the coal industry, determined by higher shipping costs and inadequate mechanization, compelled them to maintain lower production costs by either paying lower wages than competitors or demanding equal work for less pay. The operators also attempted to retain political and social control of county government and the miners in order to defeat the union's challenge to their economic position. The mine owners feared that either union or government standardization of wages and hours or elimination of local nonunion work practices threatened destruction of the county's coal industry.

The United Mine Workers sought by standardizing wages, hours, and work practices to rationalize the competitive national coal industry. Inefficient producers, who were unable to mechanize, pay adequate wages, work standard hours, pay for dead work, and maintain safety standards, were to be eliminated from the industry. After 1933, the UMW was solidly ensconced in the coal fields, but Harlan's competitors continuously threatened to terminate their union relationship unless the Harlan field was organized and forced to compete on an equal basis. Consequently, the UMW was forced to complete

175

the organization of Harlan to preserve its powerful position in the industry. After 1933, the New Deal's recovery, labor, and libertarian goals coincided with union intentions, so the United Mine Workers enjoyed the full support of national government. Without government intervention, even the powerful CIO probably could not have organized Harlan.

The Harlan operators, with the exception of prounion Black Mountain Coal Corporation, pursued individual antiunion policies. Each firm refused to hire union members, discharged and evicted from company housing employees who joined the union, and used privately paid mine guards to exclude union organizers and union meetings from company property.

The Harlan mine owners, collectively via the Harlan County Coal Operators' Association, dominated county politics and controlled the county sheriff and county judge, who appointed a large force of deputy sheriffs who were then paid and controlled by the mine owners. From 1931 through 1937, both Sheriffs Blair and Middleton used the deputies to bar union organizers from entering the county and to disrupt union meetings within the county. As long as the deputies continued their antiunion warfare, miners were afraid to join the union or attend union meetings, and union officials were unable to enter the county to recruit members, operate the grievance machinery, or service contracts. Neither the NRA's Bituminous Coal Labor Board nor the later National Labor Relations Board could halt the deputies' harassment of unionists. Only after the La Follette Civil Liberties Committee exposed the private mine-guard system, rallied public opinion against it, and forced Kentucky's governor and legislature to abolish it in 1938 was the county open to successful organization. Thus, the key to organizing Harlan County was protection of labor's civil liberties and the right to organize.

Although the union and state and national governmental bodies contended that all members of the Harlan County Coal Operators' Association engaged in a conspiracy with the sheriff and his deputies to prevent organization, the operators' purpose was probably accomplished through only a small, tight-knit conspiracy that included George Ward, Pearl Bassham, Sheriff Middleton, Deputy Sheriff Ben Unthank, and a handful of deputies, and by political consensus. Sheriff Middleton, both a politician and a coal operator, simply served his own economic and political interests by preventing the county's organization.

Although the labor-management conflict was not so bloody as one might have expected in Harlan's violent environment, it was violent enough to immortalize the county as "Bloody Harlan." Nine years of bitter labor-management warfare produced eleven deaths and twenty woundings. Law enforcement officials committed the lion's share of the violence. Deputy sheriffs killed four miners and wounded ten miners and two newsmen. National Guardsmen killed two and wounded three miners. Miners killed five deputy sheriffs and wounded three deputies and two National Guardsmen.

Deputies dealt violently with unionists because the operators paid them to prevent unionization, because the union's successful campaign to abolish the private deputy-sheriff system would deprive them of their jobs, and because the deputies developed certain personal or occupational needs that overshadowed their legal duties. Of the four miners killed by deputies, Carl Richmond, Joe Moore, and Julius Baldwin were killed more in self-defense than to deter union organization. Only Bennett Musick was killed solely for political reasons. Of twelve persons wounded by deputies, Bill Burnett, Marshall Musick (twice wounded), John Anglian, and an unnamed miner were wounded more because they defied authority or exhibited disrespect for an officer than because attacks on them would prevent organization. Jeff Baldwin was wounded because he allegedly endangered an officer's life, Carl Williams, "Rockhouse" Munhollen, and Jim Bates were wounded because they were associated in the officers' minds with "cop killing." Deputy George Lee, whose son had been killed in the Evarts ambush, pistol-whipped Carl Williams because Williams ˜was thought to have participated in the ambush. Lee beat up Munhollen after going beserk at the sight of a union rally being conducted so near the scene of his son's death. Deputies probably accidentally wounded Bates during an attack on "Peggy" Dwyer, whom the officers blamed for agitating the Evarts ambush. Only editor Bruce Crawford, reporter Boris Israel, and organizer Tom Ferguson were shot for purely antiunion reasons. The deputy sheriffs' occupational needs thus strongly reinforced the antiunion role that their position entailed.

Although union miners occasionally sniped at nonunion miners, it is surprising that no nonunionists were killed or wounded during the decade. Union miners' violence was almost entirely directed against the hated deputy sheriffs and National Guardsmen. Of five deputies killed by miners, two— Jess Pace and Owen Sizemore—were killed in self-defense. The other three, Daniels, Lee, and Jones, were ambushed—a political act. Of five persons wounded by miners, two National Guardsmen were wounded in self-defense. Three deputies were wounded in political acts, one by a sniper and two by ambushers. The miners' violence, in short, was mostly politically motivated.

The union miners viewed the deputy sheriffs as criminals, corrupted betrayers of their class, tools of the operators, enemies of the union, and cold-blooded killers—in short, as gun thugs. Much of the UMW's direct action and political effort was aimed at eliminating the privately paid deputies. Most of the miners' antideputy violence, five homicides and three woundings, occurred during the spontaneous, disorganized union campaign of 1931. That year, when deputies threatened to destroy the union by evicting, abusing, and arresting union miners, by protecting nonunion workers, and by interfering with the distribution of strike literature, union miners, ill organized and misled, sniped at and ambushed the deputies. George Burchett, a former strike leader, threatened to lead a group of Bell County miners to Harlan to "shoot them off." After 1933, when district leaders were more firmly in control of the campaign, the UMW instigated the Denhardt and La Follette investigations and a series of radio broadcasts to expose the evils of the private deputy system and rally public support for its elimination, lobbied the state legislature and the governor to end it, and finally obtained abolition of the archaic institution.

Harlan's labor-management conflict has often been used to demonstrate an oversimplified class warfare between American capitalists and their middle-class allies on one hand and workers on the other. Important divisions existed, however, within all classes of Harlan County society. While most coal operators opposed unionization, Mahan, Matthews, Hall, and Birchfield were prepared to accept collective bargaining if others did, and Asbury even if others did not. The miners, too, were deeply divided, as the Clover Fork yellow-dog strike and several UMW defeats in NLRB elections demonstrated. After 1931, a majority of miners favored organization, but a sizable minority, because of family relationships, race, loyalty to a benevolent employer, or religious or political scruples, were consistently opposed. Harlan's best-known protest song, "Which Side Are You On?," points not to the division between capital and labor but to a division within the ranks of labor. The song asks the miner, "Will you be a union man, or a thug for J. H. Blair?"

Neither was the county's middle class of a single mind. While most politicians were antiunion, several who sympathized with the miners' cause or hoped to build a labor following were either prounion or neutral. County Attorney Elmon Middleton, Sheriff Clinton Ball, Assessor John Gross, Evarts city councilman Joe Cawood, Evarts mayor Bradley Burkhart, Evarts police chief Asa Cusick and his assistant, Al Benson, were prounion, and Circuit Judge James M. Gilbert and County Judge Cam Ball were scrupulously neutral. Although most merchants opposed unionism, some, such as Milt Harbin and Joe Cawood, who hoped to destroy the company-store monopoly or to build political support among the miners, supported the union cause. The farmers, many of whom had been coal miners or had relatives who were, were of divided mind.

In striking contrast to Gaston County, North Carolina, where during the 1929 National Textile Workers Union strike the preachers had solidly backed the mill owners, [1] many vocal Harlan preachers supported unionism. Most ministers, particularly the pastors of company churches who had already alienated the miners and had no desire to estrange their wives and children as well, maintained a correct fundamentalist posture of silence and neutrality toward the issue of unionism. Until they discovered that the Communist leadership of the National Miners Union favored atheism and racial integration, Holiness preachers Finley Donaldson, Jim Grace, and Gill Green led the NMU's local organizing drive. Carl Vogel, ordained pastor of Harlan's largest and most prestigious Methodist church, Marshall Musick, a lay Baptist preacher, William Clontz and Frank Martin, lay Methodist preachers, and B. H. Moses, a Holiness preacher, contributed immensely to the success of the UMW's campaign. While these fundamentalists would have rejected the Social Gospel, they possessed a keen sense of social justice. While one might expect lay preachers to follow the lead of their working-class congregations, in Gaston County they had not. The onset of the Great Depression and the worsening of conditions in the interim, 1929–31, between the Gaston and Harlan strikes, probably fails to explain the difference, because the textile industry, like coal, had already experienced depression in the 1920s.

Thus, while Harlan differed from typical middle-class American society in its distinct absence of a large, disinterested middle class to moderate conflict between the haves and have-nots, the upper and lower classes were not solidly arrayed against each other.

For two decades, collective bargaining and World War II and postwar prosperity brought industrial peace to Harlan County. Negotiation and arbitration replaced coercion and violence in the resolution of labor-management disputes. Whereas eleven deaths resulted from labor strife in the thirties, in the next two decades, from 1939 to 1959, no one died in labor-management conflict.

The New Deal created a new balance of economic and political power in Harlan as it did throughout the nation. In 1939, the United Mine Workers counterbalanced the Harlan County Coal Operators' Association as one of the county's two preeminent economic institutions. In response to the Depression, the New Deal's labor and economic programs, and local Republicans' abuse of power, hundreds of Harlan miners forsook their traditional Republicanism and built a relatively strong Democratic party. After the thirties, Harlan normally elected Democrats to national and state offices and Republicans to local positions.[2] While neither local organization became clearly a labor party, the delicate balance forced both to become more responsive to miners' needs. Just as the New Deal extended the dimensions of labor's civil liberties throughout the nation,[3] so it did in Harlan. The abusive private deputy system was abolished, and union activity no longer resulted in suspension of a miner's rights of free speech, press, and assembly. The New Deal brought industrial order to Harlan County, and an increased share of power and liberty to its miners. In Harlan County, as elsewhere, the New Deal produced significant change and reform, not a Roosevelt Revolution.

Unionism brought significant economic and social gains to union miners. Open-shop abuses, such as the cleanup system, no pay for dead work, coal bucking, short weight, payment of wages in scrip, and the company-store and housing monopoly, were ultimately abolished; and the union wage scale steadily advanced. The union erected in the city of Harlan one of its chain of seven Miners' Memorial Hospitals, a modern facility staffed with some of the nation's best orthopedic and respiratory disease specialists, to treat the miners' ailments and provide their daughters with an opportunity to pursue nursing careers.

Few union miners—few miners of any persuasion, for that matter—survived. Because of declining national demand for coal, soaring rail-transportation costs, and inability to match its competitors' mechanization, the Harlan coal industry fared poorly with rigid regulation of both freight rates and wages. After exceeding fifteen million tons for a second time in 1942, over the next two decades annual production plunged to under four million tons. Simultaneously, Harlan miners tripled their productivity, which, coupled with shrinking production, reduced the number of employed miners from 15,864 in 1941 to 2,242 in 1961. Although the county's population plummeted from 75,275 in 1940 to 37,370 in 1970, the mass exodus to Cincinnati, Cleveland, Chicago, Dayton, and Detroit proceeded too slowly to avert widespread unemployment and poverty. In 1959, five thousand local miners were unemployed, 40 percent of the county's people were existing on union or government pensions, and more than a third of them were receiving surplus food rations.[4] Because of the area's isolation, a reputation for labor militancy, and union resistance to low-wage industry, no new industries provided an alternative to mine employment.

In 1959, declining profit margins, mounting unemployment, a Republican administration in Washington, and A. B. Chandler's second term as governor of Kentucky encouraged local operators to attempt to expel the UMW from Harlan County. The coal operators refused to renew their contract, the union struck, and Governor Chandler sent the National Guard back to Harlan for the first time in two decades. Although the major companies ultimately signed a union agreement, one man was killed and labor-management peace was again disrupted.[5] In 1964, only three major firms renewed their UMW contracts. Four large mines refused to renew their agreements, and two signed contracts with the rival Southern Labor Union, an independent union based in Chattanooga, Tennessee, that generally contracted for the federal minimum wage.[6] A UMW strike called in July, 1964, resulted in mass picketing, sniping at nonunion and Southern Labor Union miners, and dynamiting of truck ramps and mining machines. During the course of a year, more than one hundred such incidents of violence occurred.[7] By mid-1965, the UMW had only 1,250 members in Harlan, 450 miners had joined the Southern Labor Union, and 875 were nonunion.[8]

Wedded to a narrow trade unionism, the United Mine Workers did nothing to retrain or relocate displaced miners. The union relegated responsibility for technological unemployment to state and federal government, which before the Kennedy administration did nothing, and afterward did too little. The UMW, attempting to retain its organization in the face of mounting opposition, signed "sweetheart contracts," which waived all or part of a company's contribution to the union's Welfare and Retirement Fund. When dwindling membership and royalty payments depleted its welfare chest, the union canceled the membership and welfare and retirement benefits of union members who were unemployed or employed in nonunion mines.[9] In 1963, the UMW announced the closure of Harlan's Miners' Memorial Hospital, which was kept open only through the efforts of the Presbyterian Church and the Office of Economic Opportunity. The modern structure of

curved glass and steel, once the symbol of a proud and powerful union, thereafter reminded many miners of money and
confidence misplaced.

Despite the union's dwindling strength in Tennessee and
southeastern Kentucky, the tiny remnant of District 19 unionists loyally supported W. A. "Tony" Boyle's mismanagement of
their union. During the union's 1964 national convention, a
squadron of District 19 delegates, wearing white hardhats
emblazoned "District 19—Tony Boyle," employed strong-arm
tactics to suppress dissenting voices.[10] District 19 officials also
played a key role in financing and planning the New Year's
Eve, 1969, assassination of union dissident Joseph A. "Jock"
Yablonski, his wife, and daughter. William J. Turnblazer, Jr.,
confessed that he, UMW president W. A. Boyle, and District
19 secretary-treasurer and member of the International Executive Board Albert Pass planned the murder in Boyle's Washington office. Twenty thousand dollars embezzled from the union's
research fund was channeled through Turnblazer and Pass to
District 19 field representative Wiliam J. Prater, who employed
Silous Huddleston, former president of a District 19 local at
La Follette, Tennessee, to hire assassins. Huddleston and his
daughter, Annette Gilly, employed Huddleston's son-in-law,
Paul Gilly, and Claude Vealey and Aubran "Buddy" Martin to
murder the Yablonskis. Martin, Vealey, Paul and Annette Gilly,
Huddleston, Pass, Prater, Turnblazer, and Boyle were all con-
victed on a charge of conspiracy to murder.[11]

Nearly four decades after Harlan County's organization, conditions there had run full circle. Again unemployment, poverty,
social disorganization, violence, and fear cast a shadow of gloom
upon the county's future. The competitive coal industry had
until recently supplied the nation's fuel demands, had occasionally profited its owners, but had left its employees a legacy
of insecurity, poverty, hopelessness, broken health, and death.
Economic deterioration and technological advances during the
past two decades had forced more than half of Harlan's residents to join in a soul-rending exodus to northern cities, leaving in its wake a serious "brain drain" and a paucity of ideas
concerning the economic betterment of the county.[12] In 1965,
a painted plywood flag marked the United States post office

at Lynch, Kentucky. The peeling Stars and Stripes forlornly anticipated Harry Caudill's plaint, "My land is dying!"

In 1974, the UMW, under new leadership, won a prolonged strike at Eastover Mining Company, a Duke Power subsidiary at Brookside, a struggle the union viewed as the key to success or failure in its plan to reorganize fifteen thousand nonunion miners in eastern Kentucky and, subsequently, thousands more throughout the nation.[13] The victory at Eastover, widely her-alded by Barbara Kopple's film, *Harlan County, U.S.A.*, failed, however, to ignite a widespread reorganization of the union. The three-month-long strike of 1977–78 crippled the union, and the 1978 agreement, while substantially increasing wages, offers far less in the way of medical and retirement benefits to entice new members. The nation's energy crisis, which promises to worsen, augurs well for the coal industry's future. Pleas by Presidents Nixon and Carter for a tripling of coal output point to a bright immediate future. Such an unprecedented demand and price improvement could easily offset Harlan's disad-vantages in transportation and mechanization. Yet the in-dustry's hopes remain blighted by desirable, but threatening, environmental controls on both production and consumption and, more seriously, by continuing conflict between labor and management.

NOTES

1. Liston Pope, *Millhands and Preachers: A Study of Gastonia* (New Haven, Conn., 1965), pp. 324–30.

2. John H. Fenton, *Politics in the Border States* (New Orleans, 1957), pp. 23, 65–68.

3. Jerold S. Auerbach, *Labor and Liberty: The La Follette Committee and the New Deal* (Indianapolis and New York, 1966), pp. 204, 209–12.

4. Testimony of U.S. Congressman Eugene Siler and Kentucky State Senator H. Nick Johnson, U.S., Congress, Senate, Special Committee on Unemployment Problems, *Unemployment Problems. Hearings* on S.R. 196, 86 Cong., 1 sess. (1959), pt. 5, pp. 1812, 1848 (hereafter cited as *Unemployment Problems*).

5. George J. Titler, *Hell in Harlan* (Beckley, W.Va., n.d.), pp. 215–16; Victor Riesel, "Shooting Again in Bloody Harlan," *Citizen-Journal* (Columbus, Ohio), Apr. 10, 1965.

6. *United Mine Workers Journal,* July 15, 1964, p. 7; 160 NLRB 1589–95; 160 NLRB 1582–89.

7. *Harlan* (Ky.) *Daily Enterprise,* Jan. 3, Feb. 8, July 20, 26, Aug. 30, 1965; Riesel, "Shooting Again in Bloody Harlan"; Jerry Landauer, "Coal 'Sweethearts,'" *Wall Street Journal,* Sept. 23, 1965, p. 19.

8. *Harlan Daily Enterprise,* Jan. 12, July 1, 12, 1965.

9. Ibid., Jan. 25, 1965; Landauer, "Coal 'Sweethearts,'" pp. 1, 19; testimony of Roscoe Petry, *Unemployment Problems,* pt. 5, p. 1822.

10. Brit Hume, *Death and the Mines: Rebellion and Murder in the United Mine Workers* (New York, 1971), pp. 46–49.

11. Ben A. Franklin, "Boyle Accused of Murder in Killing of Yablonski," *New York Times,* Sept. 7, 1973, pp. 1, 18.

12. For the "brain drain" see James S. Brown and George A. Hillery, Jr., "The Great Migration, 1940–1960," in *The Southern Appalachian Region: A Survey,* ed. Thomas R. Ford (Lexington, Ky., 1962), pp. 68–69; for the paucity of ideas concerning economic development see *Unemployment Problems,* pt. 5, passim; for the psychological impact of out-migration see the account of Linda Mullins in Todd Gitlin and Nanci Hollander, *Uptown: Poor Whites in Chicago* (New York, 1970), pp. 258–68, and Robert Coles, *Migrants, Sharecroppers, Mountaineers* and *The South Goes North,* vols. 2 and 3 of Children of Crisis (Boston, 1967).

13. Bob Arnold, "UMW Organizing Drive in Eastern Kentucky Pivots on Strike at Duke Power Subsidiary," *Wall Street Journal,* Nov. 26, 1973, p. 12.

Bibliography

UNPUBLISHED MATERIALS

Private Papers

Banner Fork Coal Corporation Corporate Record. Ford Archive. Henry Ford Museum.
Van Amberg Bittner Papers. West Virginia University.
John Brophy Papers. Catholic University of America.
Theodore Dreiser Papers. University of Pennsylvania.
Fuson, Henry Harvey, "History of Harlan County, Kentucky: Some Chapters." Unpublished manuscript. University of Kentucky Library.
Adolph Germer Papers. State Historical Society of Wisconsin.
Powers Hapgood Papers. Indiana University.
W. Jett Lauck Papers. University of Virginia.
Philip Murray Papers. Catholic University of America.
Samuel Ornitz Papers. State Historical Society of Wisconsin.
Turnblazer, William J., Sr. "Turnblazer Scrapbooks." 2 vols. In possession of William J. Turnblazer, Jr., former president, District 19, United Mine Workers of America, Middlesboro, Ky.

Interviews

Clontz, William. London, Ky., Sept. 15, 1965.
Ridings, James W. Middlesboro, Ky., Sept. 16, 1965.
Titler, George J. Beckley, W.V., Sept. 13, 1965.
Turnblazer, William J., Jr. Middlesboro, Ky., Sept. 16, 1965.

Commonwealth of Kentucky Documents

Kentucky. Commission Appointed by the Honorable Ruby Laffoon, Governor of the Commonwealth of Kentucky, to Investigate

Conditions in the Coal Fields of Southeastern Kentucky. "Stenographic Report of Proceedings, Frankfort, Kentucky, March 25–28, 1935." Vol. 2. In possession of William J. Turn-blazer, Jr., former president, District 19, United Mine Workers of America, Middlesboro, Ky.

————. Montgomery County Circuit Court. *Commonwealth of Kentucky* v. *W. B. Jones.* Transcript of trial. 18 vols. U.S. National Archives. Record Group 60. Justice Department, General Records. Central Files. Classified Subject Files. Enclosures.

————. *Commonwealth of Kentucky* v. *William Hightower.* Transcript of trial. 17 vols. U.S. National Archives. Record Group 60. Justice Department, General Records. Central Files. Classified Subject Files. Enclosures.

United States Documents

U.S. District Court. Eastern Kentucky. *United States of America* v. *Mary Helen Coal Corporation, et al.* Transcript of trial. 48 vols. U.S. National Archives. Record Group 60. Justice Department, General Records. Central Files. Classified Subject Files. Enclosures.

U.S. National Archives. Record Group 9. National Recovery Administration. Bituminous Coal Labor Board, Division no. 1—South. Case Files.

————. Correspondence File.

————. Hearings and Decisions.

————. Record Group 60. Justice Department, General Records. Central Files. Classified Subject Files. Enclosures.

————. Correspondence.

————. Record Group 174. Labor Department, General Records. Perkins File.

————. Record Group 280. Federal Mediation and Conciliation Service.

Theses and Dissertations

Dotson, John A. "Socio-Economic Background and Changing Education in Harlan County, Kentucky." Ph.D. diss., George Peabody College for Teachers, 1943.

Miller, Glenn W. "Recent Struggles among the Coal Miners' Organizations in Bituminous Coal Fields." M.A. thesis, Southern Illinois University, 1935.

Pearce, Albert. "The Growth and Overdevelopment of the Kentucky Coal Industry, 1912–1929." M.A. thesis, University of Kentucky, 1930.

Taylor, Paul Floyd. "Coal and Conflict: The UMWA in Harlan County, 1931–1939." Ph.D diss., University of Kentucky, 1969.
_____. "The Coal Mine War in Harlan County, Kentucky, 1931–32." M.A. thesis, University of Kentucky, 1955.

PUBLISHED MATERIALS

United States Government Publications

U.S. Coal Commission. *Report of the United States Coal Commission.* 5 vols. Washington, D.C.: Government Printing Office, 1925.
U.S. Congress, House. *Congressional Record.* 71 Cong., 3 sess. (1931), vol. 74, pp. 4069–70; 72 Cong., 1 sess. (1932), vol. 75, p. 3846; 74 Cong., 1 sess. (1935), vol. 79, pp. 1202, 1860, 8987–89; 76 Cong., 1 sess. (1939), vol. 84, p. 9037.
U.S. Congress, Senate. Committee on Education and Labor. *Private Police Systems.* S. Rept. 6, pt. 2, 76 Cong., 1 sess. (1939).
_____. Committee on Education and Labor. *Violations of Free Speech and Assembly and Interference with Rights of Labor.* *Hearings* before a subcommittee of the Committee on Education and Labor on S.R. 266, 74 Cong., 2 sess. (1936).
_____. Committee on Education and Labor. *Violations of Free Speech and Rights of Labor. Hearings* before a subcommittee of the Committee on Education and Labor on S.R. 266, 75 Cong., 1 sess. (1937), pts. 9–13.
_____. Committee on Interstate Commerce. *Stabilization of Bituminous Coal Mining Industry. Hearings* before a subcommittee of the Committee on Interstate Commerce on S. 1417, 74 Cong., 1 sess. (1935).
_____. Committee on Manufactures. *Conditions in Coal Fields in Harlan and Bell Counties, Kentucky. Hearings* before a subcommittee of the Committee on Manufactures on S.R. 178, 72 Cong., 1 sess. (1932).
_____. Committee on Mines and Mining. *To Create a Bituminous Coal Commission. Hearings* before a subcommittee of the Committee on Mines and Mining on S. 2935, 72 Cong., 1 sess. (1932).
_____. *Congressional Record.* 72 Cong., 1 sess. (1932), vol. 75, pp. 5229–30, 6531; 73 Cong., 1 sess. (1933), vol. 77, p. 4580.
_____. Special Committee on Unemployment Problems. *Unemployment Problems. Hearings* before the Special Committee on Unemployment Problems on S.R. 196, 86 Cong., 1 sess. (1959), pt. 5.

————. Special Committee to Investigate Presidential, Vice Presidential and Senatorial Campaign Expenditures, 1940. *Investigation of Presidential, Vice Presidential and Senatorial Campaign Expenditures, 1940.* S. Rept. 47, 77 Cong., 1 sess. (1941).

U.S. Department of Commerce. Bureau of Mines. *Mineral Resources of the United States.* 1924–31. Washington, D.C.: Government Printing Office, 1927–33.

U.S. Department of Commerce, Bureau of the Census. *Abstract of the Twelfth Census of the United States: 1900.* Washington, D.C.: Government Printing Office, 1904.

————. *Fifteenth Census of the United States: 1930: Population.* Vol. 3, pt. 1, *Alabama-Missouri.* Washington, D.C.: Government Printing Office, 1932.

————. *Fifteenth Census of the United States: 1930: Unemployment.* Vol. 1. Washington, D.C.: Government Printing Office, 1931.

————. *Historical Statistics of the United States: Colonial Times to 1957.* Washington, D.C.: Government Printing Office, 1960.

U.S. Department of the Interior. Bureau of Mines. *Minerals Yearbook.* 1932–67. Washington, D.C.: Government Printing Office, 1934–68.

U.S. Department of Labor. Bureau of Labor Statistics. *Hours and Earnings in Anthracite and Bituminous Coal Mining: 1922 and 1924.* Bulletin no. 416. Washington, D.C.: Government Printing Office, 1926.

————. *Hours and Earnings in Bituminous Coal Mining: 1922, 1924, and 1926.* Bulletin no. 454. Washington, D.C.: Government Printing Office, 1927.

————. *Hours and Earnings in Bituminous Coal Mining: 1929.* Bulletin no. 516. Washington, D.C.: Government Printing Office, 1930.

————. "Wages and Hours of Labor." *Monthly Labor Review,* 29 (Sept., 1929), 630–79.

————. "Wages and Hours of Labor." *Monthly Labor Review,* 33 (Oct., 1931), 910–47.

U.S. Geological Survey. *Mineral Resources of the United States.* 1911–23. Washington, D.C.: Government Printing Office, 1912–27.

U.S. National Labor Relations Board. "District 19, United Mine Workers of America (Seagraves Coal Company) and Southern Labor Union, Local No. 207; Local No. 6074, United Mine Workers of America (Seagraves Coal Company) and Southern

Labor Union, Local No. 207." *Decisions and Orders,* vol. 160, Oct. 4, 1966, pp. 1582–89.

―――. "In the Matter of Clover Fork Coal Company and District 19, United Mine Workers of America." *Decisions and Orders,* vol. 4, Nov. 27, 1937, pp. 202–41.

―――. "In the Matter of Good Coal Company and United Mine Workers of America, District 19." *Decisions and Orders,* vol. 12, Apr. 8, 1939, pp. 136–59.

―――. "In the Matter of Harlan Fuel Company and United Mine Workers of America, District 19." *Decisions and Orders,* vol. 8, July 5, 1938, pp. 25–66.

―――. "In the Matter of United States Coal & Coke Company and Union of Lynch Employees and United Mine Workers of America." *Decisions and Orders,* vol. 3, Aug. 26, Sept. 11, 1937, pp. 398–99.

―――. "Local No. 7463, United Mine Workers of America (Harlan Fuel Company) and Southern Labor Union, Local No. 206; District 19, United Mine Workers of America (Harlan Fuel Company) and Southern Labor Union, Local No. 206." *Decisions and Orders,* vol. 160, Oct. 4, 1966, pp. 1589–95.

Union and Industry Publications

Coal Age. Jan., 1931–Dec., 1939.

Industrial Solidarity. June 2–July 21, 1931.

United Mine Workers Journal. Jan. 1, 1931—Feb. 1, 1941, Jan. 1, 1959—July 15, 1966.

Newspapers

Cincinnati Enquirer. Jan. 1, 1931–Dec. 31, 1939.

Courier-Journal (Louisville, Ky.). Jan. 1, 1931–Dec. 31, 1939.

Harlan (Ky.) *Daily Enterprise.* Jan. 1, 1931–Dec. 31, 1939, July 1, 1964–July 31, 1966.

Knoxville (Tenn.) *News-Sentinel.* Jan. 1, 1931–Dec. 31, 1939.

New York Times. Jan. 1, 1931–Dec. 31, 1939.

Pineville (Ky.) *Sun.* Jan. 1, 1931–Dec. 31, 1939.

Pamphlets

American Civil Liberties Union. *Kentucky Miners Struggle.* New York: American Civil Liberties Union, 1932.

American Friends Service Committee. *A Report of Child Relief*

Work in the Bituminous Coal Fields, Sept. 1, 1931–Aug. 31, 1932. Philadelphia: American Friends Service Committee, 1932.

————. *A Report of the Services and Relief in the Bituminous Coal Fields, Sept. 1, 1932–Aug. 31, 1933.* Philadelphia: American Friends Service Committee, 1933.

Costello, E. J. *The Shame That Is Kentucky's!* Chicago: General Defense Committee, n.d.

Gannes, Harry. *Kentucky Miners Fight.* N.p.: Workers International Relief, 1932.

Books

Aaron, Daniel. *Writers on the Left: Episodes in American Literary Communism.* New York: Harcourt, Brace and Co., 1961.

Alinsky, Saul. *John L. Lewis: An Unauthorized Biography.* New York: G. P. Putnam's Sons, 1949.

Auerbach, Jerold S. *Labor and Liberty: The La Follette Committee and the New Deal.* Indianapolis and New York: Bobbs-Merrill Co., 1966.

Baker, Ralph Hillis. *National Bituminous Coal Commission: Administration of the Bituminous Coal Act, 1937–1941.* Johns Hopkins University Studies in Historical and Political Science, Series 59. Baltimore: Johns Hopkins University Press, 1941.

Baratz, Morton S. *Union and the Coal Industry.* Yale Studies in Economics, no. 4. New Haven: Yale University Press, 1955.

Bernstein, Irving. *The Lean Years: A History of the American Worker, 1920–1933.* Boston: Houghton Mifflin Co., 1960.

————. *Turbulent Years: A History of the American Worker, 1933–1941.* Boston: Houghton Mifflin Co., 1970.

Bowman, Mary J., and W. W. Haynes. *Resources and People in East Kentucky: Problems and Potentials of a Lagging Economy.* Baltimore: Johns Hopkins University Press, 1963.

Brearley, H. C. *Homicide in the United States.* Chapel Hill: University of North Carolina Press, 1932.

Carnes, Cecil. *John L. Lewis: Leader of Labor.* New York: Robert Speller Publishing Corp., 1936.

Caudill, Harry M. *Night Comes to the Cumberlands: A Biography of a Depressed Area.* Boston: Atlantic Monthly Press; Little, Brown and Co., 1963.

Christenson, Carroll L. *Economic Redevelopment in Bituminous Coal: The Special Case of Technological Advance in United States Coal Mines, 1930–1960.* Cambridge: Harvard University Press, 1962.

Coles, Robert. *Migrants, Sharecroppers, Mountaineers.* Children of Crisis, vol. 2. Boston: Little, Brown and Co., 1967.

―――――. *The South Goes North.* Children of Crisis, vol. 3. Boston: Little, Brown and Co., 1967.

Condon, Mabel Green. *A History of Harlan County.* Nashville, Tenn.: Parthenon Press, 1962.

Denisoff, R. Serge. *Great Day Coming: Folk Music and the American Left.* Urbana: University of Illinois Press, 1971.

Dos Passos, John. *The Theme Is Freedom.* New York: Dodd, Mead and Co., 1956.

Dubofsky, Melvyn, and Warren Van Tine. *John L. Lewis: A Biography.* New York: Quadrangle/New York Times Co., 1977.

Fenton, John H. *Politics in the Border States.* New Orleans: Hauser Press, 1957.

Finley, Joseph E. *The Corrupt Kingdom: The Rise and Fall of the United Mine Workers.* New York: Simon and Schuster, 1972.

Fisher, Waldo E. *Economic Consequences of the Seven-Hour Day and Wage Changes in the Bituminous Coal Industry.* Philadelphia: University of Pennsylvania Press, 1939.

Ford, Thomas R., ed. *The Southern Appalachian Region: A Survey.* Lexington: University of Kentucky Press, 1962.

Ford Motor Company. *The Ford Industries: Facts about the Ford Motor Company and Its Subsidiaries.* Detroit: Ford Motor Co., 1924.

Foster, William Z. *Pages from a Worker's Life.* New York: International Publishers, 1939.

Frank, Waldo. *The Death and Birth of David Markand: An American Story.* New York: Charles Scribner's Sons, 1934.

Galenson, Walter. *CIO Challenge to the AFL: A History of the American Labor Movement, 1935–1941.* Cambridge: Harvard University Press, 1960.

Gitlin, Todd, and Nanci Hollander. *Uptown: Poor Whites in Chicago.* New York: Harper and Row, 1970.

Gitlow, Benjamin. *The Whole of Their Lives.* New York: Charles Scribner's Sons, 1948.

Graham, Hugh Davis, and Ted Robert Gurr, eds. *The History of Violence in America: Historical and Comparative Perspectives.* New York, Washington, and London: Frederick A. Praeger, Publishers, 1969.

Green, Archie. *Only a Miner: Studies in Recorded Coal-Mining Songs.* Urbana: University of Illinois Press, 1972.

Greenway, John. *American Folksongs of Protest*. Philadelphia: University of Pennsylvania Press, 1953.

Hallgren, Mauritz A. *Seeds of Revolt: A Study of American Life and the Temper of the American People during the Depression*. New York: Alfred A. Knopf, 1933.

Hays, Arthur Garfield. *Trial by Prejudice*. New York: Covici, Friede, 1933.

Hinrichs, Albert F. *United Mine Workers of America and the Non-Union Coal Fields*. Columbia University Studies in History, Economics and Public Law, no. 246. New York: Columbia University Press, 1923.

Hudson, Harriet. *Progressive Mine Workers of America: A Study in Rival Unionism*. University of Illinois Bureau of Economic and Business Research, Bulletin no. 73. Urbana, Ill., 1952.

Hume, Brit. *Death and the Mines: Rebellion and Murder in the United Mine Workers*. New York: Grossman Publishers, 1971.

Jillson, Willard Rouse. *Coal Industry in Kentucky*. Kentucky Geological Survey, Geologic Reports, vol. 20. Frankfort, Ky., 1924.

Jones, Mary Hoxie. *Swords into Plowshares: An Account of the American Friends Service Committee, 1917–1937*. New York: Macmillan Co., 1937.

Korson, George. *Coal Dust on the Fiddle: Songs and Stories of the Bituminous Industry*. 1943. Reprinted, Hatboro, Pa.: Folklore Associates, 1965.

McDonald, David J., and Edward A. Lynch. *Coal and Unionism: A History of the American Coal Miners' Unions*. Silver Spring, Md., and Indianapolis: Cornelius Press, 1939.

Marshall, F. Ray. *Labor in the South*. Cambridge: Harvard University Press, 1967.

Middleton, Elmon. *Harlan County, Kentucky*. Big Laurel, Va.: James Taylor Adams and James Taylor Adams II, 1934.

Morris, Homer Lawrence. *Plight of the Bituminous Coal Miner*. Philadelphia: University of Pennsylvania Press, 1934.

National Committee for the Defense of Political Prisoners. *Harlan Miners Speak: Report on Terrorism in the Kentucky Coal Fields*. Edited by Theodore Dreiser. New York: Harcourt, Brace and Co., 1932.

Parker, Glen L. *Coal Industry: A Study in Social Control*. Washington, D.C.: American Council on Public Affairs, 1940.

Pope, Liston. *Millhands and Preachers: A Study of Gastonia*. New Haven: Yale University Press, 1965.

Ross, Malcolm H. *Machine Age in the Hills*. New York: Macmillan Co., 1933.

Stark, Rodney. *Police Riots: Collective Violence and Law Enforcement*. Belmont, Calif.: Wadsworth Publishing Co., 1972.

Sulzberger, C. L. *Sit Down with John L. Lewis*. New York: Random House, 1938.

Swanberg, W. A. *Dreiser*. New York: Charles Scribner's Sons, 1965.

Taft, Philip. *Organized Labor in American History*. New York: Harper and Row, 1964.

Tindall, George B. *Emergence of the New South, 1913–1945*. A History of the South, vol. 10. Baton Rouge: Louisiana State University Press, 1967.

Titler, George J. *Hell in Harlan*. Beckley, W.Va.: BJW Printers, n.d.

Wechsler, James A. *Labor Baron: A Portrait of John L. Lewis*. New York: William Morrow, 1944.

Weller, Jack E. *Yesterday's People: Life in Contemporary Appalachia*. Lexington: University of Kentucky Press, 1965.

Westley, William A. *Violence and the Police: A Sociological Study of Law, Custom, and Morality*. Cambridge, Mass., and London: MIT Press, 1970.

Wolfskill, George. *Revolt of the Conservatives: A History of the American Liberty League, 1934–1940*. Boston: Houghton Mifflin Co., 1962.

Articles

Arnold, Bob. "UMW Organizing Drive in Eastern Kentucky Pivots on Strike at Duke Power Subsidiary." *Wall Street Journal*, Nov. 26, 1973, p. 12.

Barnicle, Mary Elizabeth. "Harry Simms: The Story behind This American Ballad." In brochure accompanying Folkways FH 5233, *Songs of Struggle & Protest, 1930–1950*, pp. 3–4.

"Bloody Harlan Reforms." *Nation*, Aug. 6, 1938, p. 121.

Brown, James S., and George A. Hillery, Jr. "The Great Migration, 1940–1960." In *The Southern Appalachian Region: A Survey*, edited by Thomas R. Ford, pp. 54–78. Lexington: University of Kentucky Press, 1962.

Bubka, Tony. "The Harlan County Coal Strike of 1931." *Labor History*, 11 (Winter, 1970), 41–57.

Byars, J. C., Jr. "Harlan County: Act of God?" *Nation*, June 15, 1932, pp. 672–74.

Carr, Joe Daniel. "Labor Conflict in the Eastern Kentucky Coal Fields." *Filson Club History Quarterly*, 47 (Apr., 1973), 179–92.

"Class War in Kentucky." *New Masses*, 7 (Sept., 1931), 23.

Cowley, Malcolm. "Kentucky Coal Town." *New Republic,* Mar. 2, 1932, pp. 67–70.

Crawford, Bruce. "The Coal Miner." In *Culture in the South,* edited by W. T. Couch, pp. 361–73. Chapel Hill: University of North Carolina Press, 1934.

Cressey, Paul Frederick. "Social Disorganization and Reorganization in Harlan County, Kentucky." *American Sociological Review,* 14 (June, 1949), 389–94.

Daniell, F. Raymond. "Behind the Conflict in 'Bloody Harlan.'" *New York Times Magazine,* June 26, 1938, pp. 1–2, 11.

Dos Passos, John. "Working under the Gun." *New Republic,* Dec. 2, 1931, pp. 62–67.

Draper, Theodore. "Communists and Miners 1928–1933." *Dissent,* 19 (Spring, 1972), 371–92.

Ehrich, Thomas Lindley. "Appalachian Paradox." *Wall Street Journal,* Jan. 27, 1971, pp. 1, 8.

————. "Miners 'Win Either Way.'" *Wall Street Journal,* Dec. 4, 1969, p. 36.

Evans, Herndon J. "Kentucky Hits Communism." *Kentucky Progress Magazine,* 4 (Apr., 1932), 12–15, 21, 28.

Footman, Robert H. "John Dos Passos." *Sewanee Review,* 47 (July–Sept., 1939), 365–82.

Franklin, Ben A. "Boyle Accused of Murder in Killing of Yablonski." *New York Times,* Sept. 7, 1973, pp. 1, 18.

Garland, Jim. "Harry Simms." In brochure accompanying Folkways FH 5233, *Songs of Struggle & Protest: 1930–1950,* p. 7.

Glusman, Preval. "Harry Simms—A Young Revolutionist." *Daily Worker,* May 8, 1934.

Grauman, Lawrence, Jr. " 'That Little Ugly Running Sore': Some Observations on the Participation of American Writers in the Investigations of Conditions in the Harlan and Bell County, Kentucky, Coal Fields, 1931–32." *Filson Club History Quarterly,* 36 (Oct., 1962), 340–54.

Hackney, Sheldon. "Southern Violence." *American Historical Review,* 74 (Feb., 1969), 906–25.

Hapgood, Powers. "Radio Address to Miners." *Breeze* (Ill.) *Courier,* Dec. 14, 1935.

Hardman, J. B. S. "John L. Lewis, Labor Leader and Man: An Interpretation." *Labor History,* 2 (Winter, 1961), 3–29.

"Harlan County Faces." *Fortune,* 5 (Feb., 1932), 130–31.

"Harlan Operators in Error in Refusal to Sign Up For Union Shop" (editorial). *Louisville* (Ky.) *Times,* May 15, 1939, p. 6.

Harsch, Joseph C. "Harlan on Trial." *New Republic,* July 6, 1938, pp. 242–44.

Hays, Arthur Garfield. "The Right to Get Shot." *Nation,* June 1, 1932, p. 619.

Israel, Boris. "I Get Shot." *New Republic,* Oct. 21, 1931, pp. 256–58.

Jillson, Willard Rouse. "A History of the Coal Industry in Kentucky." *Register of the Kentucky State Historical Society,* 20, no. 58 (1922), 21–45.

Johnson, James P. "Drafting the NRA Code of Fair Competition for the Bituminous Coal Industry." *Journal of American History,* 53 (Dec., 1966), 521–41.

Johnson, Oakley. "Starvation and the Reds in Kentucky." *Nation,* Feb. 3, 1932, pp. 141–43.

Keedy, Allen. "A Preacher in Jail." *Christian Century,* Aug. 26, 1931, pp. 1068–70.

"Kentucky Feudalism." *Time,* May 3, 1937, pp. 13–14.

"Kentucky Strike Call Meets Little Response; Smokeless Wages Cut." *Coal Age,* 38 (Jan., 1932), 35.

Landauer, Jerry. "Coal 'Sweethearts.'" *Wall Street Journal,* Sept. 23, 1965, pp. 1, 19.

Lane, Margaret. "Noted Woman Writer Tells the Story of Terrible Conditions Existing in Harlan County Field." *United Mine Workers Journal,* Dec. 15, 1931, pp. 11–12.

McGoldrick, Joseph Daniel. "College Students and Kentucky Miners." *American Scholar,* 1 (July, 1932), 363–65.

Margolis, Jon. "'Bloody Harlan's' Coal Mines." *Chicago Tribune,* Mar. 17. 1974, pp. 17, 25.

"News from the Front." *Survey,* Oct. 15, 1931, p. 69.

"99 Are Indicted in Kentucky Vote." *New York Times,* June 6, 1943, p. 41.

Ornitz, Sam. "Bleeding Bowels in Kentucky." *New Masses,* 7 (Oct., 1931), 3–4.

Pearce, John Ed. "Simmering Second Battle of Harlan County." *Washington Post,* Mar. 18, 1974, pp. 1, 3.

"President Green Hauls Theodore Dreiser over the Coals for His Vicious Attack on the Union." *United Mine Workers Journal,* July 15, 1931, pp. 8–9.

Riesel, Victor. "Shooting Again in Bloody Harlan." *Citizen-Journal* (Columbus, Ohio), Apr. 10, 1965.

Ross, Malcolm. "The Spotlight Plays in the Coal Pits." *New York Times Magazine,* July 14, 1935, pp. 4–5.

Spero, Sterling D., and Jacob Broches Arnoff. "War in the Kentucky Mountains." *American Mercury,* 25 (Feb., 1932), 226–33.

Stachel, Jack. "Lessons of Two Recent Strikes." *Communist,* June, 1932, pp. 527–36.

Taft, Philip. "Violence in American Labor Disputes." *Annals of the American Academy of Political and Social Science,* 364 (Mar., 1966), 127–40.

———— and Philip Ross. "American Labor Violence: Its Causes, Character, and Outcome." In *The History of Violence in America: Historical and Comparative Perspectives,* edited by Hugh Davis Graham and Ted Robert Gurr, pp. 281–395. New York, Washington, and London: Frederick A. Praeger, Publishers, 1969.

"33 Vote Officials Sentenced." *New York Times,* July 29, 1945, p. 41.

"Toothpicks." *New Republic,* Nov. 25, 1931, pp. 32–33.

"Two More Harlan Operators Sign Union Contracts." *Coal Age,* 43 (Nov., 1938), 78.

Walker, Charles Rumford. " 'Red' Blood in Kentucky." *Forum,* 87 (Jan., 1932), 18–23.

"Which Side Are You On? An Interview with Florence Reece." *Mountain Life & Work,* 48 (Mar., 1972), 22–24.

Wolman, Leo. "Labor under the NRA." In *America's Recovery Program,* edited by Clair Wilcox, Herbert F. Fraser, and Patrick Murphy Malin, pp. 89–103. New York: Oxford University Press, 1934.

Index

Abolition of private mine guards, 17, 133-43 *passim,* 178
Ages, Ky., 108, 135
Alabama coal operators, 97
Allen, James S., 76
Allen, Marion "Two-Gun," 59
Alverson, James, 58, 71, 107, 112, 115. *See also Harlan Daily Enterprise*
American Civil Liberties Union, 60, 68, 86-87
American Federation of Labor, 58, 95, 129-30, 158
American Friends Service Committee, 11, 63, 72
American Liberty League, 128, 130
American Red Cross, 33, 37, 38, 48, 70, 71
Ameringer, Oscar, 95
Anderson, Sherwood, 69
Anglian, John, 131, 177
Antiunionism, 101-3
Appalachian Coals, Inc., 104
Arnett, L. T., 134-35
Asbury, E. J., 103, 121-22, 140, 148, 179. *See also* Black Mountain Coal Corporation
Assad, Doyle, 75
Atlantic & Pacific Tea Company, 38, 39
Auerbach, Jerold, 141

Baldwin, Jeff, 60, 177
Baldwin, Julius, 60, 99, 177
Ball, Cam E., 142, 160, 161, 169, 179
Ball, Clinton, 142, 179
"The Ballad of Harry Simms," 80
Banner Fork Coal Corporation, 4
Barbourville, Ky., 79
Bardo Coal Company, 101, 152-53
Barnes, C. Rankin, 86
Barnes, Charles B., 96, 106, 119
Barton, Ann, 79
Bassham, Pearl, 40, 107, 137-40 *passim,* 149, 176-77. *See also* Harlan-Wallins Coal Corporation; Verda Supply Company
Bates, Jim, 106, 177
Battle of Evarts: planned, 42-43; fought, 43-45; causes of, 45-46, 177-78; effects of, 46-50, 108, 111, 177; unionists indicted for, 49; praised, 58; unionists plead guilty, convicted, and sentenced, 75; mentioned, 40, 57, 131, 136, 167
Battle of Stanfill. *See* Stanfill, Battle of
Bell County, Ky.: strike spreads to, 46; National Miners Union in, 62, 78; visited by Dreiser committee, 63-70; population of, 65;

199

opposes unionism, 108-9; defends operators and sheriff, 111-12, 115; criticizes Denhardt report, 115; rejoices at Laffoon's departure, 133; purchased by PV & K Coal, 165; mentioned, 27, 104, 107. *See also* Alverson, James

Harlan Fiscal Court, 71

Harlan Fuel Company, 40, 101, 144, 145-46, 151-53

Harlan Miners Speak: A Report on Terrorism in the Kentucky Coal Fields, 64, 69-70

Harlan Ridgeway Coal Company, 100-101, 117

Harlan-Wallins Coal Corporation: political corruption at, 16, 18, 107; housing at, 18; short-weighing at, 21; cleanup system at, 21; company store at, 22; miners join union, 36; discharges union miners, 34, 36, 118, 139; rejects 1933 and 1934 contracts, 101; refuses to hire union miners, 118; violates NRA code, 119; ignores BCLB decision, 119-20; requires employees to sign yellow-dog contracts, 139; bars unionists from company property, 139; uses deputies to harass unionists, 139; violates Wagner Act, 139; withdraws from operators' association, 144; signs 1937 and 1939 contracts, 144, 152, 162, 165; mentioned, 20, 39, 40, 107, 108, 111, 132, 140. *See also* Bassham, Pearl

Harvey, John, 79

Hatfield, Henry, 87

Hauck, Earl, 171-72

Hays, Arthur Garfield, 87. *See also* American Civil Liberties Union

Hays-Bablitz Commission, 16

Hazard, Ky.: coal field, 18, 104; coal operators, 159

Health care, 19-20

Hickerson, Harold, 82, 92n75. *See also* Independent Miners' Relief Committee

Hickey, John, 40, 131, 142

High Splint Coal Company, 36, 100-101, 109, 144, 152-53

Hightower, William: discharged, 36; president of Evarts local, 36; patrols stores, 39; accused of conspiracy to murder deputies, 43, 73; convicted and sentenced, 43, 75; arrested, 46, 49; refuses legal assistance from International Labor Defense, 57; indicted, 72; tried, 75; pardon, 132, 133

Hi-Lo Association, 144. *See also* High Splint Coal Company

Hirsh, Harry (alias Harry Simms). *See* Simms, Harry

Hoffman, Clare, 169

Homicides: grand jury blames deputies, 17, 112; rate of, 23; reasons for, 23-30, 177-78; incidents of, 41, 44, 60, 77, 79, 110, 135-36, 141-42, 149-50, 167-68, 182, 183; candidates for county offices promise to reduce, 99

Hoover, Herbert, 38

Hopkins, Welly K., 171-72

Housing, 9, 14, 15, 18-19, 21, 65, 181

Howard, H. H., 40

Howard, Lawrence, 138, 139-40, 149

Howard, Martha, 138, 139-40, 149

Huddleston, Silous, 183

Hudson, William, 75, 133

Hughes, Roy, 43, 45

Hunger, 10-11, 38-39 *passim,* 46-49 *passim,* 58-62 *passim,* 68-71 *passim*

Hutton, Virgil, 77

"I Am a Union Woman," 66

Independent Miners' Relief Committee, 81-83, 85, 87, 92n75

Industrial Solidarity, 46

Industrial Workers of the World, 36, 45-46, 49-50, 64-65, 74-75, 86

Injunctions, 39, 48, 76, 78

Insull Employees' Association, 144, 146. *See also* Company unions; Southern Mining Company